Praise f[...]

'Meticulously detailed ... fascinating.' *Mail on Sunday*

'Paints an evocative picture of wartime London and occupied France, highlighting the role of women's magazines in maintaining morale and disseminating government's messages.' *The Lady*

'This wonderful, minutely detailed biography is a fascinating account of a truly remarkable woman.' *Red*

'One real scoop for Summers is her discovery that it was Withers' idea to commission Cecil Beaton to take the iconic 1941 *Vogue* photograph ... Fashion is Indestructible.' *The Times*

'Summers' research is exemplary ... a saga recounted in fine detail.' **Amy Fine Collins,** *Airmail*

'A fascinating read.' *Candis*

DRESSED FOR WAR

The Story of *Vogue* Editor Audrey Withers,

From the Blitz to the Swinging Sixties

JULIE SUMMERS

**SIMON &
SCHUSTER**

London · New York · Sydney · Toronto · New Delhi

First published in Great Britain by Simon & Schuster UK Ltd, 2020
This edition published in Great Britain by Simon & Schuster UK Ltd, 2021

Copyright © Julie Summers, 2020

The right of Julie Summers to be identified as the author
of this work has been asserted in accordance with
the Copyright, Designs and Patents Act, 1988.

1 3 5 7 9 10 8 6 4 2

Simon & Schuster UK Ltd
1st Floor
222 Gray's Inn Road
London WC1X 8HB

www.simonandschuster.co.uk
www.simonandschuster.com.au
www.simonandschuster.co.in

Simon & Schuster Australia, Sydney
Simon & Schuster India, New Delhi

The author and publishers have made all reasonable efforts
to contact copyright-holders for permission, and apologise
for any omissions or errors in the form of credits given.
Corrections may be made to future printings.

A CIP catalogue record for this book
is available from the British Library

Paperback ISBN: 978-1-4711-8160-3
eBook ISBN: 978-1-4711-8159-7

Typeset in Perpetua by M Rules
Printed and bound by CPI Group (UK) Ltd, Croydon, CR0 4YY

MIX
Paper from
responsible sources
FSC® C020471
www.fsc.org

For Diane,
who has been with me every step of the way

CONTENTS

PROLOGUE

LONDON, ONE NEW BOND STREET, TOP FLOOR,

VOGUE EDITORIAL OFFICE,

THURSDAY 19 SEPTEMBER 1940, 11.15 A.M.

The editor's office had three desks: one for the editor, one for her assistant and the third for her secretary. The large windows along the south wall, hung with thick blackout curtains, overlooked the shattered roofs of the Burlington Arcade. On the wall behind the editor's desk were the layouts for the November, December and January issues of British *Vogue*, clipped to battens – the November pages fully populated, December almost complete, January with gaps for editorial and fashion. The room was full this morning as the managing editor, Audrey Withers, was in the middle of her editorial conference with the fashion and features editors, the art director and the managing director of Condé Nast Publications, Harry Yoxall.

The October issue was ready to go to the printers in Watford and would be appearing on the news stands the following week. Today their focus was on finalising November's contents. Cecil Beaton was writing a topical article called 'Time of War' about living in London under enemy attack. Audrey had asked him to concentrate on how life went on despite the constant menace of bombing and how danger brought a new perspective to life. It would feature photographs of Mrs Churchill in the drawing room of 10 Downing Street and Lady Warrender and Lady George Cholmondeley in uniform working for the Polish Armed Forces Comforts Fund.

Audrey had planned the feature to be reassuring at a time of uncertainty and upheaval. She wanted her readers to see the great and the good going about life as normally as possible and be comforted by a drawing of Lady Diana Cooper reading aloud on a terrace in the autumn sunshine or Mme de Janzé working on a Persian bedcover during an air raid. New York had sent a feature on Mrs Lydig's fastidious taste, extravagance and passion which had been legendary in New York society before the First World War. Entitled 'She had 150 pairs of shoes', the lavishly illustrated article would be followed by a piece by a subaltern's wife about how to dress in wartime – a nice juxtaposition, Audrey had suggested.

The fashion pages focused on what to wear in the town and country: wool coats for the town and tweed suits for the country with hats, gloves and sensible shoes to match. As they were about to move on to advice for warm and woolly undergarments, the alarm went up and a loud voice commanded, 'Evacuate the building immediately! Evacuate immediately!' Firefighters on the roof had spotted an unexploded bomb in the ruins of Burlington Arcade.

Audrey looked at Harry Yoxall and they both pushed back

their chairs and stood up. 'Take your papers and leave quickly but safely,' he said, as he reached for his attaché case. Audrey's mind was racing as she stuffed the papers she had been working through into a folder. What else might she need? Taking a moment to look around her, she spotted her coat and slung it over her shoulder as she edged past her desk and headed for the door.

Harry was staring out of the window to the street below to see if he could spot the bomb, but he could not. He shook his head and followed Audrey to the stairwell. The seven of them clattered down five flights of stairs, picking up workers from the other floors on their way down. Their pace slowed to a walk as the stairwell filled up with bank clerks and tellers from the ground and first floors. At last, they reached the door where an anxious air-raid warden was ushering them away from the building and down towards Piccadilly: 'Walk! Don't run! Don't panic! Move on! Get away from the building! MOVE ON!'

Clutching her folder of papers, her shoulder hunched to keep her coat from slipping off, Audrey walked purposefully at the head of her little party of evacuees. Down Old Bond Street they marched and out onto Piccadilly, past the Royal Academy of Arts and on towards Piccadilly Circus. As they were level with the entrance to Fortnum & Mason, a news photographer stepped out in front of Audrey and snapped a picture of the phalanx of *Vogue* staff striding down the centre of the street. Harry led them to his office in Fetter Lane, on the other side of the City of London, and they continued their conference as if nothing out of the ordinary had happened.

To Audrey's amusement, the picture was featured in the *Daily Sketch* the following day with the caption: 'Overdraft

Preserved. This bank staff walk happily down the road, never losing their customers' overdrafts, to new premises. Cause? Time-Bomb!' The picture appeared again as a centre-page spread to demonstrate civilian morale. It was two days before Audrey and her team could return to the editorial office and she had learned a valuable lesson. They had been unable to complete their work on the November issue as they had only managed to take with them what they could carry in their arms. From now on, she told them, each department had to have a suitcase to hand into which vital material could be shovelled at a moment's notice and carried away in the teeth of time-bombs or other dangers.

Five days later, Audrey was officially promoted to the post of editor of British *Vogue*, a role she had been fulfilling in all but name since March. Within weeks, she was at the behest of government ministers in every department, from the Treasury to the Ministry of Information, the Board of Trade and the War Office. They consulted her, as the editor of the most influential women's magazine in the country, whose readers were people of prominence and status. If *Vogue* readers could be persuaded to change the way they dressed, what they ate or how they worked, then the rest of the female population would follow. Over the course of the Second World War, Audrey Withers came to be recognised as one of the most powerful women in London.

Tall, slim and usually dressed in grey or navy, Audrey looked every bit the blue-stocking editor history has judged her to be. She had a reputation as a woman who never raised her voice but made her views known by quiet insistence. She did not stand out in a crowd, yet she reigned supreme at *Vogue* for twenty years. Beneath the monochrome exterior and the prematurely grey hair was a woman of great ambition and drive. She could be impetuous and passionate but at her core lay a great warmth, kindness and human understanding. She treated everyone with respect and was innately modest.

There is no doubt that Audrey Withers was a great intellect and a formidably capable editor, but she was so much more. She was an early adopter of new ideas in art, literature and technology, learning to use a computer at the age of eighty. She was politically active all her life, voting Labour until she joined the SDLP in her late seventies. She cared deeply about her work and even more so about the role of women at a time when they were still expected to stop work once they were married and had children. She was a co-founder of the Women's Press Club during the war and was a passionate advocate for women's rights. She believed in equality for women at work and fought hard for this in the post-war years when a grateful government wanted nothing more than for women to go back to the hearth and kitchen sink. Her management style was ahead of its time, giving inexperienced women opportunities, helping employees to overcome health and emotional problems by awarding them extra time off, and moving people sideways if she spotted they were being bullied or otherwise unhappy in their post.

She was unafraid to take on thorny issues, such as sexual harassment of her female staff, and showed spirit and backbone in spats with her star contributors to *Vogue*: Cecil Beaton, Norman Parkinson and the designer Edward Molyneux. If Audrey had a weakness it was that she was constrained by politeness. Brought up by a mother who could not show emotion, she never learned to share her innermost thoughts with anyone. At times, this could make her appear cool and distant, but it hid an inner warmth that was always there to be called upon if needed.

Audrey nurtured young talent and encouraged women to think about every aspect of their lives, from fashion to food, literature to cookery, gardening and motoring. When she joined the staff of *Vogue*, British fashion was concentrated around a small area of Mayfair. By the time she left, thirty years later, it was celebrated countrywide. She knew how much she had contributed to the world of fashion publishing, but she never wanted anyone to make a fuss about it. In her private life, she loved theatre, music and swimming, but she especially valued the company of friends and family. She continued to invite people into her home until the last few weeks of her long and productive life. She had that rare ability to reach across the generations and was as comfortable with young people as she was with her peers.

Audrey Withers' life was divided into three separate phases: her childhood and education; her working career, all but four years of which was spent working for Condé Nast Publications in London on *Vogue*; and the last forty years, when she retreated from the public arena to enjoy her second marriage and extensive travel around Russia, India and South America. This book will focus on the first two phases of her life, with the bulk of the book dealing with the war years. This was the moment when British *Vogue* emerged as a magazine fully independent of its American parent, with Audrey in control.

I

GREEN SHOOTS

'I always think of you as a bright, uncomplicated spirit in this muddy, involved world.'

— HUGH I'ANSON FAUSSET TO AUDREY WITHERS,
APRIL 1924

Elizabeth Audrey Withers was born on 28 March 1905 in Hale in Cheshire, the second daughter of Percy and Mary 'Mamie' Withers. She had a sister, Monica, who was five years older and a brother, Michael, who arrived in 1910. Her upbringing was unconventional but very happy. It helped to sow the seeds of intellectual enquiry and enthusiasm for the world around her that would be the two strongest traits of her personality in adult life.

Audrey's life spanned almost the whole of the twentieth century. She was born at a time when the man in the moon was part of celestial folklore and a mobile was something that hung above a baby's cot. By the time of her death in 2001, she had witnessed two world wars and the development of computer technology. Over her lifetime, Roald Amundsen reached the South Pole, Edmund Hillary and Tenzing Norgay stood on the summit of the highest peak on earth, and Neil Armstrong took a giant step on the moon. In politics, she saw the construction and destruction of the Berlin Wall, while in music, art and literature she witnessed some of the greatest changes of all time, including the birth and death of her favourite composer, Benjamin Britten.

At the time she was born, Audrey's father was a general practitioner and had worked in his private practice in Hale since qualifying as a doctor. Both Audrey's parents had suffered personal loss in their family lives, and this shaped them as parents. Percy Withers was born in 1867, the fourth and youngest son of John and Mary Withers. His childhood was beset by illness and he had suffered from an overwhelming terror of the dark. He wrote later of his shuddering fear of the cruelties of boyhood, 'its dirty-mindedness, its terrors and deceits. The darkness of night was dreadful to me; to be left alone with it was to be abandoned to a presence that cut me adrift from all other experiences of life.' As a child he found the company of other boys rough and crude. From them, he heard foul language and smutty tales, which he hated. He wrote,

I seem never to have known a day when ugliness and un-cleaness [sic] were not abhorrent. Something perhaps too much of Puritanism, or at any rate, a queasy sensibility, has gone with me, quietly or aggressively, thro' I believe every period of life. Nor do age and traffic with the world diminish it.

This highly strung, sickly child slipped into the terrifying territory of adolescence with a sense of wariness and often loneliness leading to blank despair. Home life was soon to be shattered by the death of first his father, when he was fourteen, and then his mother a year later, leaving the teenage boy to be brought up by his older brothers, Oliver and Sheldon, both doctors. Although there was no family money after the parents' deaths, the brothers were determined that Percy should follow in their footsteps. With considerable sacrifice on their own parts, they put him through Manchester Grammar School where he 'learned all too soon, and too grossly, the full implications of sex, and the beastliness that license, unschooled and misdirected, could make of it.' Despite his over-sensitive nature and the ease with which he was shocked by crude and base ideas, he was persuaded by his brothers to follow them into medicine, matriculating at Owens College, later Manchester Medical School, at the age of nineteen.

A decade later, he met and married Mary Woolley Summers, known always within the family as Mamie. She was three years younger than Percy and the youngest of ten siblings. Her father, John Summers, had been born in Bolton but moved to Dukinfield, 6 miles east of Manchester, where he set up as a clogger making both the leather uppers and the nails for the clogs worn by the mill workers in the area. In 1851, John travelled to London to visit the Great Exhibition at Crystal Palace, where he came across a nail-making machine, advertised by the vendors as novel, utilitarian and economical. It cost £40, every penny that he had, but John Summers did not hesitate to buy it.

Within a year, he had enlarged his business and was delivering nails all over Lancashire, Yorkshire and as far afield as North Wales. The combination of the excellent railway network in the area and John's determination to make a success of his business meant that it expanded rapidly, and by 1855 he announced a profit of £1,000. By the time his youngest daughter was born in 1870, John was forty-eight and his wife forty-two. Exhausted by eleven births in twenty years, Mary senior died a month to the day after Mamie's birth, leaving John Summers with an orphan daughter and four sons living at home aged fifteen, thirteen, eleven and eight. Mamie was brought up by her older sister, Hannah, who was nineteen years her senior, and Nanny Walker, the family's widowed housekeeper who stayed with the family until well into her eighties. Hannah was cruel, having not an ounce of human kindness, according to her brothers, and Mamie suffered from loneliness.

Hannah married and left home when Mamie was four and, a year later, John Summers died, leaving her abandoned for the third time in her short life. As a result, she grew up to be anxious and without a sense of belonging. The only happy times were when her brothers took her away on holiday to the continent in the summer. When she was nineteen, they insisted she should be educated at university. She went first to King's College London, where she was awarded first-class honours in ancient History, and then to Oxford, where her older brother William had studied. Mary was one of the first generation of female students at Somerville Hall. Her closest friend was Cornelia Sorabji, who became the first woman to study law at Oxford and the first woman to practise law in India and Britain. The two of them remained friends for the rest of Mamie's life and Miss Sorabji became Audrey's godmother.

Percy Withers set up practice in Hale and soon he felt confident enough to buy a house and consider marriage as a 'practicable and provident matter'. He knew that he would be offering his future wife a life of comfort as a GP had standing in the local community. He met Mamie at a party at her older brother's house in the spring of 1895. He had got to know the family having treated one of their relatives for alcohol poisoning a few months earlier. He fell in love with her immediately and, with customary impetuosity, proposed to her a month later. Hannah and the Summers boys organised a sumptuous wedding for Percy and Mamie in June, with four little Summers brides-maids. Mamie wore a dress of heavy ivory satin trimmed with deep Irish lace and a train borne by a tiny pageboy, her brother Harry's 4-year-old son, Geoffrey.

They spent their honeymoon in Scotland and returned to Hale to begin married life in Albert Road, he as a GP and she as his wife, with a staff at home so that she never had to set foot in the kitchen other than to agree the menu. Four years later, their first child, Monica, was born. Five years later, Audrey arrived and eighteen months after that Percy Withers was struck down with bi-lateral pneumonia and their life was turned upside down. Without antibiotics, which would not be invented for another twenty years, pneumonia was often fatal. His brother Sheldon arrived to discuss Percy's symptoms with the doctor, who refused to name the condition he most feared, simply saying he thought it unlikely that Percy would survive.

For six days during which Percy was unconscious and suffering from delirium, his two brothers, Oliver and Sheldon, with Mamie a constant nursing presence, took turns administering ice packs, oxygen, hypodermic injections and catheterisations. It was through their single-minded devotions that he woke up on the morning of the seventh day and began the long road to recovery. It took six weeks for him to be able to crawl out of bed and stagger towards a chair in the sitting room next door. It was not long after that his brothers broke the news to him that he would never again be able to return to practising as a doctor.

One afternoon while she was watching over Percy's slow recovery, Mamie received a visit from her oldest brother, James. He had come to commiserate with his sister in her new and difficult circumstances. When he left, she waved him goodbye from the front door and turned around to light the gas lamp below the mirror as the night was drawing in. It was then she noticed an envelope. She picked it up and, when she opened it, found it contained a brief note and a cheque from her five older brothers made out to her for a sum that would keep her and the children in funds and comfort for the rest of their lives.

No one has ever revealed the actual amount of the cheque, but it meant that once Percy Withers had made his slow and painful recovery, he would never have to work again and they would be able to afford, eventually, to put the children through school and university. The money also covered Percy's medical expenses, this being decades before the introduction of the National Health Service. With this one gesture of extraordinary generosity and the small annual stipend that Mary received from the Summers steel works, the family was on a firm financial footing for the future.

Once he was sufficiently recovered, Percy Withers decided that the family should sell the house in Hale and move to their holiday cottage on Derwentwater. Abbot's Bay is a tiny inlet with twin promontories that lies four fifths of the way down the lake from Keswick, towards Grange and Borrowdale. The longer promontory was crested with magnificent Scots pines and a few hardy oaks and carpeted with moss and heather. Percy had built an Arts and Crafts-inspired cottage a decade earlier, which they moved into when Audrey was eighteen months old. This is where the memories of Audrey Withers begin.

~

Abbot's Bay had neither running water nor any form of lighting or heating other than oil lamps and open fires. The house lay a good 5 miles on foot from Keswick, as there was no road along the west side of the lake. Everything had to be brought from Portinscale or Grange, the two closest villages, but each was still more than an hour's hike there and back.

The daily strain of living at Abbot's Bay was real enough for the adults, but for Audrey it was bliss. She and Monica had a governess who taught them lessons in the morning, but after lunch they were free to roam around the woods and into the low hills beside the lake. Percy taught them where to forage for mushrooms and which ones were safe to eat. Audrey loved the earthy smell of damp grass as she sought out the plate-sized field mushrooms in autumn, learning how to pick them carefully so as not to damage their gills. There was abundant wildlife around Abbot's Bay: red squirrels, birds of all kinds and otters on the lake.

Audrey came across her first owlet when she was bending down, aged about three, trying to see if there was anything in the root of a rotten tree. A pair of dark, shiny eyes embedded in a head of fluff shone out at her. She stepped back instinctively as a baby owl flew out from the hole, hooting in protest. 'Owl!' she shouted to her father in delight. 'I saw an owl!'

The acres of hillside were like a series of gardens. There were areas of Alpine flowers, of tiny, perfect roses nestling in the moss; there were herbaceous plants next to drifts of heather and swamp. Audrey learned the names of all the different mosses and ling on the promontory, and she and Monica rehearsed the names of the mountains that rose above the lake. To the north, beyond Keswick, the great riven face of Skiddaw, with Bassenthwaite lake stretching along its base, and Blencathra, the shapeliest of all British mountains, standing alongside it. To the south, beyond the oval of Derwentwater and its islands, 'the massive jaws of Borrowdale, opened wide enough to disclose in dreamy contrast with the caverned front of Glaramara and the peaks of the Scafell group.'

For Audrey, the lake was both exciting and dangerous. She learned to swim off the jetty and loved the feeling of plunging into its cold, clear water and lying on her back looking up at the promontory. In calm weather, she and Monica paddled in the shallows, watching minnows and other fry darting to and fro beneath their feet. But when the storms whipped up the water and the waves crashed to the shore, Mamie kept the girls inside. She was afraid of the power of the lake and knew from experience how it could go from flat calm to a raging sea in just a matter of minutes.

Percy Withers took risks on the lake, and many of their friends and family predicted an early, watery grave for him. They thought he courted danger, that he was absurdly brave and recklessly risky, but he was unabashed:

I risked and enjoyed. It was not a superfluity of courage; it was not fool-hardiness. The lake, and most of all the angry lake, haunted me like a passion; not one of its moods but I wished to share to the uttermost. The gentlest of them was a bounty common to lovers and strangers alike; the violent mine alone.

This was the strange mixture that made up Audrey's father. At once a brave, daring, not to say reckless risk-taker, with deep, violent passions, yet at the same time a man so puritanical and sensitive to life's vulgarities that he could not hear a rude word or a coarse expression without feeling repulsed. The effect of this contrary character on the girls was marked. Monica, like her father, was unable to countenance any form of innuendo or profanity. Audrey said later that Monica could not read novels or watch television in later life in case she came across something remotely sexual. She never married and yet she travelled all over the world and was brave, like her father, not shying away from danger or from primitive living conditions. Audrey seemed to inherit none of her father's abhorrence of sex, but she did embrace his zest for life. Her passions were every bit as strong as his and at times the euphoria she felt bubbling inside her like champagne would burst out and she would surprise people around her with her passionate exclamations of delight.

A tradition that grew up quickly at Abbot's Bay was the 5 November bonfire. Percy would start collecting wood for the fire as soon as the last embers of the previous fire were cold. This was no casual wood-collecting, but an almost industrial undertaking. Percy and Mamie would take the children and their governess out in their boat after lunch and drop them at a bay further up or down the lake to play by the shore while they began the serious task of collecting wood. After the wood had been piled onto the boat, often to a height of 5 or 6ft, Percy and Mamie would row back to the bay to collect Monica and

Audrey. This wobbling edifice would then make its stately and unstable way out onto the lake and back to the jetty at Abbot's Bay, with Percy rowing in the bows and Mamie and the children desperately trying to steady the load. This was repeated many times before the great bonfire was ready to light. The November bonfire drew people on foot, in boats, and in carriages, from miles around.

Years later, during the Blitz, when Audrey was watching London on fire from the roof of her house in Little Venice, she was reminded of the awe-inspiring power of the bonfires on Derwentwater. The crackling and hissing of the wood as it split and twisted, the sap boiling in the green stems while the desiccated needles on last year's pine branches would spit, giving off showers of sparks. She recalled the overwhelming heat from the flames as they stood in the glow of the fire, their cheeks red-hot, loving every minute of it, yet equally terrified by its intensity. Those memories returned as she watched the Blitz and she found herself both horrified and transfixed by the power of fire anew. She never told her father of this memory, nor of any others from her early childhood. She did not like to dwell on the past and always looked to the future. This was a defining trait in her character, and it meant that she was always prepared to consider something new rather than harking back to the safe and familiar.

Those early years in the Lake District were the happiest family years of all, a carefree existence where the only boundaries were those governed by nature. Audrey's parents were remarkably free-thinking for the era, and this was something that would affect her outlook on life and periodically give her problems with authority. Her parents both voted Labour and were outspoken against fox hunting. They believed in social reform and supported housing projects for workers in Keswick. They encouraged the children to be independent, to ask questions and to read widely. There were no barriers to discussion other than the delicate subject of human emotions, which was out of bounds. If Percy Withers was uncomfortable thinking about what he regarded as base human activities, then Mamie Withers was even more buttoned up when it came to feelings. She was happy to talk about any subject under the sun, but she was incapable of showing emotional affection. This bothered Audrey, even as a small child, and she was instinctively more drawn to her live-wire father, whose energy and enquiring mind she found fascinating. Years later, Audrey put her mother's lack of affection down to the circumstances of her childhood, but as a little girl Audrey missed the warmth and intimacy of the maternal bond.

Five years after Audrey's birth, a brother, Michael Derwent Withers, was born. He was quiet and absorbed in his own world, something that would become accentuated over the course of his life. It is probable that he suffered from some form of mild brain damage, but there was never a diagnosis and Mick, as he became known, was seldom mentioned outside the immediate family. With three children, two of them in need of formal education, Mamie persuaded Percy that it was time to move the family away from the blissful but isolated life at Abbot's Bay. It was with a very heavy heart that Percy agreed, and he never felt as happy again as he had done living beside Derwentwater.

The family rented property called Kylsant House in Broadway, Gloucestershire. The 1911 census lists Mary

Lucy Cranford, a governess born in Calcutta, a cook called Lilian Annie Slater and two maids, Lilian Ludlow and Nesta Longsham. The family always had a cook as Mamie could not boil an egg. She was so undomesticated that when Lilian had the day off, she had to leave pre-prepared meals for the family ready to be eaten cold, whatever the season. The attraction of Kylsant House for Percy was the long, low, cloistered room that would be able to accommodate his library of some four thousand books. The house was built in the typical style of Cotswold properties from the seventeenth century, with gables, mullioned windows and stone walls that surrounded the house on three sides. They moved into Broadway in January 1911, two months before Audrey's sixth birthday.

She was a strong little girl with chubby cheeks and fly-away blonde hair that would later thicken and darken as she edged towards adolescence. She had pronounced front teeth, like her mother, and although she was never described as beautiful, she had bright blue-grey eyes that sparkled with amusement and passion and upon which people commented even when she was in her nineties.

Of all the things the children missed most about Abbot's Bay was the lake. All her life Audrey adored swimming and she would take any opportunity to jump into rivers, lakes or the sea when she was on holiday. In Broadway, they were fortunate to find friends at the other end of the village with a pool. Percy was particularly impressed by the owners, Antonio de Navarro and his wife, Mary Anderson, who was a famous American actress. Theirs was one of the largest houses in the village and their visitors included opera singers, actors and artists, which raised them even higher in Percy's esteem. The pool, which was fed by a spring in the hills beyond the garden and larger than a standard swimming pool, was some distance from the house. The Navarros allowed Percy and the girls to swim there in the early mornings before anyone in their household was awake.

Audrey's formal education was patchy. Initially she was taught at home in Broadway by Miss Crawford, but by the age of ten her parents decided she was old enough to join Monica at a boarding school in Woking. She was puzzled later why two parents who cared so deeply about their children's minds, and who were so keen to promote discussion and enquiry, would not be more focused on what kind of schooling they should receive. After all, Broadway was close to Cheltenham, with its excellent girls' schools, but it is possible that the financial situation did not allow for two sets of school fees at the girls' college. Whatever the reason, Audrey and Monica ended up in a miserable little school with about twenty-five girls aged between ten and seventeen, learning very little other than the school rules.

Then everything changed. With the outbreak of the First World War, Audrey's life was once again turned upside down. The family moved out of Kylsant House for the duration and into a tent in the grounds of Standish Court, some 35 miles to the south towards Stroud and on the edge of the Cotswolds, where Percy was engaged as the senior doctor at a convalescent hospital. In a time of national crisis, he felt duty-bound to help as best he could, though he only worked for a year before his health failed him again. By the time Audrey and Monica arrived there in July 1915, they could see the esteem in which their father was held and for Audrey it was the only time in her life that she saw her father in paid employment.

Audrey and Monica stayed in the hospital grounds during the school holidays. Although the work was hard for Percy and his hospital staff, for the girls it was an adventure. They had to sleep in tents because all the rooms in the house were occupied by convalescing men. Audrey remembered the freezing winters, but she said they never complained about the cold because they knew the men had been in far worse conditions on the battle-fields. After the Gallipoli landings in 1915, there was an influx of Australian and New Zealand soldiers, many of whom had never left their homes before. For these men, the children were a delightful reminder of family life. They loved to chat to the girls and to see little Mick running about chasing birds and roll-ing down the slopes outside the court. For Audrey and Monica, life at Standish Court was as close to Abbot's Bay as they could imagine. They were free to roam the parkland and woods and there were coppices, hedgerows, ponds and orchards to explore.

One of the best outcomes of life at Standish was a reversal in their school fortunes. A sister at the hospital had been to St Leonards School in St Andrews in Scotland and spoke highly both of the education and the attitude of the headmistress. With his customary enthusiasm for something new, Percy announced that the girls would be leaving Woking in the summer and heading for St Andrews. This was the start of Audrey's education proper. She was eleven and would spend two years in the junior school before moving up to the senior school. Monica, already sixteen, was at a disadvantage, as she had to catch up on years of lost opportunities. Audrey always felt sorry that her sister had only ever enjoyed two years of proper schooling.

St Leonards School was founded in 1877 by an alumna of

Girton College, Cambridge, and from its inception strove to be a pioneering school for girls. Audrey moved into the senior school in the autumn term of 1918, weeks before the Armistice and her parents' move back into Kylsant House. Her housemistress was also the headmistress of the school, an exceptional woman called Mary Bentinck Smith, who was well known for her ideas on education. Audrey was under her guidance for three years, and she benefited from being in the aura of an outstanding intellectual and an advocate for equality. Mary Bentinck Smith was a brilliant scholar with a magnetic personality. She had an absolute belief that there was 'no just reason for excluding [girls] from the practice of any profession worthy of a human being's interest and devotion'. What a role model for the young and impressionable Audrey.

In her autobiography, Audrey wrote of her time at school as being one of a battle to make friends and keep faith with her independent, non-conforming, non-religious views. There was a period when she was deeply unhappy over whether she should be confirmed into the church and eventually gave in through exhaustion. It was a subject on which there was little ground given at the otherwise progressive school. Mary Bentinck Smith had a deep faith and Audrey described her as being like an Old Testament prophet when she read parts of the Book of Isaiah. Audrey was mature for her age, both physically and intellectually, and this meant that she often felt out of step with her peers. Formidably forthright, thanks to her upbringing, she was used to arguing with adults on their terms, which some of the girls who came from more traditional homes found unsettling. She wrote of how conventional the young could be, however unconventional they appeared to the older generation.

Fortunately, there was a family friend who lived close to the school who always kept her door open for Audrey. She wrote of an overwhelming sense of peace and security when she stood in the quiet hall of Mrs Robertson's house and heard her soft voice call out: 'Come away, dearie.' This was the first time that Audrey had had a female friend who neither admonished nor challenged her, but simply sat and listened while she unburdened herself. She was the older generation friend whom every adolescent needs, Audrey said later. If she was unhappy, she did not tell her parents.

Her father wrote to her in the second summer she was at school:

> We picture you radiantly happy and prosperous, you precious, and always I wait eagerly for your letters to bring this assurance. How goes the work, the music, the cricket? Tell us everything. God bless you! Heaps and heaps of love, your own Daddy.

Percy seemed to cultivate being the liberal eccentric. In another letter, he told Audrey that Chick, his nickname for Monica, had cycled into Oxford to play tennis and go dancing, only getting back home at one o'clock in the morning. 'What would your early Victorian grandmothers think of it? Even Miss Maclure [housekeeper], on receipt of the news this morning, nearly fainted away in the shock.' At a time when chaperoning was still the norm for unmarried girls, this was indeed something out of the ordinary, and Percy clearly relished that gentle flouting of the norms.

School reports show that Audrey was an active member of

her house and that she contributed a great deal. She played hockey and lacrosse with a passion, at a time when house sports were played to a very high standard. Photographs of her with her fellow team players show a strong, smiling, confident Audrey, much at ease with her peers. In May 1923, she took part in a production of J. M. Barrie's *Quality Street* and a photograph of her in costume, parasol in hand, her head thrown back in a theatrical pose, puts her right in the mix of school life. She was also head of the School Literary Society for three years, which says something about her love of books and learning.

In early 1920, the lease on Kylsant House expired and the Withers family found a house in the village of Souldern, near Bicester, about 20 miles from Oxford. The origins of the village date back to at least the twelfth century and the house that Percy and Mamie bought, Souldern Court, was early sixteenth century with many later additions. There were enough bedrooms to accommodate the household plus guests, and the gardens extended to about three acres, which gave Percy room to plant an orchard and, to everyone's delight, build a swimming pool. It was this house that became the centre of Audrey's family life.

Souldern Court was run like clockwork, to Percy's precise timetable, which even the most unpunctual of his guests began to like. The formality of lunch and dinner times belied the merriment and range of cheerful conversation, readings and discourse that happened around their busy dining-room table. Percy was at the head of everything, conducting proceedings, admonishing guests who hogged the conversation, while Mamie flitted to and fro to ensure the cook had arranged exactly the right dish to be served at precisely the correct time to each guest. She remembered that the Poet Laureate loved scones and cream, while A. E. Housman had a penchant for home-made strawberry jam.

Percy Withers' influence on Audrey's life was immense, and his attitude to parenting, at a time when little children were seen and not heard, was warm and affectionate. When she was due to come back from school the summer she had turned eighteen, he wrote of his excitement:

> Chick is here; you and Mick follow in due time. In yields – how many hundred-fold! This is outside the domain of arithmetic, outside the reckonings even of astronomy. The stars sing together, and we hear them; but other calculations to the devil!

This pulsing passion in Percy was passed on to Audrey, and she came to know the delicious bliss of uncontrolled joy and the pain of deep sadness. From the moment she could talk, he treated her as a mini-adult and it was clear to him that she had a fine, enquiring mind.

Souldern Court was a house of sunshine and poetry. It was a hive of artistic activity, with poets, writers, artists and dramatists dropping in for hours, even days – sometimes en masse, at other times individually. Percy cultivated friendships with the literati and corresponded with many of them for years. Audrey would return from school to find Laurence Binyon sitting by the pool talking to Percy while Paul Nash sketched the village pond and Gordon Bottomley mused on poetry in the orchard. At mealtimes, everyone gathered together, outside in the summer, in the dining room if it were cold, and she was encouraged to participate in discussions and share her burgeoning views and opinions with the guests. Conversation ranged from art to politics, philosophy to religion and back to poetry. Percy set great store by his friends and correspondents and wrote to her: 'such friendships have crowned a life with happiness and I love that you should have them for yours at the very start.'

Three of his friends became her correspondents and she thought nothing of pouring out her heart to them, all men, one thirty years her senior. This was the engraver F. L. Griggs, known to the family by his intimate name, Maur. She met him at a fancy-dress ball in Broadway when she was fifteen and he was immediately captivated by her, remembering later the moment when he first glimpsed her, 'seeing nothing but gleams of friendly fun in your eyes, alternately with helpful and quite enjoyable seriousness.'

Audrey told Griggs's biographer, American-born British musicologist Jerrold Northrop Moore, that she had had a teenage crush on Maur Griggs when she first met him and that it developed into a deeply affectionate friendship that lasted until his death.

There was absolutely nothing sexual in this relationship; I was simply devoted to him, and I believe he was fond of me. We corresponded for the rest of his life; and we often lunched together when he came up to London.

Her description of Maur Griggs shows her perceptive understanding of people:

I loved him for his sincerity, his heartfelt principles, and of course his charm. I felt he was utterly dependable – that he would never let down his friends, but always stand by them. I also sensed that he was very vulnerable. Though utterly firm in his outlook, he was totally unaggressive, and had to nerve himself to take up publicly a line which he held privately. I loved him for the courage with which he did that, and felt I knew what an effort it was for him.

In that same letter, she wrote about her friendship with the artist Paul Nash:

My relationship with Paul was more complicated because he himself was a more complicated character. You must remember that I had grown up in isolated villages. I had spent seven years in a girls' school in St Andrews. I knew absolutely nobody except the friends of my parents, who visited us in the country. I was only nine when the 1914 war broke out. Growing up in those post-war years it was a new experience to meet attractive and interesting men like Maur and Paul – and to find them accepting me as a person in my own right.

Of all Percy's friends it was Paul Nash who made Audrey's heart beat faster. He was at the height of his fame immediately after the First World War. He had served as a private with the Artists' Rifles at the outbreak of the war but received officer training in 1915. He was sent to the Ypres Salient in 1917 with the Hampshire Regiment, where he spent four months before he was invalided out and sent back to London. He had made sketches while at the front and these he worked up into twenty drawings, which were well received and resulted in him becoming an official war artist. After the war, despite the critical acclaim for his war paintings, he suffered from bouts of depression and financial hardship. It was during this period that he came to be a frequent visitor at Souldern Court.

Audrey was just sixteen when she first met Paul Nash and he thirty-one. She fell deeply in love with him. Her parents put it down to an adolescent crush, but the crush lasted for years and over that time they exchanged more than 100 letters. These tell a story of infatuation, certainly, but also of Audrey trying out her ideas about love, life, passions, anger and frustrations. In turn, Nash was always the gentleman, if often playful and teasing. There was no suggestion of impropriety on his part and Margaret Nash was aware of Audrey's love for her husband. But neither did Nash play with Audrey's emotions. While he teased her, he never sought to humiliate her, and sometimes he would inadvertently admit how much she meant to him. Early on in their correspondence, when she was still at school, he wrote:

> No, I don't mind how often you write to me, Audrey. So long as the parental mind does not imagine some sentimental significance in our correspondence! In which case, I should shut up with the disconcerting suddenness of a catapulted nightingale and henceforth communicate with you spasmodically thro' the personal column of *The Times*.

The only indication Audrey ever gave of her relationship with Paul Nash as something special was in her autobiography, when she wrote: 'Paul Nash was more than a friend . . .' She was quick to explain it was because he drew and painted Souldern Court, and she referred to the portrait he drew of her when they were waiting for the meal gong to go one day. She wrote with pride that it was 'almost the only portrait he ever did of anyone outside his family'. Many years later, she told Jerrold Northrop Moore, 'Paul was the first person I had met who was part of a new wave of cynicism and a kind of rebel outlook, which I found at once disconcerting and intriguing.'

When Paul Nash bounced into the peace and quiet of Souldern Court on his sporadic visits, that equilibrium was upset for Audrey. She could not react to him as if he were just another of her father's friends. He was far too amusing, engaging, dangerous even. At first, her infatuation with him was just that. She wrote long letters from school, sharing her innermost thoughts, which he found amusing and about which he chided her for her naivety.

> You know quite well that I do not think of you as contemptibly clever or the amusing plaything of an hour. You're a silly child and deserve to be spanked. All the same you wrote me a charming letter in spite of being so cross. But you weren't cross, only wounded – and a 'Blighty' at that – well I love your letters whatever they are about. No one writes me such long or such lively letters.

In a letter sent just a few days later, he wrote:

> I like your frank confessions and even your flashes of pique – but I chuckle. Yes, I suspect I shall get to know you quite

well and of course I never could resist seeing how things worked at the back. Not that your machinery is secret or very baffling. Most of your cards come out on the table – to change our metaphor – you win by being a woman, that's all.

~

Audrey's love of literature and her determination to continue her formal education after school led her to apply to her mother's old college, Somerville, in Oxford, to read English. She was turned down. It was a bitter blow, the first formal rejection in her life, and she did not like it one bit. She wrote to another of her father's friends, Hugh I'Anson Fausset, who replied by return, urging her not to let her first 'faint stumble' upset her nerves. 'You take things so dangerously, so gloriously to heart. It is the callous that succeed in the world first – and next the warm hearted who have put on the acumen of faith.' She applied again in the autumn and was awarded a place.

By the time she was due to go up to Oxford, Audrey had begun to take more interest in her appearance. She still wore her thick blonde hair over her forehead, but she took trouble over her clothes, consulting Paul Nash's sister-in-law about what she should take with her. They decided on a pale pink crêpe de Chine dress with a low waist and a long skirt, fitting the fashion of the times. Paul drew her wearing the dress and holding a fan, looking coy, with her hair over her right eye. In the college photograph, she looks shy rather than coy, and a little uncomfortable surrounded by young women clearly more confident and at ease. Audrey was unusually tall for the time, standing nearly 5ft 10 in her stocking feet, but she was light-boned and had the ability to fold herself up in her shyness so that she looked smaller than she was.

When Audrey arrived at Somerville College in October 1924, at the age of nineteen, the education of women at Oxford University was almost two generations old. Somerville Hall had opened its doors in 1879, the same year as Lady Margaret Hall and the Society of Oxford Home Students, which later became St Anne's College. These were followed by St Hugh's in 1886 and St Hilda's in 1893, but it was not until October 1920 that the first degrees were awarded to women. And, for the record, it was not until 1959, when Audrey was about to retire from her long publishing career, that all five women's colleges were granted full collegiate status.

Audrey was one of forty-nine students who came up to Somerville that autumn, three of them from St Leonards. Most of the other students had come from the famous public girls' schools, but a small number came from high schools, so Audrey felt she slipped somewhere in between the two groups. She shared her feeling of being the outsider with Hugh Fausset, but he would have none of it. Just be yourself, he told her: 'The promised land is yours! I am glad and exultant at the thought that Somerville are lucky to get you. There is nothing so lovely, honourable and infectious as this naturalness of yours.'

Oxford in 1924 was an exciting place to be, although the rules for female students were very strict. Chaperoning, the custom of girls being accompanied by an older woman when they went out, was still in force, but they were allowed to go to the theatre in fours. If they wanted to go out at night, they had to sign out of college and wear their academic gowns at all times. Curfew was 10 p.m. and woe betide any girl who was late. They would find themselves rounded up and chased by the bulldogs, as the university policemen are known.

For Audrey, Somerville was a revelation. Thrilled to be freed of the shackles of school uniforms, dormitory living and a life dictated by the ringing of bells from morning to night, she revelled in the bliss of her own small single room and the freedom to decide what she would study, when she would study and for how long. At the beginning of her first term, she was told which tutors would be lecturing on what subjects, and she could then make the decision about which lectures to attend and which she could afford to miss. The recommendation 'you may like to go' appealed to her almost as much as the tutorial system.

Unique in Britain to Oxford and Cambridge, the tutorial pits a student, once a week, against a tutor, post-doctoral student or someone with superior knowledge of the subject in question and debates a topic about which the student has delivered an essay. Every point made in the weekly essay must be defended or yielded, and there is nowhere to hide. Almost nothing could have prepared her better for a combative career as an editor, dealing with some of the largest and most voluble egos in journalism. 'One is out in the open and compelled to draw on one's powers. Intellectually, it is the equivalent of a sports training, and equally necessary to get good results,' she wrote in 1994.

Oxford never was and never has been all about academic work. Life at Somerville was full of opportunities of every kind. Audrey joined the Bach choir in her first term and sang Brahms's requiem in the Sheldonian Theatre, the 350-year-old ceremonial hall of the university built by Sir Christopher Wren. It is well-known for having magnificent acoustics and legendarily uncomfortable seating. In the spring term, the choir performed *The Planets* by Gustav Holst. Some of the students were shocked and objected to the abstract nature of the music, but Audrey loved it.

Music, theatre, ballet and art would go on to play a large role in her life, and it was at Oxford that her love of the theatre was kindled. Up to that point her experience had been limited to school productions and the pantomime in Manchester. Now, suddenly, a whole new world of drama opened up on her door-step. The Oxford Playhouse was sited less than 50 yards from the entrance to Somerville, occupying the building now used by the University of Oxford Language Centre. It had previously been a Big Game Museum and was in its second year when Audrey matriculated.

That season the Playhouse ran a series of Ibsen plays. The women's colleges magazine, *The Fritillary*, described *Peer Gynt* as a play full of surprises 'to which the English onlooker goes as a sheep to the slaughter. He sits there, helpless and surprised, while Ibsen, in a sort of joyous frenzy, pounds him with a series of wholly unexpected blows.' If the blows were unexpected for Audrey, they nevertheless landed with a satisfying thud. She was in her element. Ibsen spoke to her, and the actors of Basil Dean's repertory company equally enthralled her. John Gielgud and his brother Val were among the regulars at Oxford. Nothing could have prepared her for the raw emotion and spiritual emancipation she felt. It was as thrilling for her as Abbot's Bay had been for her father. She knew and understood that burning, private passion that great art can inspire, and it never left her.

Audrey believed she saw more quality theatre in her three years at Oxford than she could possibly have done in the same time in London. The company put on practically every play by Chekhov, Ibsen, Strindberg and Shaw and she went to every production she could. She doubted that any other student attended the theatre as regularly as she did, and she had a rotating number of friends who would agree to come with her to performances on her wish list.

Away from the theatre and all its glory, there were other entertainments to hand. The second and third years put on parties for the first-year students to welcome them to the college, serving hot chocolate and biscuits. A rather less relaxing tradition in the second and third terms was to entertain a don, one at a time, in one's room. It was usually necessary to have a fellow student along to break the ice, though Audrey often entertained alone. She was perfectly comfortable with adults and superiors. Over the course of her first year there were four dances in college. These were exceptional events when men were invited into Somerville. They danced in Hall to a live band and enjoyed refreshments in the Junior Common Room. Isabelle Watkins, who was up at Somerville in the same era, wrote, 'Doubtless the modern generation would think poorly of the sandwiches and soft drinks.'

In her second term, Audrey decided to switch courses. Her reasoning was that reading English was a luxury. She would never lose her love of literature and she would be able to go on reading for the rest of her life. Now she had the opportunity to tackle subjects that she would not be able to do on her own, at least not with the same facilities and tutors she had at Oxford. So, she switched to Modern Greats, a relatively new course that comprised philosophy, politics and economics (PPE).

It is not clear what made her choose to go down that route, but there was a young Girton graduate called Miss Rhodes who had taught economics at Somerville since PPE was introduced in 1921. Another tutor, Miss Clarke, gave sixteen lectures on British political and constitutional history during Audrey's first term. It is possible that Audrey went to some of those lectures and decided to make the change. Perhaps she entertained Miss Clarke or Miss Rhodes to tea in her rooms. We will never know, but the Education Committee records show that she switched courses on 9 February 1925 along with Miss Creswell, who only lasted until October before going back to English.

Although economics and politics were taught in college for the first year, Audrey was doing PPE, so she had to attend philosophy lectures and tutorials at a men's college. She put all her energy into her studies and took her work seriously, faced with great tomes by Adam Smith and John Maynard Keynes on economics and Descartes, Spinoza, Kant and Hume on philosophy. The sheer volume of reading required for the courses took her all the time she had during term and in the holidays. There was little time for travel during the vacations since so much of it was taken up with preparing for the next term.

One of her delights was to organise reading parties during the long summer break. Audrey's parents were usually away during June and July, so Audrey and her friends would descend on Souldern Court armed with piles of books and share long summer days lazing in the garden, swimming in the pool and walking in the fields surrounding the village with Audrey's spaniel, Bang. The dog developed a serious addiction to bull's eyes (sticky, black and white candy sweets), which Mamie would buy in seven-pound tins and leave for Audrey and her friends. 'At the sound of the tin being opened, he woke from a deep sleep and sat up instantly – and he always got a bull's eye for his pains. My friends were much taken with this trick, and Bang was ready to oblige every time.'

At school, there had been no opportunities to meet young men, and she did not appear to have a boyfriend at Oxford, but rather enjoyed the company of her female companions. It is possible that she was rather off-putting to men her own age, with her studious nature and her sudden outbursts of passion followed by periods of quiet moody introspection. Once at Oxford she began to explore more serious matters in her letters to Paul Nash, and he responded with understanding:

> You seem very earnest about human relationships – what has happened? But I'm glad about your new room with the window seat and the pyracantha . . . You wrote nicely about it so that I could get a picture of you quite clearly until you reflected upon the phenomenon of rabbits bolting at the sight of you making you ashamed – 'as if I'd done something wicked'.

Paul Nash continued to advise Audrey on everything from the way she dressed – in a little sleeveless black dress with a silver underskirt that she described to him and he drew her in from his imagination – to comments on how she was changing now that she was at Oxford:

> I warn you of one thing – you're not to get too hearty, I perceived a distressing cheery-o-ness and topholiness in

you last time, which grieved me very much. If you would enjoy the savour of life, keep to an extent quiet on the other hand, there is nothing easier than to miss it all, by making too much noise, because all the really funny, odd people who might give you a tip or two will be frightened and avoid you. Only the most obvious crude and 'jolly' people will be your companions and the weary of heart will wither away.

He immediately qualified that criticism by explaining that he knew, as 'an expert in heartiness himself', that it was a valuable disguise for one's innermost feelings but that it should never be allowed to smother one's personality. Explorations into matters of a personal nature like this continued throughout her years at Oxford. The letters came perhaps twice, sometimes three times a term, and were well thumbed and read by Audrey. Some were even smudged where her hands had held the paper tightly, with emotion.

Then one day, when Audrey was twenty-one, Paul Nash arrived at Souldern Court to find her not there.

'I suppose you'll get above yourself if I tell you I miss you – I'll risk it anyhow – I miss you very much,' he wrote, almost as if it were a surprise to him.

I have everything in my favour – perfect weather, comfort, hospitality, affection, peace. What I do lack – perhaps the feeling of adventure – do you represent an adventure – no more than an abstract sensation? It sounds a little imper-tinent but I suppose in a way you are responsible – you are a symbol as well as a self, perhaps that is why you have left such a large gap and to think too that you are one of the

quietest listeners now living – when anyone has something
to tell worth hearing . . . Oh, it's most tiresome of you not
to be here, I am in a mischievous mood – the woods and
fields invite. It is so warm – what is the use of my coming
to Oxford? No, you have messed it badly.

This marked a shift in their relationship. Earlier in the year he
had written to her saying that he would not be gushed over and
that he wanted to have their friendship on equal terms. Now
he had admitted to himself and to her that it was really she
that he had come to see at Souldern, and not her parents. He
was also aware that Mamie was no longer blind to the interest
he showed in her daughter and it worried her, not just because
Paul was already married, but because the lop-sided friendship
stopped Audrey from making any moves towards relationships
with men of her own age. He knew Mamie was concerned, but
he could not resist Audrey:

You are rather like a very young animal all over the place,
kicking up your heels and scampering round in circles,
it's charming to watch you and very tempting to run after
you but I feel it's my place to sit on a wall and say 'woa!
Steady!' – from time to time at least, especially when your
dear mother's expression rises to my mind! But I'll join in
the chase on occasions – in the future, when they're the
right occasions.

By the time Audrey left Oxford, she had worked through some
of her doubts and anxieties. The combination of Paul Nash's
loving, teasing letters that spoke to her innermost private

thoughts and the combative tutorial system that pitched her, weekly, against the intellectual muscle of Oxford, had given her a strong sense of self. She graduated from Oxford in June 1927 with a second-class degree in PPE. That year, five girls were awarded a first-class degree. Audrey was evidently disappointed to miss out and told Hugh Fausset that she felt she had let herself down. He wrote back by return: 'A second is the degree that all the really best people take. A first smacks of pedantry, a third of mediocrity, a fourth of stupidity, but a second of talent, vivacity, genius!' Whether or not she was convinced by this argument, she never said, but she asked Hugh to try to help her find an entrée into journalism.

Audrey was clear in her own mind that from now on she would have to make her own way in the world. She had lived off her parents for twenty years and she was not prepared to go home and wait for a husband to turn up. She was determined to earn her own living and fulfil a personal promise she had made to her uncle, Harry Summers, that she would never marry for money. The determination never to have to rely on anyone else for financial support in order to live was a driving force in Audrey's life. When it did once occur, it had a very bad effect on her. The only parental advice she received on leaving home was a strange remark from Percy that she should beware of the effect of the night air on sherry.

This fierce sense of independence was probably the result of watching the impressive women around her at school and university, but it had its roots in her mother's subservience to her father. One of the contradictions about Mamie that Audrey never understood was how a highly educated, intelligent woman could eschew all opportunities for self-betterment and further education that reading might offer her. Never once did Audrey see her mother reading a book, even though Percy's immense library was at her disposal. Every year during the annual spring clean Mamie would personally take every one of the four thousand volumes off the bookshelves in his library, dust them and return them to the clean shelves, but never once did she open any of those books.

Audrey joked that even as a small child she could remember her mother falling asleep in the middle of reading a book to the girls, and how she and Monica would have to wake her up to read the rest of the story. Whether this was Mamie's own, private rebellion against her overbearing husband or whether there was some other reason is unclear. Mamie was a letter-writer, however, and those letters that remain are delightful. She wrote fluently and with humour, sometimes addressing the political issues of the day, but more often giving details about the garden. She was a knowledgeable plants-woman and regularly made gifts of cuttings or plants to her friends, accompanied by instructions as to how they should be cared for.

For Audrey, the picture seemed one of subservience to her father's needs, particularly after his health began to decline again in early 1921. It started with a raging thirst that was quickly diagnosed as diabetes. At the time, this was an untreatable condition that generally proved fatal after one or two years. For over a year, Percy's diabetes dominated life at Souldern Court. He had a letter-weighing machine in front of his place at the table and he would weigh all his food in fractions of ounces.

Meals were an ordeal for us all. My father experienced – and characteristically exulted in – visions and hallucinations such as those described by fasting monks; but he became desperately close to a skeleton, and was weak and tired.

In 1922, insulin was discovered and administered to patients, and so once more Percy's life was saved by a whisker.

Audrey was aware of an underlying friction between her parents that went beyond Percy's health. As he continued entertaining and buying drawings and prints as often as he could, Mamie was responsible for the household budget that was stretched to breaking point by his activities. It is unwritten but for one mention, that the main problem arose from the fact that Percy had no income of his own and was dependent on his wife's dwindling capital and the small stipend she received from the family steel works. It would come to a head in the mid-1930s, but for now it was a matter that rumbled on quietly in the background, and one of which Audrey and Monica were aware, hence Audrey's bold statement that she would never want to be dependent on her parents for money.

The other issue that had an impact on family life was Audrey's little brother, Michael. He had some form of undiagnosed learning difficulties, which led Audrey to conclude that he was born into the wrong family. Percy always expected high standards of education and culture among people who surrounded him. Michael could not live up to this, so was a major disappointment to his father. He was sent away to school but was deemed unteachable, one school after another asking Percy and Mamie to take him away.

He seemed to have no ability to use either hand or brain in any constructive way . . . The tragic result was that a black cloud hung over them. He lived with our parents because he could not live alone. My father withdrew into himself, except for occasional outbursts. My mother was alone between them.

Audrey believed that this led to unhappiness in her parents' marriage. They could not converse with small talk over dinner with Michael present and Percy was not able to offer any form of intellectual forgiveness to his son. He shared his thoughts with his many correspondents, including Paul Nash, who once wrote to him to say: 'Mick will surprise you all one day.'

Sadly, Michael did not surprise Percy in the way that Nash had hoped, and by the mid-1930s Audrey and Monica were so concerned about the situation at home that they seriously considered suggesting their parents should separate, with Mamie and Michael staying in Oxfordshire and Percy moving to London to live with Monica. In the end, they decided against the idea, but they made sure that Percy spent as much time as he could visiting them when he made his trips to London for National Trust meetings. They took him to the cinema, which he loved, and they entertained him at home in later years. It is typical, and sad, that there is no mention of Mamie ever having come to London to see the girls. She remained in Oxfordshire with her troubled son.

NEW SHOES

'I'm fearfully, frightfully and awfully glad that you've got a job
that fits you at more than one of your many facets of taste and
ability . . . I know the paper and agree with you *Vogue* seems to
me, as a mere man, to be the best, as you say it is, and you jolly
well ought to know.'

— F. L. GRIGGS TO AUDREY,
27 NOVEMBER 1931

Audrey moved to London in the autumn of 1927, having spent
a last, long summer at home. This included a trip to Yorkshire
with her parents to witness the total eclipse of the sun, and
visits from Oxford friends to Souldern, which gave occasion to
long discussions about their futures. Audrey's degree did not
lead to any profession and her principal interest was literature.
Paul Nash was sure that the BBC or an enlightened publisher
'will know upon which sides its or his bread is buttered', but
she was keen to get into journalism. She asked Hugh Fausset to
introduce her to his professional friends, but nothing came of it.
Her father had published a book a few years earlier called *Friends
in Solitude* with Jonathan Cape. He organised an interview for

her with the publisher, but they told her that without experience there was no place for her at the company and she would be better trying to find work elsewhere, possibly in a bookshop if books were her passion. She agreed and set about trying to find a job in London.

First, she had to find somewhere to live. She moved into an unfurnished flat in Bramerton Street, off the King's Road, with three friends. The road comprised terraced villas with basements and the girls had a room each, with a tiny shared kitchen with a bath behind a curtain in the same room, on the first floor of the house. In those days, the property-owner had complete run of the premises, and Audrey had several encounters with her unpleasant landlord, who was far too intimate with his roaming hands for her liking, and she had to fend him off on more than one occasion. But life was fun and the flat alive with the comings and goings of four twenty-somethings, all buzzing with energy and excitement. They exchanged clothes and shoes regularly and discussed the short hairstyles of the day over cups of tea in the tiny kitchen. 'When our social life was in full swing, those who were entertaining at home moved one another's pans off the gas rings, while those going out pushed through to wash.'

They had all been to university or college and were part of the up-and-coming class of girls who did not belong to the aristocracy or the Bright Young Things, but were destined to spend some, or in Audrey's case all, of their lives working for a living. At times it felt a little risky after the safety of home and university, but above all it felt thrilling to be free to make their own mistakes and learn lessons from them. Audrey had no idea how to cook or run a flat, but others who had studied at Oxford were dismissive of such shortcomings:

As one of my contemporaries said, when her neighbours
were surprised that she had created a beautiful garden, she
knew how to read and there were plenty of gardening books.
We were thorough in what we did and our trained minds
proved adaptable.

Audrey never developed into a home-maker. She learned to
cook but only to feed herself and took little interest in gourmet
food until she was in her forties. She had few possessions and
fewer clothes, but her floor was always piled with books and
magazines that she had bought or borrowed from the library.
She would sooner spend money on a book than on a new dress.

She arrived in London just as the roaring '20s were fizzling
out. The Great Strike had happened during her last year
at Oxford and, being politically minded and naturally left-
leaning, she was aware of the problems facing the country. At
the same time, she was young, excited and anxious to find her
feet in her new life. London was a world away from Souldern.
There were cars, bicycles and lorries everywhere, people were
constantly in a hurry and the noise was incessant. Audrey loved
it. She felt immediately at home in the capital and it was where
she would spend the rest of her life, bar a few years in Essex
in the early 1960s.

A week or so after she moved into Bramerton Street, she
applied for a job at J & E Bumpus on Oxford Street on the
recommendation of Maur Griggs. He wrote to tell her that he
had talked to the manager of Bumpus, John Wilson, and asked
him to come straight out with whether he wanted Audrey to
work for him or not. Wilson said he was trying to find the right
department that would keep her interested and ensure that

she did not leave within the first few weeks. He also admitted he was testing her to see whether she was really serious about working there. At the time, Bumpus was one of the oldest and most famous bookshops in London, so a job there was a lucky strike and he wanted to make sure she appreciated this.

Audrey was employed on the first floor in the bound books department in October. Surrounded by wooden bookcases ten shelves high, each topped with a bust of a famous writer, she felt as if she were in an extension of her father's library. This was the department that attracted the attention of the wealthy and aristocratic who brought their clothbound books into the shop to be rebound in pigskin or calf, usually with some form of heraldic emblem. At first, she was thrilled with her new job. She wrote to Maur Griggs to thank him for introducing her to John Wilson and telling him how much she loved it, though she realised the glamour and fun would wear off a bit after a while. She described Wilson as fascinating and impish.

The work was not challenging and although she loved being surrounded by books, she found the predominantly male staff dismissive of a young, enthusiastic Audrey in their midst. She was also shocked that she was expected to bow and scrape to the customers in such an obsequious way, but the manager in charge of Bibles told her firmly that royalty and aristocracy expected to be treated as a separate class. This did not sit well with Audrey's natural inclinations and within a few months she had begun to find the atmosphere stultifying and the glamour of her job soon wore off, as she had predicted.

Her friends tried to distract her with entertainment in the evenings. Maur Griggs took her to see Gracie Fields, which they both loved, especially when she sang 'Sally', her most famous song. Paul Nash was working towards an exhibition at the Leicester Galleries, which Audrey was due to attend. Knowing that she was not happy at Bumpus, he made the effort to meet her for tea whenever he could,

> as long as it contributes to the softening of your harsh task among those repellent books. I can see that all the elderly gentlemen who serve Bibles adore you, which is a comforting reflection for what their lives could have been before you came I dare not conjecture.

She joked with Nash that she had received a pay rise of five shillings to thirty shillings a week, but that it was almost certainly in order to make sure she did not leave: 'It is comforting to hear you are more important to Bumpus by the sum of 5 bob a week but my poooooor Audrey, you must be bored with bibles!'

Audrey was indeed bored with Bibles and bound books, but she was afraid to make a move to find another job. She had confided in Hugh Fausset a year after she started work that she found it dull and he wrote to ask her whether a line of escape into a more significant landscape had opened up. She replied that she was considering broadening her mind by writing book reviews, but he advised her against it, saying he hoped that she would soon break out into some 'enormous but fantastic indiscretion'.

Nash was equally supportive, sympathising with her plight:

> Don't stand any nonsense from old Wilson. I believe he's an awful old humbug. I shall come to enquire for an old bound book the next time I am in town and I shall do my best to make you misbehave.

By now, the friendship between Audrey and Paul Nash had graduated to a more equal partnership. They began to attend concerts together and he was always encouraging her to stretch herself and take bolder steps to get out and about to meet people.

After three years of bound books at Bumpus, Audrey finally plucked up the courage to make a move. She was still focused on the idea of getting into publishing, so she applied for a job at *The Times* Bookshop, where she worked for a few months before joining the advertising department of a small publishing house in the West End. She got the job despite the fact she had no experience in advertising and told her boss openly that this was the case.

All went well until the publisher decided that what was required was a man. He was quite specific: the company needed a man. With that, 26-year-old Audrey was made redundant for the first and only time in her life, but it had a disproportionate effect on her morale. This was 1931, the height of the recession that had followed the stock market crash of two years earlier, and she had six months with no income. It was the fact that she had been told that they needed a man to replace her, not another woman with experience, that really stung. The combination of the two sent her into a period of depression, which she would later describe as being more painful than the break-up of a marriage or a bereavement.

Mamie was sufficiently concerned about Audrey's mental state that she wrote an anguished letter to Paul Nash begging him to visit her and 'throw her a lifebelt in her distress'. Nash was unable to help on this occasion. A recurrence of what he described as the introspective neurasthenic complex stopped him 'on the threshold of my purpose' from getting the lifebelt to Audrey in the storm. Her immediate financial worries were sorted out by Harry Summers, her mother's youngest brother, who came to her aid with the sum of two shillings a week. It was a deliberate move on his part to give her enough money to keep her from having to give up her London flat, but not enough on which to live comfortably. She had to find a job.

Over the course of several months she applied for every job she could find in the advertising pages of newspapers but got few replies. Then she answered an advertisement in the classified section of the *Evening Standard* for the post of subeditor at a well-known fashion magazine. She was offered an interview and it was then that she learned the magazine was *Vogue*. When her friends got back from work, Audrey was in a state of great excitement tinged with anxiety. Her aunt subscribed to *Vogue*, so she was aware of its existence, but she had no idea about what went on behind the scenes and indeed what sort of impression she would have to make.

What would she wear for an interview at such a prestigious magazine? Her crêpe de Chine dress from Somerville days was deemed too dressy and out of date, while the navy-blue dress with white collar from Bumpus days was dismissed as too bookish. Her friends all rallied round Audrey, who sat in the kitchen, astonished to be the centre of so much attention. Dresses, skirts, blouses, jackets, shoes and scarves wheeled around the room, scrutinised by the collected quartet and were dismissed or set aside for another look. This skirt was too short, that dress too dowdy, those shoes would make her too tall. Amid much laughter and loud expressions of delight or horror, Audrey was kitted out in an elegant hotchpotch of borrowed garments and delivered to One New Bond Street for her interview with Miss Powell.

Hilda Powell was *Vogue* magazine's managing editor, second in command to the editor, Alison Settle. Already over forty, Miss Powell had come to *Vogue* from the *Daily Telegraph* and had been accustomed to the cut and thrust of daily news, so that a fortnightly magazine seemed almost gentle by comparison. Her manner and appearance were reassuringly human and Audrey felt instantly at home. Audrey characterised her as an accomplished professional with a strong but calm personality, quiet humour and endless patience. The latter was a vital requisite for the temperamental characters who blew in and out of the editorial office from other departments.

Audrey remembered nothing of her interview, but she was immediately offered the job of subeditor to Miss Powell and introduced to Alison Settle, who seemed to Audrey to be sophisticated beyond anyone she had met before. That was until Madge Garland, the fashion editor, appeared in the corridor. She was the slimmest and most elegant woman Audrey had ever set eyes on. She wore long waisted dresses that accentuated her languid movements, and she spoke with insouciance and wrote about fashion with an intelligent wit that Audrey soon learned hid a very deep and fundamental understanding of the industry. Lisa Cohen, Garland's biographer, wrote:

> In her meticulous and unsentimental journalism, she grappled with this issue, grasped the world of haute couture as popular entertainment, and presented herself as a character in that story – a participant-observer, expert but amused, often self-mocking.

The world of fashion was an exacting one and tough on those who tried to enter it. Alison Settle described it as open to the well-trained but that it would only remain open to those who had the combination of fine techniques and great resilience. Audrey was on a steep learning curve, but she felt fired up as she had never done at Bumpus. Her new world was to be a place where words mattered. It was journalism at last and she was thrilled. She wrote to Maur Griggs to tell him how excited she was, assuring him that *Vogue* was the very best magazine of its kind and that 'clothes are thrilling!'. He agreed and said that the job would fit 'more than one of her facets of taste and ability'.

Miss Powell had a desk in an office next door to Audrey, who shared her room with the editorial secretary, whose job it was to keep up to speed with the copy that was produced by Audrey and others. They were located on the top floor of a brand-new building in New Bond Street with three impressive domes, each housing a director. The walls of Audrey's office were covered in spreads of the current and future issues of the magazine that they were working on. It was her responsibility to get to grips with every aspect of her new role. Audrey soon proved to be highly efficient, with a tidy mind that could hold on to multiple threads at a time. She said that her great good luck had been to land such an outstanding teacher. 'There has never been anyone to touch her since,' she wrote after Miss Powell's death.

~

When Audrey Withers walked into One New Bond Street and took the lift to the top floor for her first day at work for British

Vogue, she had no idea that she would make her entire career with Condé Nast Publications. In fact, she knew nothing of the history of the magazine, nor of the organisation behind it. All she knew as she walked past the receptionist and the assistant receptionist was that she was going to have to prove she was a fast learner.

By the time Audrey joined the staff of *Vogue*, the magazine was into its second decade in Britain and its fourth in the USA. It was, and has remained, the world's pre-eminent fashion magazine. Its dominance after almost 130 years is down to a combination of factors, but the overarching characteristic is excellence. From the beginning, it championed excellence in all areas, from drawing and photography to editorial independence and the quality of its content. It has also had the confidence to change with the times, which was a key requirement in the middle of the twentieth century.

Vogue was launched in New York in December 1892. An American publisher, Arthur Turnure, wanted to create a magazine that would establish 'a dignified, authentic journal of society, fashion and the ceremonial side of life, that is to be, for the present, mainly pictorial.' It was published weekly and cost ten cents a copy or four dollars a year. Although the magazine had an amateur quality, it had

a well-bred atmosphere that gave it a social prestige that was never questioned. No publication in America mirrored so faithfully the society and fashions of the nineties, their inanities as well as their substance, their virtues as well as their follies.

Turnure sacked his first editor, who hated fashion but was passionate about animals. Dogs, cats, donkeys and even lions appeared in the early editions.

Three years after *Vogue* started, a young girl from New Jersey, Edna Woolman Alloway, joined the circulation department. Her job was to write the names of new subscribers in the margins of the printed list and to address envelopes. Determined to work as hard as she could and make a good impression, she got more envelopes out than any other girl, but many were returned with the complaint that her writing was illegible. 'Burning with shame,' she wrote, 'I determined then and there that I would become a star in penmanship.' Edna would rise to become the single greatest influence on the content of *Vogue* worldwide over the course of the first half of the twentieth century. She was also the most important influence on Audrey Withers' career, and it was their relationship that would help to shape British *Vogue* in the future.

Edna was small in stature, with what Audrey would later describe as birdlike features, but what she lacked in size she made up for in personality. Outspoken, confident and demanding of her staff, she quickly gained a reputation for excellent editorial skills and, later, a sound understanding of business. She was also loyal and kind, something that manifested itself in her support for those colleagues who she loved and admired, including Audrey. For those who betrayed her trust, she had only scorn. One contradictory aspect of her character was her lack of willingness to support the cause of women in the workplace. Although she was fiercely independent and determined to have a career, she did not embrace the notions of feminism that were around at the time.

In 1902, Edna married Frank Chase, the son of a banker from Boston, whom she described as loveable, good-looking and irresponsible. They had a daughter, Ilke, three years later and Edna realised from the outset that the child would be entirely her responsibility. Sure enough, their marriage ended in divorce, and Edna found herself alone with a small child and an important career ahead of her.

In the spring of 1906, Arthur Turnure died unexpectedly, leaving *Vogue* rudderless but in good shape. Three years later, a new figure, who was becoming the talk of the publishing world in the United States, stepped onto the scene and bought *Vogue*. Condé Montrose Nast was thirty-six years old when he took the helm, and his name first appeared on the masthead on 24 June that year. Born in New York in 1873, he was brought up in St Louis after his father left home when he was three years old. His unusual name came from his mother's side of the family, which could trace its lineage directly back to Dr André August Condé, a military surgeon who had come from France in 1760 to establish a practice in St Louis on the banks of the Mississippi. His paternal grandfather had founded German Methodism in America. In her recent biography of Condé Nast, Susan Ronald summed him up as 'shy, meticulous, highly numerate, and driven to succeed. He had a rare aesthetic vision and a love of beauty – and women.'

After an education at Georgetown University, paid for by a wealthy aunt, Condé Nast had joined *Collier's Weekly* as he had become friends with the proprietor's son, Robert J. Collier, at university. He spent ten years working for the publication and by the time he left was being paid $40,000 a year, which was the highest salary of anyone in American magazine publishing.

Determined to make his own fortune, he left *Collier's* and began working on a pattern catalogue called *Home Pattern*. He soon realised that it was the women who did the majority of the buying and he learned to appeal to this audience. One of his innovations was clothes sizing. It seems unthinkable now, but at that time patterns were all produced to one size. He observed that neither Turnure's *Vogue* nor his other main rival, *Butterick Patterns*, had any size other than a thirty-six.

Condé Nast introduced sizing based on a study of proportions, and it became a winning formula. 'Condé's "maddening sense of detail" had made the company's and his first fortune', Ronald wrote. His other study led him to conclude that it was not sensible to follow the received wisdom, which was to build circulation to appeal to the multitudes. He understood that quality not quantity would win out in the end, especially when it came to harnessing advertising revenue. By the early years of the twentieth century, he was looking around for a publication that could fulfil his needs. Although it was not perfect, *Vogue* was the best fit he could find. Its emphasis on quality and its appeal to the upper echelons of society were a good start. He would develop the rest over the next few years.

When he took over, the staff at *Vogue* were nervous. Condé Nast had a reputation for being extremely shrewd and skilful at hiding his thoughts. Edna later described him as shy, with impeccable manners and a man devoted to party-giving. As it happened, he made few changes at *Vogue* initially, keeping the current editor in place and retaining Edna and other staff members. It later transpired that he had been focused on his passion for figures. 'He lusted over mathematics; endless pages of figures and tabulated statements and comparative statistics covered his desk.' It was only once he had fully grasped the financial situation and developed a plan for the future of *Vogue* that he began to consider the editorial side of his new enterprise.

Six months after he purchased *Vogue*, Condé Nast made his first major change. 'Beginning with spring fashion forecast number of February fifteenth, *Vogue* will be issued under a plan that will make for a bigger, a better and a still more attractive *Vogue*.' It would appear fortnightly rather than weekly from now onwards. He wanted to improve the magazine in every way, with colour covers, greatly enhanced presentation and over sixty pages of advertising. His belief was that advertising and editorial should be separated and that the magazine should sell for less than it cost to produce so that the subscribers would feel they had more than just value for money. This was at a time when advertising was considered a by-product of editorial. He was out to publish a first-class magazine that his readers could trust. To that end, he needed to be sure that the quality of the advertisements was as high as the fashion, features and editorial.

Over the next five years, Condé Nast consolidated his position, improved *Vogue*'s appearance and increased its circulation. As a result the magazine's status rose and rose. Edna Woolman Chase had been promoted from editorial assistant to managing editor, a role that encompassed all the nuts and bolts of editorial implementation but not control of content. Condé Nast admired Edna's thoroughness, her meticulous attention to detail and her preparedness to undertake the more menial of tasks if she felt it led to a better outcome. In time, he promoted her to editor and in 1914 she was listed on the masthead for the first time. When he was ready to broaden the scope of his publications and launch international editions in London and Paris, Edna was promoted to editor-in-chief and wielded her editorial pencil over all three magazines.

The First World War had an enormous impact on *Vogue*, but it had an even greater impact on the fashion world for one very simple reason: until 1914, Paris had been the default centre of fashion, scent and female beauty in general. New York and London high society looked to Paris to decide on waistlines, hemlines, bust, and every other detail in between. If Paris trussed, the rest of the world trussed with it. If French couturiers told their clients to breathe in while they tightened their corsets by an inch, the Americans and British breathed in even harder. Feathers, or no feathers; pine marten or silver fox; silk or wool. Every detail was followed, every trend scrutinised as the dressmakers in New York and London raced to beat each other to the French patterns while the manufacturers overdid themselves to make viable copies. It was a twice-yearly race for the summer and winter fashions and *Vogue* followed it all minutely. In those days, the idea of a pre-season showing was way in the future. What the press got to see were the finished models when they appeared.

In August 1914, Europe descended into the bloodiest and most destructive war in history. The lines were drawn up and ground was fought over, lost or won by feet and yards, over the course of four bitter years. Condé Nast was keenly aware of the plight of the widows and orphans in France after the first Battle of the Marne, when the French sustained 250,000 casualties, of which 80,000 died. It might seem frivolous, among the slaughter and bloodshed of the First World War, for anyone to be contemplating anything as light-hearted as fashion, but as Edna pointed out:

> In France, the *couture* is both an art and a vital industry in
> which the government has always taken a lively interest.
> The French dressmakers were caught at the very moment
> of showing their autumn collections, involving thousands
> of people and millions of francs.

This was a question that would recur over just over two decades
later, but for now it was answered by the French shutdown of
all the couture houses. The fashion trade as a whole, but particularly in New York, found itself at a loss without the stamp
of Paris's authority, and Edna had a magazine to publish.

Edna wracked her brains about what she could possibly do
to fill the pages of *Vogue* while at the same time supporting the
Allied war effort. She recalled the doll shows she had featured
in *Vogue* in the 1890s when miniature figurines had been dressed
by New York houses and photographed for the magazine. Could
this not be organised on a human scale? She proposed her idea
to Henri Bendel, who ran the smartest shop in New York. Edna
suggested that *Vogue* could organise an exhibition of original
couture designs, created by the best fashion houses of New
York, presented on living models. Receipts from the admission
charges would be sent to a French charity to support widows
and orphans. Bendel was supportive, Condé Nast scathing. A
new idea at such a time seemed ludicrous, and he was sceptical
whether members of New York society would ever agree to
support something so blatantly commercial.

Edna was not going to give up. She enlisted the support of
some of New York's most influential women and soon a committee of society's grandees agreed to select garments for the
show. However, there was the problem of mannequins. Until this

time, no clothes had been modelled on a woman who moved; they were shown on static figures, in drawings and occasionally photographs, and worn by women in society. Edna advertised for girls of a certain height, weight, age and experience. She was unsure as to whether the stringent requirements would mean they had few applications. In fact, the opposite was the case. They were flooded with applicants who almost beat down the office doors in their excitement, some more suitable than others, but all clamouring for *Vogue*'s attention. Not only did this show Edna that there was appetite for a fashion show in New York society, but it also convinced her that *Vogue* had a far wider audience than she and Condé Nast had realised. Even though the majority of those women were not subscribers to the magazine, they read it in the homes of their employers. They too wanted to dream.

The first fashion fete in history took place on 4 November 1914 and on two successive afternoons and evenings. Society women mingled with dressmakers and models, all focused on the clothes on show. The world of fashion had just taken a giant step, and one from which it could never retreat: the fashion show as we know it today had been born on American soil. *Vogue* reaped widespread praise and prestige from the event, and their advertising revenue soared. Condé Nast was the first to admit that Edna had been right all along, not least as his greatest rival, Hearst, who owned *Harper's Bazaar*, had been caught on the back foot and had not benefited from *Vogue*'s bold venture. Although the reception in New York was ecstatic, the noise in Paris was cacophonous and derisory. Egged on by Hearst, the couturiers believed that they had been abandoned by the Americans and it took a great deal of diplomacy, and the offer of a French fashion fete in New York, sponsored by *Vogue*, to reassure them. Eventually Paris was mollified and once again opened its doors to New York.

Vogue was published only in New York, but it had an eager readership in London and Paris. In the pre-war years, issues of *Vogue* were sent to Germany, to be distributed throughout the continent and to Britain, where it was seized upon by female readers from society. These were women who, like their American counterparts, looked to Paris for the latest word on fashion and had their clothes made by dressmakers at home.

Condé Nast was anxious to find some way to obtain British advertising for American *Vogue* and from 1912 he worked with an energetic British entrepreneur publisher called William Wood, who took it upon himself to get *Vogue* distributed around the bookstalls of London, especially in the West End, where high fashion was a serious topic of discussion. He promised Nast sales of 1,000 copies an issue, and that grew to nearly 4,000 copies by 1914. At the outbreak of the war, with Paris out of the picture, sales increased further. No one in New York could believe it, but Edna concluded that '*Vogue* is about women and their frills and furbelows; it is a vastly different diet from mud and uniforms, boredom and death.'

For two years, circulation in Britain maintained its high level until German submarine warfare meant that paper supplies were restricted and non-essential shipping was cut to almost nothing. William Wood travelled to New York to try to persuade Condé Nast to go the whole hog and produce an edition of *Vogue* in Britain along with British advertising. The case was well made and Condé Nast agreed. Thus, London *Vogue*, or *Brogue* as it was always referred to in the New York office to differentiate it from its American parent, was born. At the outset, New York shipped over fashion material and a little editorial with the idea that gradually local material would feature in *Brogue* with articles on society, shops and entertainment in much the same vein as it did in New York. When Condé Nast launched the French edition of *Vogue* in 1924, it was known as *Frogue*, but this got shortened to 'Frog', which was understandably not popular with the French and was soon dropped.

Like its American counterpart, *Brogue* was published fortnightly, but unlike American *Vogue* it was losing money hand over fist and Condé Nast considered more than once, and with great seriousness, closing down his London venture. It had suffered from an unsatisfactory run of editors from the US perspective. The first, Elspeth Champcommunal, edited *Brogue* from 1916 to 1922, when she returned to France to work as a fashion designer in her own right. She believed that *Brogue* should be more than just a fashion magazine and should contain articles on more than just beauty, society and entertainment, but also on health, sport and travel as well as containing opinion pieces. The person on whom Elspeth Champcommunal relied was Madge Garland, who had started at *Vogue* while William Wood was still in charge. She worked as a messenger, tea girl, stamp buyer and general run-around, but under the editor she also learned a great deal about the world of fashion.

Elspeth Champcommunal was succeeded by Dorothy Todd, who many credit with transforming the magazine into 'a tour-de-force of fashion, art, literature and journalism'. She had briefly edited *Vogue* in 1916, but now she was in charge and determined to make her mark. Edna had a different take: 'The atmosphere she created was lofty and she was browsing happily in rich pasture. Unfortunately, from our point of view, it was the wrong one.'

Todd and Garland were a dynamic duo, openly gay, and celebrated by the Bloomsbury set. It was they who discovered the artist and photographer Cecil Beaton while still a Cambridge undergraduate, who was desperate to get his work shown in *Vogue*. He told Madge Garland that a new edition of *Vogue* was regarded as an event of importance, eagerly awaited by him and his friends in Cambridge. Madge encouraged him and in time he would meet Edna Woolman Chase and become the most significant artistic contributor to *Vogue* in the first half of the twentieth century.

Condé Nast had set up a branch of his corporation in London and in 1921 he appointed a very able ex-army officer with a distinguished First World War record, and an American wife, to be the managing director of Condé Nast Publications Ltd. Major Harry Waldo Yoxall MC and bar was twenty-five years old and had no interest in fashion, but he had a shrewd mind and a good understanding of figures. He said years later that his favourite scent was the printer's ink. He had been working in the promotion department at *Vanity Fair* in New York when Nast cabled him from London and asked him to take charge of his ailing publication: 'I say "asking" but really it was commanding; he was a Napoleonic type.'

Harry Yoxall was the ideal man to take responsibility for Condé Nast's business in the UK. He had the ability to focus on detail but keep in mind the bigger picture, which is exactly what Nast appreciated. Yoxall was a stickler and resisted all attempts to Americanise the language in *Brogue*. On one occasion, an employee received a memo from him saying that if the man ever used the word 'finalise' again, 'I will finalise your appointment with Condé Nast Publications.' Despite a gruff voice and, at times, an austere appearance, Harry Yoxall had a gift for making friends and putting people at their ease. Even in the 1950s, when he had been at Condé Nast Publications for thirty years, he commanded respect and admiration for his human touch with his employees. If a member of staff went off sick, he would telephone and arrange a visit, arriving with a bunch of flowers and a kindly word for the patient. He was unfailing in his generosity towards people with personal problems, and only when they seriously threatened the magazine's future did he act.

In September 1926, Harry Yoxall fired Dorothy Todd on Condé Nast's instructions on account of her editorial shortcomings. She threatened to sue. They both attacked her morals in public and she backed down. The affair had a dramatic impact in Bloomsbury, with people springing to her defence. Vita Sackville-West wrote, 'So poor Todd is silenced since her morals are of the classic rather than the conventional order.' Some staff resigned in protest and contributors stepped away, but Edna got to work immediately to find a new editor and to transform her into the right image of a *Vogue* representative. Madge Garland was dismissed at the same time as Dorothy Todd, but would later return as fashion editor.

Todd's shoes were filled by Alison Settle, who was appointed by Edna to move British *Vogue* more into the mainstream and to expand the magazine's readership to encompass more middle-class women. Britain in the 1930s had a burgeoning middle class who tended to live in the suburbs and were married to teachers, civil servants and professionals. The wives often had university or college education, but above all they had time and money. They were a natural target for *Vogue*, which helped to nurture women's dreams and aspirations. Edna kept a very close eye on the direction of Alison's editing and was frequently caustic. On one occasion, she launched what Harry described in his diary as a violent attack against Alison's work: 'The old bitch has some right on her side, but the manner of her addressing it is inexcusable.'

One issue dominating the behind-the-scenes situation at *Vogue* was finance. In the Wall Street crash of 1929, Condé Nast, one of the richest men in America, had lost almost all his fortune. In the end, the British newspaper publisher Lord Camrose bought shares in Condé Nast and formed a holding company that retained his name and therefore his apparent control. Lord Camrose also gave Condé Nast a free hand in the management of Condé Nast Publications Ltd. It is fascinating that the British ownership of such an important American company was kept secret, even from Fleet Street, where Camrose had his offices in the *Daily Telegraph* building. By the time he bought out Condé Nast, he was the joint owner of Allied Newspapers, which owned the *Daily Dispatch*, the *Manchester Evening Chronicle*, the *Sunday Chronicle*, the *Sunday News* and the *Sunday Graphic*, as well as a string of other newspapers across Britain. Harry Yoxall was summoned to have lunch with Camrose once a year, in total secrecy, to report on the progress of the British company.

By the time Audrey Withers arrived at British *Vogue*, the magazine was into its fifteenth year and in new offices, away from the traditional publishing district around Fleet Street, to be close to the fashion houses, shops, manufacturers and beauty firms where most of their departments operated. Miss Powell believed in letting people learn on the job and she encouraged Audrey to shadow her. Within a few weeks, Audrey was working independently on correcting proofs, measuring type to make sure captions fitted perfectly, and looking out for every tiny detail. Get a turn wrong, that is to say, the page number for the continuation of an article in the back of the magazine, and Mr Yoxall would have something to say about it, she was warned. She learned never to allow a 'widow' to get through, that is a word on its own on a line, and she soon realised that the art editor, James de Holden-Stone had strong feelings about the shape of capital letters at the beginning of a caption. He did not like the first word to start with what he regarded to be a weak letter, such as an 'I'. All this detail had to be absorbed and put into practice with no mistakes. Audrey recounted a tale against herself when, early on, she had written a caption for underwear. She had marked the word 'knickers' to be split after the second k instead of before it. The printer rang the office and said to her, 'Those knickers of yours, Miss Wivvers, they won't split where you want them to.'

Audrey was soon responsible for writing all the captions in the magazine and often other copy as needed. She would be given a description of a photograph and expected to come up with the exact number of words to describe the image and in precisely the space dictated by the art director, who in turn knew the limitations of typesetting. It was at once creative and limiting in equal measure, and it appealed to Audrey's love of detail.

One thing she learned early on was the discipline of working with a writer's copy. Miss Powell told her that under almost no circumstances should copy be altered without an explanation to the writer. This was partly out of respect but also because altering copy could change the sense of an article. It was a valuable lesson and one that she would stick to for the rest of her editing days, even though there were times when she found herself at odds with a contributor over a word or turn of phrase.

The other lesson she learned was the question of *Vogue*'s editorial independence. This had been handed down from New York and had been part of the DNA of the magazine from its inception. Edna, now the editor-in-chief of all three *Vogue* magazines, was fastidious about this. In the early days, she had had heated discussions with advertisers who wanted their work to be included in editorial or with artists who had opinions on how their work should be featured. Audrey would come to have a major disagreement with the fashion designer Edward Molyneux in the early 1940s. She would look back on this training and find it reassuring to know that it had been part of her early education under Miss Powell.

Audrey settled happily into her new life as British *Vogue*'s most junior subeditor. The fortnightly edition gave rhythm to her life and she enjoyed the hustle and bustle in the few days leading up to printing. One of her roles was to go to the printers to oversee the final layouts of the proofs for the next edition. This involved a long day out of the office when she and an assistant from the art department would be holed up in a room at the printers going through every page to check captions, turns, pictures and so forth. It was not unusual for them to get a last-minute change to a layout hurriedly phoned through from the office either by Miss Powell or by Alison Settle's secretary, which would require a frantic juggling of images and text and then a last thorough check and sign-off before the proofs could be released for printing.

This was the most nerve-racking aspect of the job, and to begin with it set Audrey on edge. For days, sometimes weeks, she had looked at the walls behind her desk to watch the spreads for the upcoming issues taking shape. Often an article would be scheduled for one issue but be delayed by a fortnight, four weeks or even longer. Yet once the hard copy was in front of her, it was as if she were seeing it alive and for the first time. This would change over the years and she soon learned how to keep at least three editions in her head at any one time.

On the home front, life was busy and enjoyable. Audrey had moved out of Bramerton Street when two of her flatmates left to get married and rented a flat at 23 Paddington Green with a friend. She loved dancing and would often go out to meet friends at Olympia, where the hall was so vast that two bands were needed to fill the space, or to Covent Garden where the stalls of the opera house were boarded over for part of the year so the young and not so young could dance the evenings away.

Soho was a popular haunt for Audrey and her friends. It was a place of contrasts and excitement. In Berwick Street Market, she would see women in fur stoles jostled past the market stalls by suave young men in silk scarves and wearing eye make-up, while a cockney salesman in a cloth cap would shout out his wares from his small stall selling stockings. Around a corner she might have stumbled on an escapologist trying to impress a small crowd of men, or show girls from the Windmill Theatre. She and her friends would meet up for a glass of wine prior to the theatre or a concert, or simply sit in a café and watch the exotic members of the brand-new Caravan Club, advertised as London's greatest bohemian rendezvous, drifting past the windows. Her other passions were classical music and of course the theatre. Here she had a stroke of luck. Her flatmate was a theatre costume designer who worked as a freelancer, so she got to know a lot of people in the theatrical world. They were regular visitors to West End productions and Audrey was often invited to the dress rehearsals, which suited her budget.

While she was living in Bramerton Street and working for Bumpus, she would go to classical concerts on her own, and this continued in her *Vogue* years. On one occasion, she was sitting alone in the gallery in the Queen's Hall during the interval of a promenade concert when she was spotted by one of the Bumpus sales' staff, a young man called Jock Stewart. They chatted and realised that they shared a passion for the same sort of music. Over the next months they met regularly at concerts and then at dances. Jock was tall, fair-haired and good-looking, with fine facial features and was so charismatic that men and women were equally drawn to him. Audrey would never have been described as beautiful and had recently taken to wearing her hair tied back off her forehead, which made her look more imposing than before. But she had eyes that sparkled when she was animated and made her face light up.

Jock, whose full name was Alan Hay Stewart, was two years younger than Audrey. His father was a professional musician, playing double bass in a London orchestra. Jock had been brought up in the city in straitened circumstances but on a diet of Beethoven and Brahms. He and Audrey made a handsome couple and they were always amused when people mistook

Jock for the actor, Rex Harrison, and approached him for his autograph. What at first was a draw for Audrey, who adored her handsome boyfriend, would later become a problem.

Jock and Audrey's love of music, books and travel brought them ever closer and their friendship blossomed into a happy partnership. He had not been to university, as his father's career meant that there was little family money, and Jock had left school at fourteen to earn a living. Audrey knew that he was intelligent, but he was unhappy about his lack of education, and had a chip on his shoulder. He disliked his job at Bumpus, even though he was regarded as one of the brightest young stars on the sales team. His lack of formal education meant that he did not feel confident to pursue his ambition. What he wanted more than anything else was to be a publisher. He discussed it with Audrey, and later with Harry Yoxall, but this dream eluded him for his entire career.

By 1933, they had been seeing one another for two years. Jock had visited Souldern Court and had been warmly welcomed by Audrey's parents. Initially he found Percy terrifying, but he liked Mamie from the outset and he developed a rapport with Michael, which delighted Audrey. In April, Jock asked her to marry him and they set the date for September that year.

In her autobiography, Audrey dismissed her wedding to Jock in two sentences:

> Our friends had assumed that Jock and I would marry, and one day we did. From my parents' point of view, it must have been an unsatisfactory affair, to a man they had never taken to, and not in church but at a registry office.

In fact, quite the opposite was true. Percy wrote to Maur Griggs a month prior to the wedding of his delight in Audrey and Jock's forthcoming marriage. Griggs wrote back to say that he believed Audrey was one of those fortunate people who married wisely and well.

The night before the wedding, Percy and Mamie threw a large party at Souldern Court for all their friends from Oxfordshire and beyond who would not be able to attend the London event. Maur Griggs was one of the guests and he wrote to Audrey two days before the party asking her to let him know what he could get her as a wedding present:

> You know, dear Audrey, that in terms of mere money I should need to be a very wealthy man indeed to be able to send you something expressive of my love and regard for you, but our values, thank God, are not measured in terms of cash, and it is still possible for me to send you something for yourself and your home which will have some value in your eyes. So will you tell me, if you can?

She was delighted and wrote back asking him to give her one of his engravings, which he duly did.

A. E. Housman wrote her a letter of congratulation and, to Percy's boundless satisfaction, sent her a first edition of *A Shropshire Lad*. Laurence Binyon sent warmest good wishes to the little girl he had known for nearly twenty years, and others showered her with praise and gifts. Percy, always keen to score a point, was especially delighted when one of his correspondents, the American actor Edward Sothern, arrived for the party. It says something about her father that he described

Sothern's arrival and his present of a bouquet of flowers to Audrey, but made no mention of the party itself. Only Paul Nash did not attend either the Souldern Court party or the wedding on the following day. He offered his profound congratulations but signed the letter formally: 'Yours ever, Paul'. It was the last letter he would write to her for nearly a decade.

Jock and Audrey married on 2 September in a London registry office with a reception at Percy's club, the Savile, for 100 guests. The fact that they got married in a registry office was not of the remotest concern to Percy, who was a professed atheist. Mamie might have been disappointed, as she had developed religious beliefs over the past few years and would have liked Audrey to get married in a church, but it was a very happy event that was followed by a four-day honeymoon in Brighton. Audrey and Jock moved into her Paddington flat and his parents moved into the maisonette above so the Stewart family in its full complement of four adults filled the three-storey house.

Audrey was the main wage earner with a salary of thirty-six shillings a week, which was increased by half again by the income from shares in the company of John Summers & Sons, gifted to her by Harry Summers as a wedding present. Jock, by comparison, was still earning a salesman's wage with bonuses. Audrey's salary covered the rent and most of the expenses, which meant that her parents-in-law lived rent free in the maisonette above them.

As she was not interested in domestic matters, Audrey left the running of the household in Paddington Green to her mother-in-law, Elsie. In those days, shops had not opened by the time she left for work in the morning, and they were shut by the time she returned home. Hours at *Vogue* were long, and she was frequently expected to stay well beyond the end of the day if there was a rush job on an issue or something major had cropped up that would affect the workload. She wrote later that she was grateful to Elsie for helping out at the flat. She took the long hours in her stride, but it did not go unnoticed at work and Harry Yoxall was particularly impressed by her dedication to the magazine.

3

STEPPING UP

'I have worked now for almost twenty years, nearly ten of
which have been happily spent in your service. I have never
worked with any group of people anywhere for whose abilities
I had greater respect or for whom I had more affection.'

— BETTY PENROSE TO CONDÉ NAST,
9 AUGUST 1938

1935 was a momentous year for Audrey. In March, she turned
thirty years old and in September she would be promoted
from sub- to managing editor at *Vogue*. Miss Powell, who
had employed Audrey four years earlier, had been diagnosed
with stomach cancer the previous summer and had undergone
surgery. The loss of Miss Powell was a bitter blow on both a
professional and personal level for Audrey. She had been in post
for nearly a decade and was one of the most trusted and diligent
of all the editorial staff in One New Bond Street.

Miss Powell recovered sufficiently to work for *Vogue* on
specific editorial projects, such as editing the cookery books,
but she would never again return to full-time employment.
She retired to a cottage in Dunmow in Essex, but she was not

abandoned by her old employer. Condé Nast Publications in London continued to pay for her medical care right up to the end of her life, which was a full eighteen years after she retired, and she received frequent visits from members of the *Vogue* editorial staff even in the last weeks of her life. She belonged to the *Vogue* family and it was in that spirit of warmth and generosity that she continued to feel a valued member.

It was an unsettling time at the magazine as Condé Nast and Edna were unhappy with the editorship of Alison Settle and they made their views clearly felt. Meantime, Condé Nast had sent a very able editor, Elizabeth 'Betty' Penrose, to shadow Alison and see if she could work out what was going on in London. Audrey was downhearted at the change of managing editor. She naturally would have been Miss Powell's successor, but Betty Penrose took over the role as she continued to shadow Alison Settle and Audrey remained subeditor. For fifteen months after Miss Powell left, it was business as usual, but Audrey found herself having to carry all the responsibility for her own job, plus the majority of the work that Miss Powell had done before she left, with neither a salary rise nor any acknowledgement of her increased workload. Or so she thought. Betty Penrose had indeed noticed, and she wrote a long, confidential letter to Nast a year after her arrival giving an appraisal of the editorial and fashion staff in London.

She praised the staff overall and singled out four key people who made the place run, although 'given a freer rein and the opportunity to use their own initiative their performance would, I am sure, be immeasurably improved'. The first of the four to be named was Audrey. 'Formerly Miss Powell's assistant but has, ever since I've been here, done practically single-handed all the work that it formerly took both her and Miss Powell to accomplish.' Although it would have been Betty's job to be more hands-on managing editorial content, she told Nast that what with shadowing Alison Settle and listening to everyone's difficulties and complaints, she barely had a moment to herself to write a caption or correct a proof. She went on:

> Withers has a ready pen – writes practically every caption and title – edits or re-writes most articles – knows everything about the mechanics of the printing of the book – the ordering of foreign material – plus the miscellaneous details, such as payment slips for outside work done, dealing with our own accounting department on the cost of each issue, making out credit lists for our own advertising department etc. She makes all proof corrections and literally knows everything about the thousand and one things that go into the business of getting the issue out and running the editorial room. I don't think anybody but me realizes how much she does or how well she does it.

She went on to describe how she tried to work alongside Audrey until late hours most nights in the lead-up to an issue going to press, helping as best she could, but admitted,

> I couldn't in a life-time duplicate her performance on detail, at which she is an absolute wizard . . . Her judgment is excellent and her capabilities such that I do not feel you could ever quite replace her. She is the kind of person who is so essential that if she is gone from the office for a day it seriously handicaps things.

After this fulsome praise, Betty sounded a warning bell for Condé Nast: Audrey 'is tremendously good in her job, but at the same time, disheartened. She has been overworked and overlooked so long I'm sure that if she got a better offer she'd leap at it.' Signing off, Betty concluded, 'She's extremely co-operative and easy to work with and she and I get on like sisters.'

It would be hard to find a more generous assessment of Audrey's abilities or, indeed, of her contribution to the magazine at the time. 'With the above, plus an adequate supply of secretaries, there is no reason why, in my opinion, British *Vogue*, under an able and stationary editor who was always on hand to direct and decide, couldn't beat the world.'

Alison Settle had been in post for nearly a decade and although she had an excellent eye and was respected for her in-depth knowledge of the fashion industry, she was autocratic and often difficult to deal with. Edna had picked many fights with her over editorial direction. Although Alison had succeeded in turning *Vogue* away from the Bloomsbury-led direction of her predecessor, Dorothy Todd, the magazine was still losing money. Eventually Alison was demoted and moved to work on special editions. Betty Penrose was promoted to editor and this created the opportunity for Audrey to advance at last. She was invited to cocktails at the RAC Club by Harry Yoxall on 25 September to be told that she would now be *Vogue*'s managing editor in London.

To his surprise, Audrey seemed upset at Alison's demotion, as she had been one of the members of staff who had protested most against Alison's methods, sharing her thoughts with Betty. Nevertheless, she was excited to be confirmed in her new role and she celebrated her promotion and her second wedding anniversary with Jock at a dinner at the Criterion.

As managing editor, she moved towards commissioning, not in her own right but as Betty's right hand. From now on, she met with contributors who wrote about fashion, who produced regular features such as advice on shopping on a limited budget or beauty, but she also began to interact with the men and women who wrote for the society pages and with the artists and photographers. The photographer was king, Audrey wrote later, and with some feeling. For it was this heady mix of brilliant but temperamental stars that breathed unique life into *Vogue* and at the same time made the lives of those who worked with them difficult.

The editorial corridor was a hive of activity, especially in the lead-up to an edition going to press. Editors, contributors, photographers and artists all made their presence felt. Some wafted past Audrey's open door in fine fashion, smelling of perfume and cigarettes. Others scuttled or marched, depending on the nature of their request to the editor or their appeal to Harry Yoxall, if they could not get what they wanted from Audrey or Betty.

Raised voices, quick conferences about a picture or a piece of writing and then a last-minute tweak to the spreads that had to be conveyed down the line from the art editor to the setters and then to the printers. She liked the buzz and pressure of signing off the final proofs and she prided herself that she now knew exactly what the magazine would look like, down to the last line, when it appeared in print a few days later. The last thing she wanted was a surprise.

What actually went on behind the scenes at *Vogue* in order

to produce an edition of the magazine? And what was Audrey's role now that she was managing editor? The hierarchy at *Vogue* in London matched that of New York. The editor had overall control over the magazine and would consult with the managing director about direction of travel. Below her was the managing editor, who kept the wheels turning and who would commission certain photographers and models to undertake photo shoots. She would also co-ordinate all the copy that came in from the features editors (fashion, beauty, social and so on) and be the editor's eyes and ears.

Years later, Audrey described the role as one for a person 'who should by all means invent stories and methods of presentation, but who must get them carried out by the outside staff or contributors, as she herself has so much office responsibility'.

A managing editor's job cannot be handed to anyone on a plate, but is one in which the individual must make a great part of the job for herself through gaining the confidence of the staff, finding the ways of getting the best work out of people, getting them to talk things over with her before taking in a final proposal to the editor, and so on. I think I was able to do a good deal of this sort of work for Betty, and it is what I should like done for myself.

Below the managing editor was the subeditor, who was responsible for writing captions, checking proofs and doing whatever she was asked to do by the senior staff. There were secretaries in each department with a dedicated secretary for the editor and managing editor as well as one each for the features editors, who were frequently out of the office gathering material for their pieces. At a time when everything had to be typed on mechanical typewriters, accuracy was key, and time would be wasted if a secretary introduced typing errors or missed out words.

In 1937, British *Vogue* celebrated its twenty-first birthday and Audrey had been in the role of managing editor for two years. In the first June issue, she had to deal with one of the knottiest questions of the day, so we will examine this edition in detail to lift the veil on how the magazine came together.

The front cover is a painting by Eric, *Vogue*'s long-standing illustrator who worked for the magazine from 1920 to 1958. His full name was Carl Erickson and he came originally from Illinois but moved to New York and then to Senlis in France with his wife, who was also a fashion illustrator. Eric depicted a model in a pink two-piece suit in a garden with a black Scottie dog at her feet. The caption on the masthead reads: 'Pink, once connected chiefly with baby jackets, comes of age in Creed's Tussore suit – audacious with its burnt orange lapels, yet basically simple and perfectly tailored. Eric drew it. Goodbrook has it.' This was written by Audrey and had exactly to fit the five lines allocated to it. She had to split the word Tussore over two lines. It was one of the aspects of her work that depended on her ability to condense or expand not only words but the shapes of letters to fit a space. Today we have software that makes this easy. In 1937, she had learned to do it by eye.

At this time, *Vogue* appeared in twenty-six editions each year, every two weeks on a Wednesday. As Condé Nast had impressed upon New York, so he told London that the magazine should be produced at above cover price. The shortfall would be carried by the advertising revenue and by the late

1930s there was a healthy stream of regular advertisers who took slots in *Vogue*. The first sixty pages of the total 124 for this issue comprised advertisements for high-end shops such as Fortnum & Mason, Debenham & Freebody and Lillywhites, who sold clothing and fashion accessories.

The advertisements were the domain of a separate department from editorial, but they were scrutinised in the same way as features to ensure they were of a suitable standard for *Vogue*'s readers. It was not possible for the magazine to show an advertisement for a model that could not be purchased in the shops. A member of staff would have checked with Debenham & Freebody that the 'Model Tea Gown' shown on page four, costing 18½ guineas, was available. The same would have applied to dresses from Nicolls or shoes from the London Shoe Company.

Lillywhites advertised summer golf clothes opposite a dreamy-looking model in a long, opaque nightdress by Celanese. Wolsey had a double-page spread for their crochet knit wool '*directoire* knicker', which was a new introduction from the continent that boasted 'More freedom, more generous stride, and a really slendering fit (note that!).' There were smaller advertisements for Cyclax stockings, Gala lipstick, Berlei corsets as well as for hair products, perfume and cold creams. The cosmetics industry was still young and the move from stage make-up to everyday foundations, lipsticks and creams had only taken place in the past fifteen years, when Elizabeth Arden and Helena Rubinstein moved into mass-market production.

In among these pages advertising expensive goods made with expensive materials are advertisement features on travel to the Dolomites, Le Touquet (for golf) and the Cornish coast. The masthead gives the details of the edition, the index of Special Features, London fashions, Paris fashions, Society, Travel, House and Hostess and Limited Incomes. The layout was similar in each issue and Audrey's role would have been to allocate the pages and turns for each feature so that they made sense for the readers. The bottom of the masthead is key, listing the three *Vogue*s: British, French and American. Elizabeth Penrose – editor of British *Vogue*, Michel de Brunhoff – editor of French *Vogue*, and Edna Woolman Chase – editor-in-chief of the three *Vogue*s. Edna's name is in type twice the size of that for Penrose and de Brunhoff.

Now we are in Audrey's domain. For weeks, the double-page spreads of the contents of the issue had been hanging above her desk in her office next to more spreads for the following edition due to appear two weeks later. These were fixed with bull-dog clips onto wooden battens on a huge noticeboard. Sheets of paper with a page number in either corner would be arranged in order with handwritten notes, such as 'Paris Collections' or 'Fashion is How You Wear It' or 'Shophound'. These would be moved around at the editorial conference, chaired by Betty Penrose, where all the editors – features, fashion, social and beauty – would pitch their ideas.

Once the rough layout of the magazine was decided, it was down to Audrey to allocate illustrators or photographers and writers. As deadlines came, and sometimes went, Audrey would have to chase up contributors to ensure that the art department received the material in time to work on the layouts. Scissors and glue were the tools most often used by the art editor and his assistant.

Betty Penrose would have a set of spreads in her office as well, and these would become populated, like Audrey's, with more detail as the issue deadlines approached. Sometimes features or ideas would be moved from one fortnight to the next if there was a need to rush in a feature for a particular date, as happened in this issue. It centred around one of the most contentious characters of the day: Wallis Simpson.

Edward VIII had abdicated the previous December and married Wallis Simpson six days before this issue of *Vogue* hit the newsagents' shelves. This points up the great difficulty *Vogue* had in reacting quickly to the news as a bi-weekly magazine. At this stage, *Vogue* still boasted a social editor and the man in London with that job was an American, Johnnie McMullin. He was one of the best-connected men Audrey had ever met. Impeccably dressed and in high demand by the highest of society as an escort, he was closely acquainted with Mrs Simpson, so *Vogue* had had a ringside seat to the drama of the abdication.

Audrey would have been working on this issue for weeks, and at that time Wallis Simpson was not yet divorced, so although it was widely known that the Duke of Windsor wished to marry her, there was no date set. The divorce came through on 3 May and after that there was a frenzied to and fro between New York and London. The Americans were fascinated by the love affair between the former king and his twice-married mistress and wanted to splash it all over *Vogue*. The British press had maintained almost complete silence, so strongly was the public against Mrs Simpson.

When Edna suggested to Betty that Cecil Beaton's photographs of Wallis Simpson from the previous summer should feature in *Vogue* and *Brogue*, there was understandable reluctance in London. Even Johnnie McMullin had warned Edna against pushing too hard, as Americans were 'damned unpopular for the moment'. Betty and Audrey discussed the problem with Harry Yoxall and telegrams clattered back and forth across the Atlantic arguing, protesting and eventually agreeing a way forward.

To a large extent, the London office was still in thrall to New York, and to refuse utterly a request to include the story would have been impossible, but they also knew how badly a large feature on Mrs Simpson would be received in Britain. In the end, there was a compromise: New York published six luscious double-page spreads of Beaton's magnificent, romantic photographs of Wallis Simpson, which he had taken at the Château de Candé the previous year, accompanied by a long, gushing article by him about her charms and contradictions.

London published seven photographs with Audrey's minimal captions: 'Exclusive photographs taken for *Vogue* by Cecil Beaton at the Château de Candé' and 'Château background for the Duchess of Windsor, photographed by Beaton'. One can almost sense her holding her nose as she wrote those words. The following month she was appalled to see photographs in the newspapers by Beaton of the Duke and Duchess at home in Paris and to spot symbols of the Duke's royal past throughout the furnishings, including the three feathers of the Prince of Wales on their bedhead. 'Even the waste-paper baskets simulated the drums of the Brigade of Guards,' she wrote in disgust.

The key element of the magazine was the fashion material. At the time, the fashion editor was Madge Garland, who had been in post for five years, and although she was widely respected in the industry, Harry Yoxall and Betty Penrose doubted she was as committed to *Vogue* as she should be. They did not think she produced strong editorial, so there were discussions going on behind the scenes between London and New York about whether to renew her contract or to let her go. Audrey would not have been aware of this, but the role of the fashion editor at *Vogue* would be one that was not satisfactorily settled until the appointment of Pat Cunningham more than a decade later.

On a personal level, she liked Madge Garland very much and enjoyed her spontaneity and good humour around the office. She admired her cultured outlook and intelligence, but also the fact that Madge did not rely on a husband to keep her housed and fed.

The fashion pages from the Paris and London collections came not from the *Vogue* studio in London but on large plates from New York. These could be printed directly, with text and captions added in London. A magnificent double-page spread showed three models in black staring up towards a single star against a black background in a studio shot by the French photographer André Durst. Audrey's captions were appropriately dramatic:

Sky-rocketing across the horizon is black tulle. Left, Lanvin's vaporous dress with tucked band of tulle aslant the shoulders tying in a great bow behind. Next, a swirling skirt with zigzag bands of horsehair stiffened tulle, and shirred bodice: Molyneux (London).

The sheer elegance of the models and the quality of the photographs would have taken the readers' breath away.

In contrast, a spread of fashion photographs taken in America show the limitations of outdoor photography at the time. The colour photographs by Toni Frissell are out of focus and look woeful in comparison to the exquisite spreads on previous pages. This has more to do with the printing than the original prints themselves, but it looks amateur in comparison to the professional studio shots. At this time, photographers had begun to experiment with taking the model out of the studio and into the countryside, but it was another few years before it became an art form, which for *Vogue* reached its peak under Audrey's watch when Norman Parkinson carried out fashion shoots on his farm in Worcestershire during the war.

For Audrey, the fashion pages needed only her eagle eye for spelling or grammatical mistakes in the accompanying texts, whereas she had much more to do on the subsequent features, one of which was called Down with Diets. It was accompanied by illustrations of lobsters at Ascot and tea at the Garden Party and derided 'unbalanced, crank diets' that are easily given up. Audrey was an unfussy eater. To the end of her time at *Vogue*, she would prefer to eat sandwiches at her desk at lunchtime rather than going out to a restaurant, so she would have been entirely in tune with this feature.

By 1937, the features editor was Lesley Blanch, the traveller and novelist, whose brief was to write about anything but fashion. Features are what interested Audrey most and in future she would go on to expand *Vogue*'s ambition to address any subject relevant to the day. For now, she was getting to know Lesley Blanch and keen to encourage her to write about the arts, both good and bad. Lesley was an eccentric personality with unrivalled connections in the theatre, cinema and the fine arts. Her pieces are perceptive and witty, though not always kind if she found a show boring, but she welcomed new talent and featured young actors and actresses alongside familiar, famous names of the time.

Lesley Blanch and Audrey were the same age and although they could hardly have been more different, they got on well. Audrey described her as

the most completely individual character that you could meet in a lifetime. She was a free spirit, really, in a period when it wasn't at all as easy as it would be now. She was uninfluenced by anybody, let alone anybody's opinions.

Lesley married three times over the course of her life, the first time for love, the second time for money and the third for pleasure, wrote her biographer, Anne Boston. She was the type of person who liked to rewrite her past to make it seem more romantic or better suited to her narrative. She was no team-player but that never bothered Audrey, who appreciated her fresh, original thinking and her inquisitive, knowledgeable mind.

Lesley Blanch lived in her own melodrama, missing a bus could become a black tragedy and she had only extravagant praise for her friends and vitriol for her enemies. She wore exotic clothes, inspired by the Russian ballet, and was devoted to cats. She was fearless and undeterred by social strata, Anne Boston wrote, and 'above all, the most determined resistance fell in the face of her charm – true charm, unfeigned and irresistible.'

Betty Penrose, now in the editing chair, was content to leave Audrey to handle Lesley Blanch's contributions and articles poured onto Audrey's desk about everything from celebrities and aristocratic society to the bohemian demi-monde in which Lesley felt so at home. In her Spotlight column, she bucked the accepted trend by featuring productions that she did not enjoy, as well as those that she considered worthy of her praise. In one of her early columns for *Vogue*, she launched a fierce attack on summer open-air-theatres, which she described as a torture for shivering actors, sodden scenery and programme girls hiring out rugs. 'Why not hot-water bottles too?' she suggested in brackets. She took a pop at Vivien Leigh's performance in *The Dark Journey* and was scathing about a tubby tenor who played the part of the rake-thin Paganini. Anne Boston wondered whether Audrey despaired of the wayward beam of Lesley's Spotlight, but on the contrary, Audrey liked her features editors to be provocative, believing it was one of *Vogue*'s roles to challenge its readers and to ensure there was no intellectual complacency.

An important feature in *Vogue* from the outset had been aimed at women of limited means. It had various titles over the years but at this stage it was simply known as Limited Incomes. Bargain of the Fortnight featured a linen beach frock while instructions for a ruffled bed jacket appeared on the Knit Your Own page. *Vogue* patterns were available for women who wanted to make their own clothes, including a one-piece bathing suit and a pair of slacks, something seldom worn in Britain at the time and then usually only at the beach.

Once all the material had been signed off by Betty Penrose, laid out by the art director and edited by Audrey, it was time to send it to the printers. At the time, Harry Yoxall had been experimenting with different printers and had settled on the Sun Engraving Company in Watford. Audrey would personally take the proofs down to Euston Station by taxi and put them on the train to Watford, where the printers would check the layouts and prepare to print them. Audrey read every feature, caption and editorial three times before the magazine went to print: once in manuscript form, once in the layout stage and finally in the edition itself to make sure that no errant comma or incorrect turn had slipped in. It was something she continued to do once she became editor.

Betty Penrose was making an impact on the editorial front that was noticed and appreciated by Condé Nast and Edna. Nast wrote to compliment her. 'It is a matter of record,' he wrote,

> that in the years prior to 1937, the criticisms of British *Vogue* editorially on the part of Mrs Chase and myself were constant and caustic and they continued to be caustic during the first period of your management, but it is the opinion of Mrs Chase and myself that during the past year British *Vogue* editorially has improved tremendously, and as you say, can be compared favourably with American *Vogue*. British *Vogue* now looks like a periodical that comes from the same organization that produces American *Vogue*.

He went on:

> Particularly during the past year there has been a very definite improvement in the aesthetic standard of British *Vogue*, and without qualification, during your Editorship, there have been achieved a well-organized office, a good system and a high standard of efficiency.

While British *Vogue* was winning plaudits from Condé Nast and Edna Woolman Chase, Audrey was concerned with domestic matters. The lease on the house on Paddington Green was about to expire and the landlord did not wish to extend it, so she was forced to look for another rental property for her, Jock and her parents-in-law. By great good luck, she was able to find a four-storey terraced house in Blomfield Road, just opposite the pool of Little Venice, where the Grand Union Canal meets the Regent's Canal.

Today the houses are in private ownership and exchange hands for vast sums of money. When Audrey and Jock took on the lease of 31 Blomfield Road, it was a council-owned property which she described later as a tenement block. This was another of Audrey's understatements when it came to describing her private life. The handsome house is a magnificent stucco and brick mansion with a private and communal garden. It was one of nearly thirty that were built in the middle of the nineteenth century and converted from single dwellings to flats in the early twentieth.

The house was generously proportioned with large rooms on the ground and first floors and a commodious basement that served as a kitchen. It stood in a curved terrace of six properties, each with a sizeable garden that backed onto the gardens of the houses on Warwick Place behind, so that the swatch of green between the houses filled with trees offered a welcome lung in the polluted streets of that era. It is true that Little Venice was not as upmarket as neighbouring St John's Wood, and there was a running joke that this was where the staff and the mistresses of St John's Wood inhabitants lived. That would have suited Audrey, who never wanted anyone to think she had airs and graces.

Number 31 was divided into three flats and by the following year was occupied by Charles and Elsie Stewart, who had the basement, Jock and Audrey, who had the first floor, and Margaret Cockburn, a housing estate manager, who lived on the top floor. Jock and Audrey shared the ground-floor rooms with his parents and his mother continued to run the household and organise the cooking and cleaning. Miss Cockburn was a day younger than Audrey and the National Register of 1939 shows that the two of them volunteered for the Women's Auxiliary Fire Service as drivers, which leads one to suppose that she and Audrey were on more than nodding terms and quite possibly friends. In that same register, Elsie Stewart's personal occupation is listed as 'unpaid domestic duties', while Audrey, or, more correctly, Elizabeth A. Stewart, is listed as a journalist and Jock's entry reads 'Assistant Manager, Bumpus Ltd (bookseller)'.

Blomfield Road was a step up from the maisonette in Paddington. There was plenty of space on the walls to hang her growing collection of prints and drawings and visitors appreciated the quality of the art in her stairwell and front room.

Audrey had developed a keen eye for art over the course of her teenage years and, encouraged by Percy Withers and Paul Nash, she had begun collecting prints and drawings. Paintings were beyond her budget, but she went to a summer exhibition at the Redfern Gallery that year and bought a little drawing of a town square from 1898 by Picasso. She paid £60 for it and sold it for several hundred twenty years later. At the same time, she bought a large Renoir lithograph, which she gave to Jock as a birthday present.

The list of works she bought over time, including Henry

Moore, Barbara Hepworth, Graham Sutherland, Gwen John and David Jones, shows that Audrey was always keen to look for something interesting in the present, rather than settling on the safe territory of the past. It had led her to Ibsen and Strindberg in the Oxford Playhouse in the mid-1920s and it would lead her towards Benjamin Britten operas in the future.

The outlook over the canal basin from No. 31 offered Audrey a view of the waterway traffic, which she never tired of. The pool of Little Venice was a wide-open triangle of water surrounded by white Regency houses and full of moored boats and barges. The small island in the middle of the pool was named after the poet Robert Browning and the towpath alongside the canal basin led toward Camden. Today it is described as the canal that 'tiptoes through the capital'. On Sundays and in the summer, pleasure boats would take tourists up to Camden Lock and back but in the winter the scene was quieter and much of the traffic was commercial. Audrey wrote of how she loved to watch the huge barges, loaded with cargo or London's rubbish, moving off in procession up the canal. She described how the crews would open their umbrellas in rainy weather and the whole scene would resemble a Japanese print.

Life in Blomfield Road was comfortable and home life was happy. She and Jock had a busy social life and at weekends would take a train into the countryside to go exploring. Often they would end up in Oxfordshire for lunch or tea and, in summer, a swim in the pool. They went to the theatre and concerts whenever they could and were sometimes accompanied by Percy on one of his periodic visits to the capital for meetings. He loved to stop by the house and see Audrey at home. At thirty, she remained childless but ambitious for her career at *Vogue*. She was energetic and full of enthusiasm for the way her professional life was going. This showed in the new and confident way she now wore her hair, which already had streaks of grey in it, pulled back from her forehead in a loose bun. She wore lipstick and nail varnish but no make-up or rouge on her pale skin.

Her colour of choice for clothes was blue or grey and she often wore striking jewellery, combining new designs with antique pieces she had inherited from her mother's family. She was tidily dressed rather than glamorous and that was a style she cultivated from then on. She was Miss Withers to everyone but Betty Penrose and Harry Yoxall, who called her by her Christian name. Few people at work, apart from Harry, knew anything about her private life, and that was how she liked it to be.

Harry had met Jock professionally when discussing the publication of the *Vogue* cookery books and they occasionally had lunch together. He was aware that Jock was increasingly dissatisfied with his work at Bumpus. Even though he had been promoted to assistant manager, Wilson gave Jock little opportunity to take on responsibility himself. It was deeply frustrating for him and he came to bitterly resent his role. Audrey's background, with her buttoned-up mother and her eccentric, self-centred father, gave her little experience of how to deal with a discontented husband. She buried herself deeper in her work, often not getting back to Blomfield Road until after 8 p.m., and it was not unusual for her to be even later in the build-up to an issue going to press.

One of Audrey's passions beyond literature, music and work was travel. She had travelled widely with her parents as a child and adolescent, visiting Egypt, France, Switzerland and Italy. With Jock, she continued to visit the continent each summer. They were excited by the possibilities that air travel offered and made the most of their one-week breaks to go to Palermo, Dubrovnik and other cities. They also enjoyed walking in the countryside, and Jock's postcards to his father-in-law describe sunbathing beside lakes in Switzerland and swimming in rivers in southern France.

~

In recognition of her hard work, over the summer of 1937 Audrey was offered the opportunity by Betty to go to Paris for the autumn collections. Betty was anxious to get better communication between London and Paris, and she wrote to Condé Nast justifying her decision.

> With the consistent grind and detail that falls to her lot, I felt very strongly that a refresher in Paris with an opportunity to see the Exhibition and the inside of the Paris office would do her a world of good. This it accomplished and it accomplished an enormous amount in my attempt to get a better system between us and the Paris Office. Incidentally, it also accomplished this – that Audrey now has a very good grasp of the way things go on in the Paris Office.

Audrey stayed at the Hôtel de Crillon, a majestic eighteenth-century building overlooking the Place de la Concorde. It was more luxurious than anywhere she had ever stayed before and she revelled in the delight of being on her own in the beautiful city. It was the first of many visits to the French capital for the fashion shows and she wrote enthusiastically to her father about the thrill she felt at being there on business. Back in Britain she told Betty that she and Jock had made up their minds to take a holiday in America the following summer and suggested that she should perhaps visit the New York office while she was there.

Betty was already convinced of the value of sending key staff to visit *Vogue*'s overseas offices. She immediately wrote to Condé Nast reminding him of the benefit British staff had reaped from spending time in the New York office, getting to 'sense the general atmosphere of America, but more especially the atmosphere of *Vogue*'s New York office'. She went on:

I now learn that Audrey Withers and her husband are hoping to go to America for a holiday next Spring and to this end, are saving all their shillings madly. I am frightfully excited at the prospect of Audrey making such a trip and extremely anxious to do anything that I can to make it come off. Audrey is a woman of enormous ability. She is the single indispensable person in this office and if any great crisis arose, I fully believe that she would be able to put out, single-handed, an issue of *Vogue*. It seems to me a great waste of an opportunity for Audrey simply to go to New York on holiday and to have no chance of getting an inside view of American *Vogue*.

Condé Nast agreed, although he had another Briton on his mind at the time and this one was causing him a severe headache.

Of all the regular contributors to *Vogue* at that time, the most valued on both sides of the Atlantic was the photographer, illustrator and writer Cecil Beaton. He was one of those extraordinary human beings whose life was his own artistic creation and he himself the centre of that creative act. His ambition from the time he was at Cambridge in the 1920s was to be famous, and it was his life's work to make that happen. Beaton had been taking photographs since he was a little boy. He had an excellent eye and a singular ability to stage his photographs to the maximum benefit of the sitter, with whom he would flirt and joke in order to create the best pictorial outcome. He loved being a photographer, his biographer, Hugo Vickers wrote, because it 'nourished the actor in him'. Eventually this would be the strand in his career that would help to finance the rest of his life.

In 1925, Beaton met Dorothy Todd and Madge Garland, whom he immediately liked. They encouraged him in his photography and were soon praising him for producing the best photographs but were unable to use them because they always arrived too late. 'Do try and get them out sooner,' Garland told him. Two years later, he had his first professional break. Edna Woolman Chase was in London and met Beaton, whom she described as 'our blessing and our trial'. He walked into her office, 'tall, slender, swaying like a reed, and very young. The aura emanating from him was an odd combination of airiness and assurance.'

At first, he drew caricatures for *Vogue* and they were immediately popular. His fashion drawings and photography came later and were equally well received, though Edna could not believe that he worked with such a small camera. When she asked him who did his developing, as he had no studio, he replied, 'Oh, Mrs Chase, Nannie does it for me at home, in the bathtub.' Edna wrote of him:

He, more than any other photographer or artist who has ever worked for us, seems to have become inextricably entangled in our lives. In one way, I suppose, I am responsible, because Cecil came to us when he was very young and I inevitably developed a maternal feeling for him. One way and another, between his talent and his temperament, his affectionate nature, his shrewd eye for what is good for Cecil, and our appreciation of his ability, matched by our need to keep him down to size if we are to run the magazine in business-like fashion, we have whipped up quite a saga.

Beaton was so highly regarded by *Vogue* that he was a regular visitor to New York, a city he took to immediately, loving every last minute of the glamour, society and culture. Soon he was not only drawing for *Vogue* but writing theatre reviews and articles about the New York nightlife. He also did freelance portrait work, being sagely advised to charge very high prices so that he could stay in the smartest hotels and make the right impression. It turned out to be good advice, but Beaton had a flaw: he always spent his gross salary, not calculating the impact of tax, so that he was in a permanent state of financial embarrassment and thus dependent on the regular, well-paid work from *Vogue* to keep him afloat.

One of the advantages of Beaton to *Vogue* was his contact with British high society and the aristocracy, right up to and including the royal family. This had led to the successful photo shoot with Wallis Simpson, which had been such a triumph for American *Vogue*, and he was favoured by all the types of people who featured in the society pages of the magazine. When Audrey first met Cecil Beaton, he had been working for *Vogue* for fifteen years and his reputation was as great in London as it was in New York.

However, in early 1938, just as Audrey was finalising the plans for her trip, an episode occurred that caused a terrible rift between Beaton and *Vogue*. He spent the winter in New York, working under extreme pressure, drawing, designing, photographing and attending parties day in and night out. At the end of the previous year, he had submitted a series of drawings to illustrate the borders of an article by Fran Crowninshield in *Vogue* entitled 'The New Left Wing in New York Society'.

The sketches included a lavish fireplace with a burning fire and a chandelier above, boxes of bouquets and a table with books and knitting needles. In the bottom right-hand corner was a small collection of sketched press cuttings, and within these Beaton had buried an anti-Semitic word. It was so small that it could only possibly have been spotted by someone actively searching for it with a magnifying glass. But it was there, and the damage was done.

Beaton received a handwritten summons from Condé Nast as soon as it had been noticed. When he arrived at 1040 Park Avenue, he found Condé Nast waiting for him. He said, 'We're in a tough spot . . . I could not mind more if I were losing my own son but I can see nothing else but to ask for your resignation.' Beaton's first reaction was to feel a sense of freedom and elation, but that was soon crushed. The reaction to his sketches was dramatic and furious. He was denounced as an anti-Semite and Condé Nast had to distance himself from him formally in a press statement.

Sixty thousand copies of *Vogue* with the offending sketches had been printed in New York and distributed before the caption had been spotted and production stopped. Condé Nast estimated that it had cost *Vogue* $36,000, and now none of Beaton's work could be published in any of his magazines. An offer of work for Orson Welles was withdrawn because the backers were Jewish, and other contracts were cancelled. Beaton wrote in despair in his diary: 'I was reduced to pulp. I felt as if I had committed a murder.' He returned to London with his tail between his legs and found that he was as unwelcome there as he had been in New York.

Although anti-Semitism was rampant in Hitler's Germany, it was also present in Britain. Confined in the main to Oswald Mosley's British Union of Fascists, who daubed slogans against the Jews on walls in the East End and shouted abuse through loudspeakers, there was nevertheless casual anti-Semitism throughout society. Under the terms of his contractual agreement with *Vogue*, he could not work for anyone else until 1939, so he decided to spend the summer travelling. By the time Audrey arrived in New York, the Beaton saga had subsided to some extent, but she knew that his name was so toxic that it was not safe to bring it up in the *Vogue* office.

When senior *Vogue* staff, such as Harry Yoxall, sailed to New York, their expenses were paid, but this was not the case for people in Audrey's position unless they had received a specific request to spend several months in America. Betty knew that, so she appealed to Condé Nast to make a contribution to Audrey's ticket aboard a 'fast boat' from Southampton to New

York. She also asked him to pay Audrey for a month's leave in New York so that she could spend time getting to know the New York office before Jock joined her for the holiday part of their trip. She signed off her letter: 'I would be eternally grateful to you if you can see eye to eye with me in this matter and I am sure, if you can, you will, in the end, be eternally grateful to me for having brought the matter up.' Condé Nast agreed by return.

By February, the plans had been firmed up and Betty told Condé Nast that he and Edna should do everything in their power to make the month she would spend on the New York staff 'a real benefit to us all'. Audrey was excited. She wrote to Condé Nast, addressing him as 'My dear Mr Nast'. In a letter bubbling with delight and anticipation, she wrote of her conviction that a really close co-operation between the offices 'is needed if the organisation you have built up is to function as an international unit; and it is such a help if the various staffs can have a working knowledge of one another's methods'. She thanked him for his generous contribution towards her ticket and a month's pay as well as three weeks' holiday. She enthused about seeing him and Edna again, as well as meeting other staff in New York who she knew by name but not in person. This letter brims with all the enthusiasm and excitement that is familiar from her earlier letters to Paul Nash from Oxford.

Percy Withers was as excited as if he were going there himself, writing to her,

it is delightful to think you have the thrill of the American prospect in your hearts ... and Jock's month – with you – in USA and positively we rejoiced too exuberantly

98

to remember to fling our caps in the air! Never was a more impossible dream, or a more glorious one, by way of being realized. My own delight couldn't be greater.

The next few weeks were spent in an excited whirl of planning and anticipation. After Jock joined her, the two of them would be taking a train trip across America, and the itinerary for this, accompanied by colourful brochures full of alluring pictures of mountains, deserts and the sea, was the most thrilling of all. It would be the first time Audrey had spent a month on her own, away from the office, away from Jock and away from the nagging feeling in Britain that Europe was a dangerous and unstable place. When she sailed on the *Ile de France* on 8 April 1938, German troops had completed their occupation of Austria and the annexation or *Anschluss* had been declared three weeks earlier.

After a calm crossing, the *Ile de France* sailed into New York. Audrey stood on deck, windswept and excited, her hat held firmly in place with her right hand, gazing at the Statue of Liberty and the great towers of downtown Manhattan glinting in the April sunshine. She could make out the Chrysler Building with its distinctive spire and the Empire State Building further uptown, rising dramatically over the rest of the skyline. Her arrival in the 'Wonder City' was every bit as thrilling as she had anticipated. She was picked up by a family friend and driven through Lower Manhattan, past skyscrapers larger than anything she had ever seen before. Thirty, fifty, a hundred storeys high, they towered above her, breathtaking and overwhelming.

Edna had organised for Audrey to be looked after by Jessica Daves, her assistant editor at *Vogue*, who would go on to become editor after the war. There would be none of the razzamatazz that was accorded to visitors like Beaton or Harry Yoxall, but Audrey would have been overwhelmed by any kind of fuss. She was happy to stay in a modest hotel and walk five blocks to 420 Lexington Avenue every morning to *Vogue*'s offices.

She was struck by how much more elegant the offices were in Lexington Avenue than those in New Bond Street. She was taken with Edna's desk, which had a yellow painted top and grooved legs picked out in blue. She had never seen anything like that before in a working office. She learned that it had been Clarissa Nast, Condé Nast's first wife, who had decorated the offices, bringing pale colours and light textures to the box-like architecture of the rooms. Edna reassured her that life before the refurbishment had been very basic and cramped, but Audrey could not imagine that now. Everything impressed her.

For four weeks, she shadowed Jessica Daves and Miss Pineles, *Vogue*'s managing editor. She had conferences with Edna, with Dr Agha, the art director, and with Frank Crowninshield, Condé Nast's right-hand man. Edna encouraged her to talk to everyone she could, on the editorial side, in the art department and in production. Condé Nast took her out to lunch and pumped her for as much information as he could on the abdication. It was the question on everyone's lips: what would it mean for the future of the royal family? He formed the impression of an intelligent woman who understood not only how to edit a magazine but most importantly how to edit *his* magazine, *Vogue*, and that sat well with him. Despite his enormous success and standing, Condé Nast was not an outgoing man and Audrey found him quiet, charming and very serious about his business. She could relate to that and was grateful that he listened to her ideas.

Edna took Audrey under her wing and lectured her on the history of the tricky relationship between *Vogue* and *Brogue*, especially since the Beaton affair. She found Audrey enthusiastic and charming. She liked her work ethic and was impressed by how quickly she absorbed the culture of the New York office and how she took note of everything going on around her. She also liked her on a personal level, enjoying her wide-eyed enthusiasm for everything new. Audrey was equally taken with Edna. They had so much in common: both had had unusual upbringings – Edna in a Quaker family where people were addressed as Thee and Thou – and both attached great importance to their own work and independence. Although Edna was almost thirty years older than Audrey, her lifetime of experience of friendships with older people made for a comfortable relationship that would grow ever warmer.

Audrey's attention to detail was impressive, Edna told Betty Penrose, but she feared she did not have that spirit of daring that Jessica Daves had, 'of willingness to take a chance on the unproven, provided they scent possibilities'. In this, she was wrong. Audrey may have come across as cautious and fact-based, but when it came to dealing with the unfamiliar on her own territory, she would prove to be undaunted and undauntable.

Audrey made the most of her time in New York, going to concerts in Carnegie Hall close to her hotel when she had free evenings. She spent her days in *Vogue* listening, watching and making friends with the staff. She also got to see first-hand the production of the shells that would be sent to Britain for use in *Brogue*. On one occasion, Edna and Condé Nast took her to Greenwich, Connecticut to visit the Condé Nast printing press, a state-of-the-art facility built in 1924. He had become dissatisfied with the quality of printing he had been able to get, so he had opened his own premises. It printed not only Condé Nast publications but also other magazines, including the *New Yorker*.

In comparison to Sun Engravings's small premises on the outskirts of London, where British *Vogue* was printed, Greenwich looked to Audrey like something out of the future. The size of the plant was impressive, but so were the surrounding gardens, which had been sumptuously laid out and included fountains and sculptures imported from Italy. Condé Nast told her that it was all to do with his message to the millions of people who had to drive between two vast columns engraved '*Vogue*, *Glamour*, *House and Garden*, Condé Nast Publications'. It was proof of the wealth and achievement of Condé Nast Publications and it was part of his advertising psychology.

What struck Audrey on this visit was Condé Nast's taste and his attention to detail. She made one brief visit to his 22-room, two-storey rooftop penthouse at 1040 Park Avenue. She was there to see where many of the famous *Vogue* photo shoots that had been used in *Brogue* had been staged. Known simply as 1040, this apartment, decorated by the famous New York interior designer Elsie de Wolfe, was luxurious beyond Audrey's experience. Every room she popped her head into, including the Chinese Chippendale ballroom, looked as if it were a photograph from one of Condé Nast's magazines come to life.

Three and a half weeks after her arrival, Jock's ship docked and Audrey was now on holiday. They spent a few days in New York together, sightseeing in Manhattan and visiting the museums and art galleries on Fifth Avenue and around Central Park. Jock wanted to enjoy the glamour of the city that never sleeps, and the two of them enjoyed going to restaurants and dance venues that she had not been to when she was on her own. Their favourite was the Rainbow Room, a stunning roof-top club that had opened three years earlier and was said to be in a class of its own. 'So great is the room's prestige,' the *New York Evening Journal* exclaimed, 'that ace performers will work there for much less than salaries they command elsewhere.' It was here, in this exotic and beautiful atmosphere of New York's nightlife, that Audrey was introduced to a Russian émigré, Victor Kennett, whom Jock had met on the *Manhattan* when he sailed from Southampton. She could not have known it at the time, but it was a meeting that would change the course of her personal life.

For now, there was America to explore. Audrey and Jock set off by train from Grand Central Station to Chicago, from where they boarded the Super Chief, a train that ran from Chicago to Los Angeles along the southernmost transcontinental route, passing through Kansas, New Mexico and Arizona. The train was large and comfortable, with a viewing platform at the rear and dining and lounge cars for relaxing. Audrey and Jock took the opportunity to step down from the train whenever it stopped to take on water or fuel at a station. Arizona fascinated her and she marvelled at the sunset over the desert.

Two days later, they arrived at Los Angeles and were disappointed. It seemed to them to have no heart but just go on and on. From LA, they caught the Coast Daylight to San Francisco, a brand-new service that had been running for just twelve months, described as the most beautiful passenger train in the world. It ran over the Santa Lucia Mountains and along the Pacific coastline for over 100 miles. The carriages, known as streamliners, boasted 'enormous showcase windows 5ft wide, soft foam rubber seats, fluorescent lighting, a low-voiced public address system to announce station stops and points of interest, baggage elevators and air-conditioning'. Little could have been further from the rickety old rolling stock that ran between London Paddington and Banbury, which Audrey was accustomed to.

She and Jock arrived in San Francisco on a Friday afternoon and were immediately enchanted. They spent the weekend walking around the bay and riding trams up and down the steep hills, drinking in the views of the Golden Gate Bridge, Alcatraz and Marin County beyond. She described San Francisco as 'surely the most beautiful city in the world'. From there, they took a car to Yosemite, where they were astonished by the scale and grandeur of the extraordinary landscape and the colossal rock formations that cluster around the valley floor: El Capitan, 3000ft of vertical rock, with its then unclimbed 'Nose'; Half Dome and Bridalveil Fall, where the water cascades nearly 620ft, vaporising into tiny water droplets on its way down.

At Yosemite, they witnessed a traditional bonfire, where blazing logs were pushed over the edge of a cliff to create a magnificent fire fall. California was undoubtedly the highlight of their twelve-day train journey across the USA, though the trip through the Rockies and across the rich farmland of Minnesota impressed upon them the enormous scale of the country. They arrived in New York from Chicago on 4 June and, two days later, they boarded the *Normandie* and set sail for Southampton.

It would be seven years before Audrey next set foot in New York. By then the world had survived the most destructive war in history and she had become the most powerful woman in London.

The passenger list named Jock as 'Bookseller, England' and Audrey as 'Elizabeth Stewart, Wife'. Also on the list was Victor Kraminsky, an engineer from London, travelling unaccompanied. Kraminksy was Victor Kennett's Russian name, which he changed after fleeing from Russia in 1917. He told Audrey that as soon as he learned that she and Jock would be sailing on the *Normandie*, he had rushed down to the travel agent and booked his passage on the same voyage.

When they arrived in their cabin, Audrey and Jock found the largest bouquet of flowers she had ever seen; they were from Victor. Jock was pleased to have Victor on board and asked him to take care of Audrey while he explored the delights of the ship on his own. Victor was ten years older than Audrey, sophisticated, confident and passionate. Whereas Jock was slim, tall and good-looking, Victor was smaller and stockier with dark hair, a dark moustache and a scar above his left eye. His magnetism was extraordinary and his Russian accent made his tales of life in pre-revolution Russia and his escape to Switzerland sound all the more exotic. She was swept off her feet. While Jock was good fun and a good companion, Victor was worldly and had far wider interests. He and Audrey became almost inseparable immediately.

Audrey wrote later of how Victor had absolute and extraordinary confidence that the two of them were destined to spend the rest of their lives together. He had already made up his mind to get her to leave Jock and join him before they had boarded the ship. Audrey was attracted to Victor, flattered by his attention and excited by the underlying passion that seemed to exist like an electric charge between them. He was separated from his wife, he told her, and was desperate to secure Audrey's promise to join him before they parted in Southampton. But she was not as brave as he was and felt helplessly vulnerable as she listened to his entreaties and then weighed them against what she knew to be the shame and ignominy of divorce in Britain. She made him no promise, but neither did she turn him down.

When she saw her parents the weekend after she arrived back in Britain, her father could tell there was something wrong. Eventually she confessed that she was in love with Victor and planned to leave Jock. Percy was horrified. He stamped on it there and then, condemning a love affair on an ocean voyage as something that would happen in a cheap novel and could not possibly be conceived of as viable on dry land. She was shaken by his vitriolic disapproval and promised to think about it. She cared for her father's approval more than anyone else's and to incite his scorn left her feeling cut adrift.

She took herself off to a London hotel, where she was bombarded by letters from Victor as well as from Jock, who implored her to stay with him. 'Later I realized that Jock was desperate at the thought of supporting his parents alone.' This was written in 1994, long after both Victor and Jock were dead. It is more likely that Percy Withers' opinion prevailed and the thought of creating a scandal that might also affect her work caused Audrey to lose confidence and to tell Victor that she could not make the brave leap he had begged her to make. When she confronted him with her decision, he fell to his knees and wept. It was the first time she had seen a grown man cry and it made a very profound impact on her.

However, it did not sway her resolve. She turned her back on happiness and threw herself with increased energy into her work.

> Of course if there had been nothing else in my life, it would have been unbearable. But how seldom does anyone have everything? And if something is missing, the gap can be filled with something else, which, for me, was absorbing work – probably too absorbing for the good of a marriage, especially to a husband who disliked work and longed only to retire.

The affair caused a rift but they worked hard to rebuild their relationship and remained married for the next thirteen years. To their friends and the outside world, they looked like the most glamorous couple, but Jock had begun to take more of an interest in other women.

By the time Audrey returned from New York, the coronation of George VI had taken place and the political situation had begun to consume more of people's time than ever before. On the continent, Adolf Hitler had been making bellicose speeches threatening to destroy Czechoslovakia. In a speech during the tenth Nazi Party Congress, Hermann Goering referred to the Czechs as 'a miserable pygmy race' who were 'harassing the human race'. This would lead inexorably to the Munich Crisis of September 1938, when the British prime minister, Neville Chamberlain, met Hitler four times over a period of fourteen days, acting as a negotiator between Hitler and the Czech president Edvard Beneš. On the fourth occasion, Hitler invited Italian duce Benito Mussolini, French premier Edouard Daladier and Chamberlain to one last conference in Munich. The Czechs were not invited and the resulting agreement, which gave Chamberlain the confidence to declare on his return to Britain that he had secured 'Peace for our time', led the following day to German troops marching into the Sudetenland.

As 1938 came to an end and *Vogue* looked forward to the spring collections, Audrey reflected on a year of changing fortunes and emotional upheaval. If she regretted her decision not to leave Jock that summer, she never mentioned it again. She spent Christmas in Banbury with her parents, who were now living at Epwell Mill, an early eighteenth-century stone house on the outskirts of the village of Epwell, 7 miles west of Banbury. Souldern Court had become too large and expensive to run. The Mill was a smaller property that better suited their financial position. Percy's strength was declining, and she had become aware of how dependent he had become on Mamie. It was a worry that she and Monica would have for the next few years.

Audrey and Jock returned to London and she was back at her desk at *Vogue* the following day, ready for what the New Year would bring.

4

VOGUE UNDER FIRE

'The war cannot last forever and our experience in the last
war was that even in such times, one of the reasons for *Vogue*'s
popularity was the fact that it still retained its standards
of beauty and of taste, which, in a devastated world, was a
pleasing relief.'

— EDNA WOOLMAN CHASE TO HARRY YOXALL,
30 NOVEMBER 1939

In the summer of 1939, war was imminent and the atmosphere
in Britain and on the continent was febrile. In August, Germany
announced the formal military occupation of Slovakia, breaking the guarantee of independence Hitler had promised in
March. Audrey and Jock had been following the news from the
continent with increasing anxiety. They read all the daily and
Sunday newspapers and became more concerned by the week
about the probability of all-out war. At work, Audrey was as
busy as ever. She had been to Paris in August and had returned
with news of a return to wasp waists, big shoulders and high-
heeled sandals emerging from the fashion houses. Naturally
she had discussed the political situation with her colleagues

and they all predicted Hitler's demand for land from Poland.

It was an unsettling time for *Vogue*. If war came, would the magazine have to shut down? That question hung in the air for weeks, and the uncertainty was inflamed by the absence of Harry Yoxall's steadying hand. The crisis had arisen during Edna's visit to London in June. Harry had been called to New York by Condé Nast, 'who was in grave, even urgent, need for help'. He needed Harry for at least a year to help him run the worldwide organisation. It would mean leaving *Brogue* in the hands of the advertising manager, Bill Davenport, in whom Betty Penrose had no confidence. She told Edna that she had no intention of staying after her contract had expired unless she was paid substantially more.

Betty wrote a six-page letter to Condé Nast outlining the gloomy situation that faced them:

There is a possibility of the managing director [Harry Yoxall] switching to New York; the advertising manager is due to leave in a year, an old and experienced art editor [James de Holden-Stone] is on his way, while an admittedly talented, but at the same time, extremely difficult man [John Parsons] in the matter of time and production replaces him; the fashion editor [Madge Garland] cannot be regarded as a permanency; the extremely important post of social editor [Lady Patricia Ward] falls vacant at the end of this month; our number one photographer [John Rawlings] is required in New York as soon as we can release him. Over and above all this is the fundamental fact that conditions in Europe are, to say the least, unsettled.

This level of anxiety was exacerbated by the political situation that blew up on 1 September, when the Germans invaded Poland. Two days later, Neville Chamberlain told a fearful nation that the country was now at war with Germany.

The first edition of *Vogue* to appear after the outbreak of the Second World War included one of the greatest fashion images ever taken. Horst P. Horst had photographed a model in a corset by Detolle for the American designer Mainbocher. The model is sitting on a wooden bench, with her back to the camera, her slender torso curved to the right, the corset partially tied with ribbons draped over the back of the bench and the model leaning her head in towards her right arm, which is raised. It reveals nothing, yet it is one of the most beautifully suggestive images imaginable.

How extraordinary that this ethereal creation appeared at such a time of fear and trepidation. Of course, the issue had been planned weeks in advance and the coincidence is just that, but it is a reminder that although the war had been expected and had now broken out, there was a strong feeling that life should go on. Whereas Paris had buckled and shut down in the face of the immediate and horrific slaughter of the First World War, this time it would be different and the couture houses either side of the English Channel determined to keep going whatever the circumstances.

Such was the fear of an all-out attack by the Luftwaffe on London and other major British cities that the government had made provision for the evacuation of mothers and babies, unaccompanied schoolchildren, the elderly, disabled and infirm. Hospitals and nursing homes were moved wholesale to safer parts of the country, and all but essential businesses were asked to consider relocating. Max Factor cosmetics found a home in Pulborough in Sussex. All cinemas, theatres, concert halls and other public venues were ordered to close. Race meetings and sporting fixtures were cancelled, and people were discouraged from gathering in large numbers, though church services were still permitted.

The shutdown lasted for just two weeks, but it had the effect of changing the perception of normality for the general public. Life on the home front had been completely disrupted by the outflux of people from London and other cities. This was the beginning of the period that would become known as the Phoney War, and it would run until the spring of 1940.

In the strange atmosphere of the autumn and winter of 1939, Audrey learned to get used to being at war, although no fighting was taking place anywhere close to home. Like many women of her age, she could sense there were opportunities in wartime. Although she could not know yet what these would be, she was determined to be a part of it.

At the time of the Munich crisis the previous year, she had joined the Auxiliary Fire Service and had taken driving lessons during her lunchbreaks. By September, she had her HV (heavy vehicle) licence, which gave her permission to drive a fire engine. To her disappointment, she never got to drive anything larger than an ancient taxi when ferrying officers between fire stations. In the early days of the war, the greatest fear was not of bombing but of a gas attack on Britain, so every member of the public had to carry a gas mask. When Audrey was driving fire officers, she was ordered to wear her mask. Street lighting had disappeared, traffic lights were blacked out, and car headlights had a cross-slit showing only a glimmer. They had not yet received the sensible advice to rub the inside of their gas mask lenses with soap in order to stop them from fugging up, so Audrey once drove more or less blind into the path of a London bus, which also had minimal lighting. Fortunately, they were both driving so slowly that there was no crash, just a brief stand-off as Audrey reversed out of the bus's way.

As she was working at *Vogue* all day, her AFS duties took place at night, and after her shift she would walk home along the canal towards Little Venice. London was a different city at night in the blackout. Gone were the garish neon advertising signs and street lights, now replaced with softer shadows and grey outlines. The city was clothed in a mantle of black and white, but it was still strangely beautiful: 'You see everything lovely and the ugly things are hidden.' A diarist wrote, 'At night, London does seem, not like a deserted village, but like a beautiful city in a trance.'

Nights with a full moon were especially lovely, the city quiet with little traffic and fewer people out and about. The barges in Paddington Basin that Audrey had found so colourful and evocative that summer moved like great, shadowy creatures over the oily surface of the black water. The bargemen were silent and the bright umbrellas had given way to dark oilskins, while their dimmed torches gave off faint glows. By day, the scene looked more familiar, but Audrey loved the view of the canal at night with its unseen energy and the quiet determination to keep London ticking. Truly there were some compensations despite the inconvenience and danger of the blackout.

The outbreak of the Second World War came as the major fashion houses in London and Paris were about to bring out their new collections, and for several weeks there was disruption as no one was quite clear what to do. Some houses closed, others abandoned the autumn shows they had been working on for months, not because they feared the bombs but because the majority of their London clients had moved to the country.

Although some people returned after the first panic, the picture was messy, so the designers decided to be proactive and take their work out of the capital and to the country. Digby Morton was the first to set up a travelling show. A Dubliner by birth, he had been living in London since 1923 and was widely regarded as one of the most influential designers of the era. Successful in New York as well as London, he was known for his exquisite tailoring of women's suits. He teamed up with Woolf Brothers (the furriers), the Elizabeth Arden Beauty Salon and Aage Thaarup, the Danish-born milliner who, like Morton, had been successful in the decade leading up to the war and named the queen among his most notable clients.

Starting in Bristol in November, they took four models plus six large dress baskets, ten hat boxes, ten make-up cases and some £4,000 worth of furs. One hundred and fifty people, including a handful of men, watched models show off thirty-six gowns with an average price tag of eighteen guineas. This tour gave a clear signal that the fashion industry was able to react quickly to whatever the situation demanded, and it set a precedent for a working relationship with the Board of Trade over the course of the coming months and years.

Vogue naturally celebrated the travelling show and an article appeared in the November edition under the title 'Brisk Action on the Mayfair Front'.

Official communiqué No. 1 from the Mayfair front reports the ranks of British Designers to be holding their position resolutely. Material advances have been made and each day's action further secures the ultimate objective of economic victory . . . We are not surprised, but inordinately pleased, to learn that so stern a thing as the will to conquer can be made of such fragile stuff as a frock.

After this somewhat tongue-in-cheek opening, the article went on to list the ways in which the different couture houses were coping with the new conditions.

Some, such as House of Worth and Norman Hartnell, one of the Queen's favourite designers, were sending sketches to clients and cutting material on request; others were joining forces to show their work around the country. Hardy Amies, Audrey's favourite designer, who later became dressmaker to Queen Elizabeth II, was continuing to design for his clients at the same time as carrying out his duties in the Fire Brigade. Amies would go on to have a most interesting war with the Intelligence Corps, working in Belgium with various resistance groups and organising sabotage assignments.

Meanwhile, Harry Yoxall had made up his mind to return to Britain from New York, leaving his wife Josephine and his two children with her family in Ohio. It was a heart-breaking decision for them, but he felt certain that his presence and his experience of the First World War was needed in London more than it was in New York. He sailed on 3 September, the day war broke out, and was back in the office by the eleventh with a publishing plan thrashed out by him, Condé Nast and Iva Patcévitch, Nast's personal assistant, who would succeed him in 1942.

A fortnightly magazine was always going to be at a disadvantage against weeklies, and both would be overshadowed by the daily newspapers, which pumped out story after story of the goings on in European cities that many people in Britain had never heard of. Betty Penrose and Harry Yoxall called a conference to discuss how *Vogue* should function in wartime, what its message should be and how best it could keep going while fulfilling the government's very strong message of propaganda.

Condé Nast was pulling strings from New York and Harry found himself dancing on a pin head as he tried to keep the various parties happy while also ensuring that printing and distribution kept going. Betty Penrose's first war editorial appeared on 20 September.

> In accordance with the government's wish that business should carry on as far as possible, *Vogue* will continue to be published during the war, but as a monthly magazine . . .
> The next issue will appear October 25. Look out for it, subsequently, on the last Wednesday of every month.

It was a gamble and the board decided to take it because they knew that there would be restrictions on everything from paper for printing to petrol for distribution. As a result of the transport problems – petrol was the first commodity to be rationed immediately after the outbreak of war – *Vogue* would be available only via subscription and would be delivered to specified newsagents.

The editorial went on to promise that *Vogue* would offer helpful, practical advice as well as the 'usual charming, civilised articles on fashion, manners and other things besides'.

We believe that women's place is *Vogue*'s place. And women's first duty, as we understand it, is to preserve the arts of peace by practising them, so that in happier times they will not have fallen into disuse. Moreover, we believe that women have a special value in the public economy, for even in wartime they maintain their feminine interests and thus maintain, too, the business activity essential to the home front. *Vogue* found this to be true in the dark years of 1914 to 1918, during which it was born and throughout which it mirrored women's many sided activities . . . So once more we raise the 'carry on' signal as proudly as a banner. We dedicate our pages to the support of important industries, to the encouragement of normal activities, to the pursuit of an intelligent and useful attitude to everyday affairs – and to a determined effort to bring as much cheer and charm into our life as possible. This, we are convinced, is the best contribution we can make to national defence.

Although appearing as the editor's words, it is almost certain that Audrey wrote this piece. It smacks of her spirited determination not to let a mere war get in the way of publishing a magazine that was dedicated to keeping up morale and encouraging women to be brave and to do their duty. It might seem out of character that Audrey continued to work for *Vogue* rather than leaving to take on war-related work. However, for the first nine months of the war it was unclear what women could do other than volunteer alongside their normal activities. By the time the Phoney War had ended, Audrey was already convinced that *Vogue* had a role to play and she was in constant contact with the Ministry of Information and other government bodies who wanted to influence women's thinking. She realised that *Vogue* could be a powerful weapon of war in its own right.

~

Audrey adopted a Siamese kitten the week the war broke out. She heard that a cattery in Maida Vale was closing down for the duration and several litters of kittens were due to be put down if homes could not be found for them. It was one of the sad facts of the early weeks of the Second World War that pet owners in major cities, fearing the effect of bombing, decided to have their pets put down, later to regret their hasty decisions. Over the course of the first few weeks of the war over 650,000 animals were destroyed and vets all over the country were unhappy at having to put healthy cats, dogs and other small animals to sleep.

Harry Yoxall met Timmy when he arrived at Blomfield Road a month after the war broke out to pick up Audrey and give her a lift to see her parents. As a cat lover, he was delighted to see such a pretty Siamese, but as an art lover he was even more interested in Audrey's pictures, which he described as 'good and well displayed. She had a nice Utrillo of the same period as ours'.

As they drove out of London and towards Oxford, they marvelled at the magnificent autumn colours. It was a lovely warm day and Audrey felt a weight lift from her shoulders as they left the capital. Harry wanted to talk to her about the disruption that the war had caused and would continue to cause *Vogue*. Paper rationing had already been introduced and the cost of a ton of paper had risen by 30 per cent. Deliveries of patterns and shells from New York would be limited and delayed as shipping was restricted and he had been instructed by Condé Nast to cut the staff at One New Bond Street. This last act affected Audrey directly and he wanted to talk to her about how the work could be spread out between the remaining staff, which was already smaller thanks to two men signing up to serve in the army and a couple of junior women being evacuated to the countryside with their families.

Audrey took the news in her stride. A monthly edition of the magazine would put less pressure on the small staff but it would also mean that it would be more difficult to react quickly to news. Like everyone in the office, she had been braced for the outbreak of war. Harry had been running air-raid practices since April and had impressed everyone by being the fastest to get from the top floor of One New Bond Street to the base-ment, down six flights of stairs, on every occasion. He had also drawn up a plan for succession in the event of his and Betty Penrose's deaths, which left Audrey in charge of *Vogue*. Madge Garland, who at that stage might have seemed like the most natural successor given her long-standing relationship with *Vogue*, was at the bottom of the list.

Condé Nast had demanded staff cuts at *Brogue* in order to compensate for what he believed would be serious wartime losses on the magazine. He told Harry he wanted the salary bill to be reduced by a third. Some of the cuts came from natural wastage, but some staff would have to be made redundant. Bill Davenport returned to America in October and would not be replaced.

The main problem that faced the office in the first few months of the war was the limit on working hours. Whereas before the war it had not been uncommon for Audrey to work until after 8 p.m., once the blackout was introduced at the beginning of September the office hours were restricted to the time between 9 a.m. and 5.30 p.m., with a compulsory hour for lunch when the office closed so the air-raid wardens would know where people were at any given time. The blackout affected every aspect of life. While it was inconvenient for the staff in the editorial and administrative offices, it was even more difficult for the photographic studio and the printers, both of which relied on lighting after dark and had large windows to cover.

In New York, Condé Nast and Edna were wondering anxiously what was going to happen at *Brogue*. Although the September figures were disappointing, sales of the pattern book held up and Harry reported that they had just about broken even despite the increased costs of production. Things looked up in October after *Vogue* switched to monthly editions and Harry took the plunge to print an extra 10,000 copies 'over and above what the blasted newsagents ordered' for the November issue. To everyone's surprise, the magazine sold out in the first ten days. That month he was able to report a healthy profit after taxes for the last quarter of the year. This was to hold up for the entire war, and two years in he was able to write to Condé Nast to tell him that his prediction had been correct and that the war would be good for *Vogue*.

Three issues into 1940, there was a change at One New Bond Street. At first, it seemed temporary, but, with time, it became permanent and represented the greatest change in Audrey's working life. Betty Penrose had arranged to take a holiday in Italy before spending an extended period in the United States to visit her elderly mother and ailing brother. While it might have seemed a strange time to take a long break from London, it was not clear in the spring of 1940 what direction the war would take. In addition, Betty was involved in a wrangle about pay that she was unable to resolve in London, so she was keen to be in New York to discuss terms personally with Edna and Condé Nast. Her demand was for a 50 per cent pay rise over three years. With her departure, Audrey remained in post as managing editor but acted under Betty's long-distance guidance as editor in everything but name.

History has judged this to be a turning point in Audrey's life, but in truth it was the start of a protracted six months of negotiations between London and New York. It had always been the intention for Betty to return to Britain in the summer and she had a passage booked for early June. A month before she was due to sail, Hitler launched the Blitzkrieg against the Allies and invaded Belgium and neutral Holland.

Just over two weeks later, with the British Expeditionary Force in full retreat, new prime minister Winston Churchill ordered the most ambitious, if desperate, seaborn evacuation of British forces in history. Over a period of five days, more than 338,000 Allied soldiers, mainly British, and a handful of civilians, were picked up from the beaches of Dunkirk, many by a flotilla of little boats, and brought back to Britain. It was a miraculous event for the country and a mighty relief for the personnel who escaped, although technically a military humiliation. A month later, France fell, and with that everything changed.

Britain stood alone on the edge of Europe, though shored up by support in kind and on the ground by Polish and Czech forces as well as the Norwegian mercantile fleet, Danish gold and the presence of several governments-in-exile who stood by Britain for the duration. As fears of invasion escalated over the summer, Harry Yoxall was in constant contact with Edna and Condé Nast over the fate of Betty Penrose.

Should she risk the submarine-infested waters of the Atlantic or an uncertain flight via Lisbon to London, or should she remain in the safety of New York? If she stayed, could she continue to edit *Vogue* remotely? And if not, who could replace her? Harry Yoxall cabled Edna in despair, explaining in the staccato language of telegrams his dilemma: 'better decide now whether Betty returns soonest possible or stays America indefinitely STOP doubt my ability continue bear editorial advertising.' Half an hour later, he sent another urgent message: 'Conditions may soon make quality product impossible and Betty's return likely involve her danger STOP She must decide personal problem you whether willing risk mediocre editorial.' At this point, Harry did not appear to consider Audrey a possible successor for Betty Penrose.

Edna and Condé Nast sent a joint telegram in reply to say that they would let Betty come back at the end of June, or, failing that, the middle of July if there were a cancellation aboard a vessel leaving New York, 'meanwhile full confidence staffs ability produce better magazine than competition and resigned to inevitable lapse quality in face insuperable difficulties profound sympathy gratitude.'

While Harry was mulling over what would happen if Betty Penrose were not to return, things were hotting up on the war front. In early July, the Germans launched their *Luftschlacht um England*, or the Battle of Britain as it became known. The objective was to force Britain to enter into a negotiated peace settlement. It was the most dangerous period of the war to date, and everyone, from Churchill down, feared that an invasion of Britain was imminent. The spirit of despondency did not last for long, however. The Royal Air Force, aided by pilots from the Polish and Czech air forces who had escaped to Britain after the fall of France, fought with bravery and determination. A nation held its breath as the mighty Luftwaffe tried but failed to overwhelm the RAF.

Audrey was having none of the defeatist talk about the quality of *Vogue*'s output. Her July issue, which was published just days after the fall of France, was dedicated:

> To the gallantry of the French: the couturiers who mean, evacuated somewhither, to maintain their vital export trade; *Vogue*'s Paris staff, who support and report them . . . to the spirit which lets off gay cracks, like squibs, among more frightening fireworks . . . a spirit we hope we may claim to share.

For the first time, Audrey brought the war directly into the pages of *Vogue*. Up to now there had been articles on women in the services, but they had been focused on duty and uniforms, training and preparedness. She was now taking a step away from cheerful, morale-boosting editorials and features to real war reporting. Sandwiched between an article about the beauty of the English countryside and a piece about nurses, drivers and organisers – women working in France, to treat the wounded in hospital lorries – was a piece of first-person narrative from an invaded country. She published an article by Lee Erickson, the wife of Eric, *Vogue*'s fashion illustrator, from Paris. She gave a bleak picture of their family's flight before the Nazis:

> Flight is too swift and easy a word to describe so dreadful a thing as this. Exodus is better – slower, heavier, more pain-ful. This sluggish river of tragedy filled the road as far as the eye could see. It was moving slowly along all the lovely roads of France in the bright sunshine, like slowly flowing blood.

She described how, in the four and a half hours it had taken them to reach Paris, 50 kilometres to the south-east, she had seen only one woman weeping. The rest of her fellow travellers were stern-faced and patient. 'A few hours after we left Senlis, a bomb fell 30 yards from our house and blasted our doors and windows across the rooms. The wife, mother and daughter of our butcher were killed. The butcher has gone mad.'

Bringing the war to her readers mattered to Audrey, and from this point she took control of editorial despite Betty Penrose's insistence on having the last word and Harry Yoxall's misgivings that quality could not be guaranteed. She had a sup-porter in New York at the highest level. Condé Nast had long argued that his editors in New York, Paris and London should bring the news of the moment to *Vogue*. It was his belief that a keener news sense, a stronger feeling for timing and a livelier talent for dramatising material would lead to an increased circulation.

He had suggested that the editors in every department should read their morning, evening and Sunday newspapers with the interest of *Vogue* in mind. If they found anything that would come within the sphere of interest for *Vogue* readers, they should mark it up and put it on the desk of the managing editor.

Audrey took this to heart. Long concerned that she was editing a magazine in wartime that dealt with the peripheral matters of fashion and furbelows, morale and duty, she could see a clear way that she could make *Vogue* more relevant for the time. Not only would war reportage, sporadic at first, bring the war closer to the lives of her readers, it would also help to make the articles on matters to do with fashion, beauty and, later, Make-Do and Mend more relevant. She could run pieces on the economics of wartime fashion, on the role of the fashion industry in earning valuable foreign currency and, eventually, on the prosecution of the European war itself.

For now, she was still in no-man's-land in terms of her formal role, but at the beginning of July they heard officially that Betty Penrose would not be coming back to Britain. Harry Yoxall told Edna of his misgivings about Audrey's fitness to work as editor given her lack of experience among the movers and shakers in society. Edna shared his concerns, but Condé Nast did not. He was categorical in his support for Audrey. 'I would rather have an editor who can edit than an editor who can mix with society,' he told Edna.

In September 1940, Audrey was officially named *Vogue*'s London editor, coinciding with the start of the Blitz. She was thirty-five years old and burning with ambition. The war had given her a special sense of purpose, and it seemed to others around her that the more difficult things became, the better she coped. She saw the opportunities for *Vogue* and she was determined to embrace them with her usual energy.

The new role came with a place on the board of Condé Nast

but no pay rise, and her name did not appear on the magazine's masthead until 1942. This was not a slight but simply because there was no masthead for two years owing to the shortage of paper. The war would shape her editorship from now onwards and she very quickly earned Harry's full-hearted support and admiration. She proved him and Edna wrong and Condé Nast right.

The first Luftwaffe bombs fell on London on 24 August 1940. Two weeks later, on 7 September, the sustained attack on the capital began in earnest. Three hundred German bombers and 600 fighters flew up the Thames and dropped their bombs on Woolwich Arsenal, a power station, a gas works, the docks and the City.

London was bombed for the next fifty-six nights consecutively. The reaction of the public went quickly from one of alarm and horror – over 400 people were killed and 1,600 badly injured on that first night, and thousands more made homeless – to defiance and acceptance. It became known as the Blitz spirit.

Audrey was typical of many who adjusted quickly. In the first week of the bombing, she and Jock slept downstairs for safety, but they soon gave that up and returned to their own bedroom on the first floor. She found the war exhilarating, not because of the fighting and bloodshed but because it gave her life a new value: 'I woke up every morning with the delighted consciousness of being alive and with a strong sense of purpose. Everyday affairs – usually carried out unthinkingly – became a challenging obstacle race that one rejoiced at winning.'

This challenge thrilled not only Audrey. It was reflected in the work of the photographers and writers working on *Vogue* and other magazines. The travel writer Rosita Forbes was one of those who spoke up for people who took up the challenge to keep going. 'It is the ordinary men and women of Britain who will win the war,' she reminded the readership in *Women's Own*, and she was critical of bosses who insisted their staff were protected during air raids.

I know it is not your fault when you are hustled into cellars by the heads of your businesses. But remember this war may go on for three or four years. There may be one or two or half a dozen air-raid warnings a day during that time. Hitler, after his success of the last weeks, will certainly do his best to go on slowing down our work – because he cannot otherwise defeat us. So every one of you should make up your mind that you won't stop working – just to please Hitler! . . . If you have nothing serious to do, by all means take shelter. But if you are on a job of work, you are a soldier.

As the bombs fell and the warning sirens sounded once, twice, sometimes three times a day, the editorial staff became frustrated by the inconvenience of having to leave their offices. They had firewatchers on the roof at One New Bond Street who had a panoramic view of the surrounding buildings, including the Burlington Arcade diagonally opposite, and these men would warn them if they had to evacuate. Early on in the Blitz an unexploded bomb caused an exodus from the building, and that day Audrey learned the lesson that she should always be certain that everyone working on the next issue had all vital papers to hand. The two days they were forced to spend away from the office were wasted and she knew they could not afford that in future.

As everyone got used to the bomb alerts, Harry agreed that rather than leaving the building, the editorial staff could use the basement to work during daytime air raids. The cellar was fitted out with desks for layouts, chairs for the secretaries and subeditors, as well as the accoutrements of an air-raid shelter: stirrup pumps, emergency ladders and gas masks, and a large sign over the door said, 'No Smoking'.

Audrey asked the photographer Douglas Slocombe to take a series of shots of *Vogue* in the bomb cellar, which she could use to illustrate an article for New York to show how the magazine was persevering despite the bombing. In one shot, Audrey and the art director, John Parsons, study a photograph while an assistant art editor appears to be busy sticking cut-out photographs onto a new spread – the glue, rulers and other tools of his trade scattered over the desk. In front of them sit two secretaries, one with a portable typewriter on her knee, the other subediting copy. Her chair is a deckchair and on the back of it hangs her gas mask in a fashionable print bag. The men are wearing suits and Audrey, as usual, is wearing a hat. Her black-and-white checked coat is the same one she was wearing when a photographer snapped the *Vogue* staff on Piccadilly three weeks earlier.

Another image shows eight young women with papers or notebooks on their knees and in the background three behatted older women, one knitting, who are indisputably the fashion editors, including 55-year-old Gertrude Pidoux wearing a severe black hat pulled firmly down over her ears. What is striking about the images is the air of calmness and normality they manage to capture.

While the editorial team was planning, writing and laying out the next editions of *Vogue*, the studio photographers had moved into a wine cellar basement in a Hungarian restaurant next door to their premises on Rathbone Street. Shoots were carried out among huge wooden casks and boxes of Pommery champagne from France. Harry Yoxall once spent a morning in the cellar with the photographers when he was caught out by an alarm on his way to Fetter Lane. That day, he recorded in his diary, there were six air-raid warnings. After he escaped from Rathbone Street, he made his way to New Bond Street where Audrey was holding the fort, ignoring the air-raid warnings: 'there are so many alarms now that one can't stop for them. Audrey is a tower of strength.' They worked through the next warning until it was time to go home.

The following day was 18 September. John Lewis department store had been hit, as had Bourne and Hollingsworth. Audrey heard that the photographic studio had lost all its windows in the blast that had accompanied the bombs but no one had been hurt. When Harry arrived for an editorial conference at lunchtime and there was another alarm, they decided to take cover in the shelter and hold their conference there in safety. On her way home that evening, Audrey walked along Oxford Street with Harry to survey the damage. They did so in silence, subdued by the sight of debris in every direction. Clothing models were strewn on the street, some limbless, others curiously intact. It made for a macabre sight.

There then followed the most intense bombing of their area of London to date. Audrey rang Harry from the office the next morning to say that there were unexploded bombs reported in the St Regis Hotel close by, so she was sending all essential staff home and would make her way to Fetter Lane with a nucleus who were preparing to put the final touches to the November edition. Two days later, Harry took Audrey out to lunch and noted matter-of-factly in his diary, 'Lunched Audrey: our usual haunt, the St Regis, has been bombed, so we went to the Café Royal. Much destruction in Regent Street at that end as well.'

That afternoon they heard the news of the sinking of the *City of Benares* in the middle of the Atlantic. Seventy-seven children on their way to safe homes in Canada died in the explosion or of exposure in the lifeboats before they were rescued. Audrey learned that evening that Digby Morton and his wife were on the ship with their children but were fortunate to have been rescued. It was one of the worst civilian disasters of the war and it put a stop to government-backed evacuation schemes to Canada and other Dominion countries.

That weekend Audrey learned that Condé Nast had agreed to give the nucleus of staff who had kept going in the shelters during the worst raids an additional week's salary in recognition of their bravery and commitment. It was accompanied by a glowing letter of appreciation from Betty Penrose for the standard of the work in *Brogue*.

A week later, One New Bond Street was hit during an air raid. Fortunately, nobody was in the office and the damage, though extensive, was superficial. Audrey, Harry, Vera Selfe (Harry's secretary) and a couple of others arrived early in the morning with brooms and dustpans. They spent the day cleaning and clearing up as best they could and then set about rearranging the departments that had to do immediate work, finding corners for people whose offices had been too badly damaged for reoccupation. The difficulty was that there was a time bomb in Regent Street, by Austin Reed's, so they had to put the black-out material up over the office windows that had not been blasted out and provide lights where people were working, in case another explosion shattered the glass.

Audrey was pleased to show her readers both in Britain and America that *Vogue* was carrying on, cheerfully. 'Here is *Vogue*, in spite of it all!' she wrote on a page of the November edition. She published six images of the bomb damage, two from outside showing the crater in the street below, a pair showing the interior with offices strewn with broken glass and two labelled 'Beneath', which show work carrying on in the bomb cellar. '*Vogue*, like its fellow Londoners, is put to bed in a shelter.'

Condé Nast and Edna had been horrified by the news stories of bombing in London and were concerned for their British workforce. Worry soon turned to pride, however, and the letters and memos from New York showed how much the Americans admired the British for their determination to carry on and get the job done. In a four-page spread with turns, New York published an article by Audrey entitled 'British *Vogue* Weathers the Storm'. The first quarter-page photograph showed Harry Yoxall in his bomb-blasted office, the floor covered in glass and shredded papers, on one of the two phones on his desk, pipe firmly in his mouth, with Vera Selfe silhouetted against the window. She has her shorthand pad in her left hand, her right resting casually on the back of a chair as if this state of affairs was entirely normal. The article was preceded by a comment from the editor, Jessica Daves:

This account of the difficulties of publishing in a *Blitzkrieg* was written in an air-raid shelter by the managing editor of

British *Vogue*. It is a further example of the courage of British workers, whose first thought is not for their own safety, but for the job they have to do.

It is interesting to note that although Audrey was officially editor now, America still stuck by her former title.

Although a prolific producer of captions and essential copy, Audrey had never contributed an entire article to *Vogue* in her own name. This lent her the opportunity to give American readers a sense of the drama of life in London during the Blitz, but also the new type of normality that they soon created at *Vogue* and of course at countless other offices and businesses in the capital. She tried to achieve a balance between bravado and pathos in the descriptions of how the staff were coping.

The greetings we exchange when we arrive seem to belong more to a hospital than an office. 'How are you?'... 'What kind of night did you have?'... There have been some sad mornings. One of our staff was killed when a bomb hit his flat, killing his mother also and injuring his sister.

It was not only death and injury but loss that she described: staff members had been bombed out of their flats and houses, all their possessions lost. One of those was Lesley Blanch who now had almost only the clothes she stood up in. Audrey wrote about how some staff had moved to the country but came in by train daily, while others stayed with friends and relatives, often sleeping on floors or in air-raid shelters.

In this 3,000-word article, there is no boasting, merely a

word picture of the changed circumstances, with delightful detail: every morning, once all the staff were accounted for, someone went down into the cellar to retrieve the big laundry basket, which contained all their 'treasures'.

> Every night it is packed up and every morning unpacked again. If the siren goes work goes on until the alarm warns that planes are overhead or that guns are firing with the result that we now take shelter less frequently but more rapidly.

She described the flight down into the cellar on such occasions:

> We grab work and paraphernalia, descend six flights of stone stairs to the basement. We look as if we are going on a peculiar picnic: coats slung around our shoulders; attaché-cases with proofs, photographs, layouts, copy, mixed up with gas-masks, sandwiches and knitting. The Art Department men carry under one arm a stack of drawings and layouts; and under the other, a stirrup pump, a pick axe or a shovel. It's a peculiar picnic all right.

Audrey had always worked behind the scenes and not pushed herself forward. Only in her editor's notes and the Withers to Chase memos would the voice of the British editor be heard clearly. This was her opportunity to tell the world how she was steering her magazine through the choppy waters of the Second World War. She described living during the Blitz in unsentimental terms:

Many people have moved down to the ground floor of their houses, and are living in one room, which is cosy and warm, although the guns outside are deafening and the shells whiz up and the bombs whiz down, and the house shakes as though a thousand poltergeists had been let loose.

She wrote of the gallows humour that prevailed: 'a feeble joke makes us laugh, and we're glad of the chance to laugh at anything; and on the other hand, you get oddly insensitive and callous, and are amused by incidents that normally you would have found macabre.' She described how two fashion models in a taxi were being driven back to the office and the driver told them with glee that the lorry behind them was transporting an unexploded bomb.

Audrey wrote about how her editorial staff worked to get hold of the material that would make up the next issue. It was still necessary for them, even in wartime, to be in touch with fashion, social and entertainment activities of all kinds:

And there's the rub. Shops have been bombed, stocks injured or destroyed, time-bombs have caused temporary evacuation of premises, explosions have shattered acres of shop-windows. And besides these more violent effects of war, every firm with which we deal suffers from the general dislocation: air raid warnings reducing hours of business; production slowed down; mails held up; telephone communications uncertain; customers evacuated.

Fashion models were scarce and sittings were constantly interrupted by late deliveries of clothes and air raids. When the alarm sounded, everything had to be bundled up, including the models, and taken down to the wine cellar. She illustrated the point with a photograph of the beauty editor escorting a model, wrapped in a towel, who had been in the middle of a photo shoot when the warning went off. The model's face is covered in cream and her hair in a turban.

Once all the various threads of the magazine had been drawn together, the next worry was engraving and printing. And then distribution. Everything was a problem, but every problem was soluble. Audrey told American readers that the October issue had come out on time and November, after the offices had been bombed, was only one day late.

> Each issue is a new hurdle in a steeplechase. We gather all our forces as we approach it; the difficulties pile up threateningly; one last spurt – and (so far) over she goes! And no owner leading in his steaming horse feels prouder than we on the day when all the book-stalls are hung with the new *Vogue*.

In bringing this detail to American readers, she was also painting a picture of life in London such as it can no longer be imagined today. She commissioned Beaton to write an article for her about London after the bombing. In 'Time of War', published in November, he described how London continued to function despite the nightly raids:

> The siren's wail and the terrible crumps bring useless unhappiness and filthy turmoil. The windows rattle with the explosion and a sinister wind blows the curtains into coils,

but the worst has happened here and we now know we can prevail; such reckless bullying cannot dash our spirits . . . The birds panic in the air and soar in circles at the approach of the desperate invaders, and the rabbits remain quivering on their hindlegs, shell-shocked for hours after the explosion, but the Londoner was uncowed.

He ended on a defiant note:

To spite Hitler and in spite of him, the garden catalogues arrive, and we order not only the beans and the potatoes and the spinach and cabbages and beehives that thrive so well in London gardens, but the fibre and the bulbs of hyacinths that will enliven the darkest day at home.

After the bombing of London, new vistas opened up and strange juxtapositions could be seen everywhere. As buses trundled through the ruins of Oxford Street, the sound of hens clucking and ducks quacking could be heard, while pigs slept in neighbouring Berners Street in makeshift shelters next to bomb ruins. Where once the Burlington Arcade had stood, there was now a vast reservoir that the fire brigade used to store water to fight fires. From Audrey's office window, the scene below resembled a lagoon beside a deserted fortress, and she found it strangely beautiful.

While Audrey was keen to impress on America how well business continued to function in London and how morale was still high, despite the relentless bombing of the capital and other cities, she also had her eye on the situation in Britain. It was difficult to justify working on a high-end fashion magazine during the Blitz when people around them were suffering death, injury, loss and devastation. It begged the question as to why fashion magazines were even tolerated by the government, who were already imposing quotas on all publishers, whether newspapers, magazines or books, for paper.

What was *Vogue* for? What, indeed, were any of the women's magazines for? There were several answers, but two of them were overwhelming and explain why someone like Audrey, with her strong sense of public duty and desire to support her country in a time of crisis, would continue to work on a fashion magazine. The first was that women's magazines had a special place in government thinking. Ministers in every department, from Health, Information and the Treasury to Agriculture, Food and Fisheries and the Board of Trade, needed to have access to every aspect of women's lives and to influence their thinking on food rationing, clothes, savings, spending, health, evacuation, education, hairstyles, stockings, entertainment – in fact anything and everything to do with a functioning society with a strong female workforce. They had already realised that it was more effective to appeal to women through magazines that they trusted than through the pages of the daily papers, which could be ignored.

Secondly, targeted features on every aspect of the war from its prosecution to its economy would drive home continuously the government's various messages. In the early months of the war, it was important to the government that people should not stop buying clothes. *Vogue* encouraged its readers to buy for their autumn wardrobes rather than holding back: 'every time you hold back from buying, you knock the national economy a fraction off its balance. Multiply that by millions, and it becomes a considerable punch on the very chin which the dress trade is trying to keep up.'

This was a message from the Treasury, and would have been delivered to Audrey and other editors at one of the hundreds of press conferences they were to attend over the course of the war. Ministers realised that a large female workforce meant more female spending power than ever before. It was important to ensure that women who were working had a few luxuries on which to spend their money as well as on routine food and clothing.

In a curiously symbiotic way, the world of women's magazines and the Ministry of Information formed a working relationship that, though strained at times, functioned well for both groups. Audrey reckoned that the women's magazines, from *Vogue* to *Mother and Home*, *Harper's Bazaar* to *Weldon's Ladies Journal*, reached over 90 per cent of women in the country. As *Vogue* was read by influential and affluent women, the ministry regarded it as a key platform on which to campaign in Britain.

Although Audrey had been formally appointed editor of *Vogue* in September 1940, Betty Penrose continued to manage her as best she could from New York. Condé Nast had made Betty editor of his newest magazine, *Glamour*, but she found it hard to give up on her beloved *Vogue*. A series of memos followed over the autumn including detailed instructions on the mechanics of dispatching material to New York. The memo system existed between departments rather than between people, so that those from Withers to Chase could be sent from Audrey (fortunately she always initialled her memos), from her secretary if the message was perfunctory, or from an editor or subeditor who had been asked for a particular piece of information. In the same manner, Chase to Withers memos were sent from the editorial office in New York but not always by Edna herself. Jessica Daves, the editor of *Vogue* under Edna's role as editor-in-chief, always deferred to Chase as the nomenclature for her correspondence with London.

For the rest of the autumn, Betty continued to try to guide Audrey's hand instructing her in detail how to use the material she was forwarding from New York. But she also acknowledged Audrey's vital role in sending material to America that would keep American *Vogue* up to date on the news from London week by week.

Sometimes her requests seemed completely out of tune with the situation on the ground. On 14 October, received the following day in London, Betty asked Audrey to find out the truth behind a small notice that had appeared in the *New York Times*. It had reported that the queen and other female members of the royal household, as well as their ladies-in-waiting, were practising shooting on a twenty-five-yard rifle range in the grounds of Buckingham Palace. She said she did not imagine it would be possible to get news photographs of this activity, but any titbits from the story would be lapped up in New York. The article had singled out the queen as the best rifle shot among the women in the royal household, but also that the Duchess of Kent was said to be a crack shot with an automatic pistol.

That night a German bomb had penetrated a London street and exploded in Balham underground station, killing sixty-eight people. The picture in the papers the next morning was of a red double-decker bus nose down in a vast crater. Betty's memo remained unanswered for six weeks. When Audrey asked her assistant, Brenda Hall, to reply, it was terse and to the point. There was resistance to it being known that any of the royal ladies knew how to shoot and it was impossible to send anything to add to the story.

~

After the fall of France, a number of British designers who had been working in Paris managed to escape and get to London. The arrival of Edward Molyneux and Charles Creed had a positive effect on the couture houses of the capital. Molyneux was regarded as the most influential British designer working in France between the wars, and his return to Britain gave Harry Yoxall the impetus he needed to call the British fashion elite together and encourage them to work not as individuals but under a loose umbrella organisation to capture the American market. It was obvious that the whole fabric of British life would change, but it was also clear that as a group or society the designers could better fulfil the government's ambition to offset enemy propaganda and prove that Britain could deliver the goods.

After an editorial conference with Audrey, Harry gave a cocktail party at the Berkeley and invited Norman Hartnell, Victor Stiebel, Elspeth Champcommunal and others to discuss co-operation. He told Edna that he felt like

a kind of mid-husband at the birth of a body where all the limbs . . . are kicking in different directions. But I feel that the couture boys and girls here will never get anywhere unless they form some kind of professional association and maintain as a permanent policy the temporary unity which was rather precariously achieved for the South American collection.

Audrey had met many of the British designers over the course of her work at *Vogue* but Molyneux was as yet unknown to her personally, though no one in London fashion could have been unaware of his reputation. Molyneux had begun his fashion career working for the society couturier Lucile in 1910 as a sketcher, and had moved to Paris in 1911 to work as an assistant designer at her Paris branch. During the First World War, he fought with the Duke of Wellington's regiment, attaining the rank of captain but losing his sight in one eye in the Battle of Arras in 1917.

He returned to Paris and opened his own fashion house, expanding to Monte Carlo in 1925 and London in 1932. He was known for the refined simplicity of his designs and was the couturier to whom the fashionable woman would turn if she wanted to be dressed absolutely correctly but without being predictable in the interwar years.

When the Second World War broke out, he remained in Paris, but shortly before the fall of France he escaped to Britain via Biarritz on a coal barge, arriving in London a few days later. He set up a salon in Grosvenor Street and let it be known he was open for business both in Britain and abroad. The Captain, as he was known, was in equal measure brilliant and demanding. Although he refused to attend the cocktail party thrown by Harry in late 1940, he assumed, correctly as it happened, that he would be made president of the soon-to-be-formed Incorporated Society of London Fashion Designers, known thereafter by its shortened form 'IncSoc'.

Audrey's first spat with Molyneux came in October during the Blitz. He had rung Audrey to tell her that he was not prepared to allow his designs to be included in *Vogue* unless he had been permitted to pass the photographs in advance. This was completely against *Vogue* policy and Audrey was having none of it. Despite the Captain's reputation and cachet in the world of haute couture, she was determined to stick to the *Vogue* line of independence at all costs. What is striking from this first of many letters that Audrey wrote when laying down the law to the great and the good of London and New York was the note of confidence she sounded in her writing:

> Now I must put it to you that such a procedure would be quite inconsistent with our editorial policy, and would create a precedent that could not but destroy the balance and harmony of the magazine. The value of *Vogue*, to the dress houses and to its readers, lies in the fact that it is a completely independent fashion magazine: and it is to our mutual inter-est that this independence should be unimpaired.

She went on to remind him of the dozens of pages devoted to his designs over the years and told him she was lining up Cecil Beaton to photograph his mid-season collection. 'Never, how-ever, has any edition of *Vogue* submitted a fashion photograph, in advance of publication, for approval to any outside party, however eminent.'

Predictably, Molyneux was furious, and over the next few weeks and months he tried everything he could to get her to change her mind, including involving the president of the Board of Trade. When that didn't work, he tried to suggest that Condé Nast had, at a pre-war meeting, agreed to the couturiers seeing their illustrations in advance of publication in French *Vogue*. Audrey and Harry consulted on this question and came to the conclusion that he was at best misremembering what Condé Nast had said. It had always been *Vogue* policy that editorial control should be absolute and final. The row rumbled on.

At one stage, Molyneux refused to allow any of his designs to be shown in *Vogue*, but he backed down and later told Audrey that he had never wished for publicity during the war. He had merely allowed *Vogue* and *Harper's* to show his designs to help keep the magazines going. Audrey had a challenging interview with him in Grosvenor Street when Molyneux insisted that Audrey's refusal to give him editorial control of his images to be shown in *Vogue* was a piece of 'gross discourtesy' on her part. Harry heard about this and told Edna how proud he was that Audrey had stood up for *Vogue* and for herself, not allowing Molyneux to cow her. 'I think Audrey, while showing a very proper firmness in this matter, has handled a difficult situation with the most perfect politeness and unlimited patience.'

The problem was that the government and the Board of Trade, who had little interest in couture beyond its potential to earn much-needed foreign currency, defaulted to Molyneux on anything to do with fashion. Molyneux had considerable influence as chairman of IncSoc, but 'because he has great power, and has fallen in love with the exercise of it, this is no reason for us to give way'. It was the first of many difficult conversations Audrey would have with people who were determined to put their cases before her with great force.

Whatever she felt personally about the row with Molyneux, she kept her cool. Later she confessed to Harry that the Captain had waged a long war on her nerves. It was one of her striking qualities that person after person who talked about Audrey would mention: she never lost her temper, however much she was provoked. One keen observer, Pam Makin, watched Audrey at editorial conferences. 'She had absolute authority when it came to editorial decisions. But she exercised it quietly. She knew better than anyone what was right for *Vogue* and when it came to it, she got her way.'

Eileen Toll (née Batson) who used her middle name, Sheila, while she was at *Vogue* because there were two other girls named Eileen on the staff, remembered Audrey's high standards:

> In the build-up to an issue going to print, there would be sub-editors going in and out of Audrey's office. If something wasn't right for *Vogue*, she would reject it and I would see the girls coming out of her office with long faces. But if she liked it, they would have a spring in their step and would be all smiles. That is how much people respected Audrey's standards and that is how much it meant to them.

Audrey never raised her voice and she did her utmost not to be dictatorial but to achieve results through consensus. She had once heard Alison Settle asking what the point was of being editor if she could not get her own way and remembered thinking at the time that this was no way to achieve a happy outcome. She explained later that she had tried to make the fashion and art departments and editorial people work together, like a committee, so that features grew up in general agreement. She only ever over-ruled people whose judgement she respected when she felt it really necessary.

She endeavoured to keep her personal taste out of decisions when, for example, the sheets of contact prints did the rounds, showing the initialled choices of the photographer, the editor-in-charge, the art editor and, finally, of herself. 'I knew that all of them cared about what was chosen, and would have been no good at their job if they hadn't cared.' If she felt that there was good reason to go with her choice as opposed to another's, she would always try to give an explanation, and they would usually be along the lines of the probable impact on the reader or arguing for clarity of information.

An example of her high standards was demonstrated in the early months of 1941. Betty Penrose had commissioned an article from an American author for Audrey to reproduce in *Brogue* but it was not of the quality the British editor required, and she said so bluntly, describing it as 'thin' and of just the type that appeared constantly in the daily press. 'The subject for us really has to be handled from some specifically *Vogue* view-point. The upshot is that Harry has arranged to sell parts of it to the *Star* for 3 guineas, and the rest will have to go down as "killed".'

Everyone knew that Audrey's opinion was the one that mattered, and they knew that behind the scenes Harry stood by her decisions. He described her in his autobiography as the example of devoted professionalism. He knew of her left-wing leanings and he praised her ability to show her personality but not her prejudice in *Vogue*, editing what was essentially a capitalist magazine with complete objectivity.

During the second year of the war, it became ever more difficult to fulfil New York's requests for society photographs and features. People were scattered around the country and often popped up in London with little or no notice, so that to arrange photographic sittings or interviews proved all but impossible. And besides that, Audrey was aware that there was a psychological resistance on the part of women in high society to being photographed and publicised in new clothes. She noticed that fewer people than ever wanted to have their pictures published in *Vogue*. When Jessica Daves requested a feature on women in London society, Audrey proposed Lady Audrey Stanley, one of *Vogue*'s feature writers, to do it. Lady Stanley was well-connected and she was more likely to have success approaching the aristocracy than anyone else at *Brogue*. Audrey suggested that the women should be photographed in new clothes but that the captions should refer to their war work. This approach was only partially successful because when the women went to the couture houses to choose their garments they all chose evening outfits.

Five months of negotiations with Mrs Churchill over the reproduction of some of her husband's paintings for New York came to nothing, to Audrey's intense frustration. She told Edna she had tried every possible avenue but felt that she had shot her last bolt. This unwillingness to co-operate with *Vogue* was part of a wider anxiety in Britain during the war about being seen to do anything that might appear to be frivolous or unpatriotic, even if the photographs were to be by Cecil Beaton.

By the time Audrey took over the reins at *Vogue* officially, Beaton had been out of favour with New York for the best part of two years. The furore over the anti-Semitic comments in the margins of the Crowninshield article had had a long fall-out, far longer than Beaton had imagined. Edna and Condé Nast had realised the loss of Beaton to *Vogue* was serious and they felt that he had been sufficiently punished by being left out in the cold. They had begun using images by him unattributed, though they feared that his style would be recognised by a rival publication. It would be humiliating to admit they had used his work anonymously, but in the end only one magazine editor noticed and no comment was made.

At the beginning of the war, Beaton had made a significant comeback in London when he was invited to Buckingham Palace to photograph the queen. In one image, reproduced in *Vogue* in the October edition, the queen is pictured in a long, white, sequined off-the-shoulder dress against a background of an eighteenth-century romantic landscape and surrounded by white roses, hydrangeas and heliotropes. He had captured his sitter in a regal but intimate setting. Seldom had such a relaxed portrait come from the royal household, and it was immediately seized upon by admirers of both Beaton and the queen as representing a stunning return to form.

Beaton's biographer, Hugo Vickers, observed a significant change in the tone of Beaton's diaries at the outbreak of the war. Gone were self-obsessed thoughts and personal hopes, and in their place was a deep concern for Britain. During the Phoney War, Beaton tried to work out what role he should take. In the spring, he began to work for the Ministry of Information and over the course of the next few months he photographed ministers and war leaders for the ministry. Some of these images accompanied articles in *Vogue* by Lesley Blanch.

As soon as Edna agreed to reinstate Beaton, Audrey used as much of his material as she could. Although she had been as disgusted as anyone by his anti-Semitic views, she recognised his significance to the magazine. She also understood that the war had inspired an intense patriotic loyalty, and he was spurred on to produce some of his finest work.

Beaton was a great improviser in the tricky circumstances of blitzed-out London. Material for photo shoots was hard to come by and had to be made of shatter-proof materials such as wool, paper and wire. When Audrey asked Beaton to photograph the French journalist Eve Curie, he brought props from his house, including pictures, miniatures, pots of ferns and draperies. He arrived in a state of high amusement because a sympathetic taxi driver had asked him whether he had just been bombed. He photographed her wearing Molyneux models, which she had chosen for her American lecture tour.

As the second year of the war drew to a close, the bombing continued unabated. Audrey's message to her readers in the December issue was encouraging rather than exhorting. She urged them to seize the passing moment and make Christmas memorable and happy, whether they kept it 'in the nursery, the cellar, the Anderson, or billets'. The Christmas festival should be celebrated 'even with tuppenny toys in twists of coloured paper'.

Their own Christmas was to be greatly cheered by a shipment of presents, mainly food, from Condé Nast personally. It included Virginia hams, chocolates and tins of fruit as well as silk stockings for the female staff, a rare and welcome gift after the British ban on the sale of silk stockings two months earlier. He also sent money to be given to every member of staff in recognition of their fighting spirit during the difficult months of the autumn, but also in case of future bombing where those who had been spared might not be so lucky.

The staff had already done exceptionally well, as Harry was able to show Condé Nast at Christmas. In the thirteen months since the start of the war, for which time he had figures, *Vogue* had averaged forty pages of advertising per issue, whereas *Harper's Bazaar* had only managed to secure thirteen pages per issue. This was of great satisfaction to Condé Nast on every level. He was always keen to score a point off his rival publisher, Hearst.

For Audrey, her first three months in charge of *Vogue* had been exhausting. The perpetual threat of bombing and the disruption to her office routine had made life difficult, but she was proud that the magazine had come out each month. Her staff were proud too, and just before Christmas Lady Stanley wrote to Condé Nast:

> We went through such a transitional stage and we did not know exactly what to strive for as everything was so precarious and atmosphere and feeling was as fickle as the wind, but now I really think a comprehensive pattern has come out of it all. Audrey Withers is a remarkable person. She has such balance and tact and we all admire her enormously as being editor just now must be a difficult job.

5

FASHION IS INDESTRUCTIBLE

'It is wonderful for us here to know how bravely England
is holding its ground, and a particular inspiration to us on
American *Vogue* to witness the incredible way in which British
Vogue continues to function.'

— CONDÉ NAST, 31 OCTOBER 1940

Wartime propaganda was a vital part of the prosecution of total war, that is to say a war in which there are no non-combatants. From the outset, the British government had recognised the importance of filtering information through a lens of their design. Raw news was seen as potentially bad for morale and certain stories were suppressed in order not to alarm the public. An example of this was the sinking of RMS *Lancastria* on 17 June 1940, with the death of up to 6,000 British nationals and troops. It was the largest loss of life in British maritime history, and though the government attempted to suppress it, the story broke a month later.

The Ministry of Information was the most active department in the government in dealing with propaganda, but the War Office, the Ministries of Health, Agriculture and Food all had vitally important messages that they had to get across. They frequently called together representatives of the major women's organisations, including the Women's Voluntary Service, the Townswomen's Guild and the National Federation of Women's Institutes, and editors of all the leading women's magazines for briefings and to get their advice.

Early in the war the government had been keen to get women and children out of the cities and into the safety of the countryside. This had resulted in a poster campaign directed at mothers telling them bluntly that their children were safer in the country. One particularly sinister poster showed two little boys sitting under a tree next to their mother with a shadowy figure of Hitler whispering 'Take them Back!' in the mother's ear, pointing towards the city behind him. The strapline below read: 'Don't do it, Mother – leave your children in the safer areas.'

During the Blitz, posters urged families to open their doors to passers-by or to contact a policeman or air-raid warden if they were bombed out and had nowhere to go to. The Ministry of Food wanted families to dig for victory and win the war on the kitchen front. These messages and others urging women to consider volunteering for war work appeared in all women's magazines. *Vogue* encouraged readers to plant vegetables in their borders and prepare for the winter by bottling, pickling and preserving fruit and vegetables.

The pressure on Audrey and other editors was intense, and it would escalate with ever more detailed messages on every aspect of home life. By the middle of the war, the government had so much control over people's lives that they could stipulate the width of the gusset in a pair of women's knickers.

If Audrey had been preoccupied by the drama of the Blitz on London in the autumn, by the end of the year she was focused on the future. She spent Christmas with Jock, her parents and Monica at Epwell Mill. Despite wartime rationing, they had been able to buy a capon from the farmer next door and Mamie's home-grown vegetables added a delicious freshness that Audrey and Jock had missed in their daily fare. The only thing that was missing was brandy butter to accompany the 2-year-old fruit and suet pudding, which they all decided was even better than the 1-year-old one they had enjoyed last year. Audrey and Jock returned to London on Boxing Day and she came straight back to the office to distribute presents to the staff with Harry Yoxall, a long-held *Vogue* tradition.

Audrey's editorial in January 1941 was entitled '*Vogue*'s Eye View of Britain's Future'. It chimed with the mood in Britain. The contrasting illustrations were Ford Madox Brown's 1852 painting *The Last of England*, depicting a couple aboard a crowded vessel sailing for Australia to start a new life. They stare ahead, stony-faced, ignoring the White Cliffs of Dover. This is set against a photograph of Mr and Mrs Churchill on a boat on the Thames entitled *The New England 1941*.

She wrote:

Ford Madox Brown's emigrants looked back at the port despairingly, because their life in England had fallen into ruins. Mr Churchill looks at the riverside grimly but hopefully, because it is only the buildings that are ruined, and life in Britain begins anew . . . We may be poorer financially, but it will only be our fault if we are not richer spiritually . . . The world we fight for may not be a Brave New World, but it will be a New World for the Brave. Luxury and ostentation will be gone, but quality and taste will survive . . . and so *Vogue* looks into 1941, confident of our victory, confident that beauty and graciousness will still keep breaking in.

Her optimism was premature. The war was not going in the Allies' favour, and things were about to get worse, not better.

In this same issue, Audrey ran a feature entitled 'American Aid for Britain'. She wanted her readers in Britain to know just how much their American counterparts were in sympathy with them and to what lengths they were going to show that. Betty Penrose had sent thirty-five photographs with extended captions detailing the energetic efforts of New Yorkers in supporting the British war effort. She told Audrey that barely a day went by when she and others were not besieged on the streets of New York by volunteers collecting funds for Britain. She described the whole of New York as being covered with pins, brooches, clips and vanity cases all bearing the Union flag. Audrey used fourteen pictures in a double-page spread with a cheerful introduction:

America is going flat out to help Britain. Every day and in every way they back us up, 100 per cent. Clark Gable's popularity pales beside that of Winston Churchill, whose fighting speeches and epigrams are quoted enthusiastically. There are no more large private parties – only 'Help Britain' benefits in all their many guises.

The photographs display the great and the good of New York at 'work and play for Britain': Condé Nast is shown at dinner at

New York's most famous Polish restaurant, while Edna dined with Mrs Arturo Toscanini at a party that raised over $20,000. There are pictures of women at work on behalf of Britain. One group is shown making surgical dressings and the caption informs readers that the Red Cross and similar relief funds had raised over $5 million for Britain. Furniture, bedding and food sent from America was handed out by willing helpers to the bombed-out homeless of London and other cities under the umbrella of the British War Relief Society that co-ordinated charitable donations.

Audrey was keen to celebrate the immense generosity of the American people towards Britain, but she did not want her readers to feel that Britain was not able to cope, so she published an upbeat feature called 'The Way Things Are', which reminded her readers how people in the cities and in the countryside alike were coping. Illustrated with sketches of life at the Dorchester Hotel with fire-watchers on the roof and high society dancing in the ballroom or sleeping in the lounges, it provides a portrait of high society at play even during the Blitz.

This feature serves as a reminder that one of *Vogue*'s pre-war focuses was on the comings and goings of high society. It was one of the last features of its kind under Audrey's watch. She was happy to show duchesses and dowagers doing their bit for the war effort, but she was not interested in featuring the same women dressing up to dance to Lew Stone's band three floors down while the bombs fell above.

In the January issue, she included a report from Paris on the strange life under Nazi occupation. The pictures chosen showed quiet street scenes with horse-drawn vehicles, carts or cycles, and the Champs Elysees deserted: 'The trees are still there, and the roof tops, but in the street, nothing moves; the silence is only broken by a military band or car.' It concluded: 'London at war is livelier than Paris under the armistice that passes for peace: more traffic, more shopping, more shows. Our scarred city leads a more normal, civilised life than the scatheless but stunned capital of France.' In her editor's note, she wrote that this material had come to *Vogue* via New York. It was easier to get news of life in occupied France across the Atlantic than it was across the channel. That state continued for the next three and a half years.

$\sim$

On the night of 12/13 April 1941, Fetter Lane, which housed the *Vogue Pattern Book* and other publishing enterprises, was destroyed by a fire bomb. Harry Yoxall wrote in his diary: 'the Fetter Lane business is my creation. Also, it was by far the most profitable side of our business. Henceforth our finances will be shot to pieces.' Audrey was woken early on the morning after the fire and immediately called her staff photographer, Lee Miller, to go and photograph the remains.

American-born Lee Miller had been working for *Vogue* since 1940, and she would go on to be a vital member of Audrey's war team in the future, but for now she was working for the *Vogue* studio on a variety of assignments. She took several pictures of the first-floor pattern factory. In order to get the best view of the smouldering ruins, she climbed into what was left of a six-storey building opposite, which itself was still on fire, and while firemen played hoses around her, she stood among the smoking debris to get her pictures.

Crowds of people watched the firemen fighting the fire, which burned for thirty-six hours. Some of the men managed to get into the ruins of the pattern factory 'where they found the steel bins still standing full of charred bits of paper which were once *Vogue* patterns; down in the flooded basement, the safe was burst open while it was still red hot, and the water-logged banknotes were taken out and put to dry'.

Audrey was relieved to report, in the same memo, that Ginger the cat, who Harry had brought in as a kitten four years ago, had been found 'undamaged' at the back of the building two days after the fire had started. 'He is still determined to go back and live in the ruins, and has to be kept locked up for his own good.'

This last detail appealed to Condé Nast, who had been applauding British *Vogue*'s achievements under fire. In a letter to several dozen key publishers, businessmen and advertisers in New York in February, he had written of his pride at the dramatic story of

> how our British staff is carrying on under fire . . . bringing out issue after issue, usually on time, in the teeth of bombs that have made its offices, on two different occasions, unin-habitable . . . scurrying to underground shelters at the cry of roof spotters . . . dodging 'no entry' signs at battered buildings . . . getting and photographing the new fashions, in spite of traffic tangles and bombing of our own offices and those of our clients.

He described how *Vogue*'s circulation in Britain in the first nine months of the war had increased by 8 per cent over the previous nine months and was now at its highest in its history. Condé Nast's pleasure in relaying this to his American audience is evident:

> One of the amazing things about this war is the way civilised life goes on in England, in the midst of devastation. Not just bread-and-butter life, but life with its graces stubbornly maintained . . . incredibly courageous . . . incredibly efficient.

The losses at Fetter Lane were significant: 350,000 patterns and 450,000 cheap DIY knitting leaflets were burned to oblivion, but Harry Yoxall had kept duplicates of all the master patterns and one of each cutting machine in his house in Richmond. Thus they were able to restart the *Vogue* pattern books more quickly than anyone had believed possible.

Just down the road from Fetter Lane, the twelfth-century Temple Church and other buildings in the Inns of Court were badly damaged in the same bombing raids that had taken out the pattern building. A few weeks later, when Beaton was back in London, Audrey commissioned one of the most famous photographs of the war. Entitled *Fashion is Indestructible*, it shows a model standing with her back to the camera, in the ruins of Temple, reading the sign on the building that tells its history. Two arches remain intact but the rest of the building had been reduced to rubble.

On 4 July, Audrey wrote a memo to Edna headed: 'Elizabeth Cowell in Digby Morton Suit'. Enclosed were a series of poses of Beaton's model. She explained that the church had been chosen for its historic interest at the heart of the British legal establishment. The model, Elizabeth Cowell, was one of the first two television announcers at the BBC and, besides having a lovely voice, Audrey wrote, she was also very good-looking.

The suit, by Digby Morton, was in a black-and-white lightweight herringbone tweed with a black velvet collar and fastened with silver studs rather than buttons. 'The skirt is straight and narrow, as we feel all skirts will be in future owing to the rationing of materials. Hat by Hugh Beresford.' In that prophecy, she would turn out to be right.

The most significant aspect of the memo, however, and indeed of the photo shoot as a whole, was that it was Audrey's idea.

> I had long wanted to get Cecil Beaton to do a photograph of a smart girl against some such background, as I felt this would show so dramatically how it is possible for *Vogue*'s entire world to carry on even amid such wreckage.

When the photograph was published in *Vogue* and *Brogue* in September 1941, it was widely admired, not just for the quality of Beaton's image, but for what it said about Britain's defiance in the face of continued bombing. It has become one of the most enduring images of determination to come out of the war and history has judged it to be one of Beaton's most memorable wartime photographs. No one, until now, has appreciated that it was Audrey's idea. It is proof of her instinctive understanding that a powerful image could tell a compelling story.

Still reeling from the shock of the fire at Fetter Lane and the huge damage done to London in the spring Blitz, Audrey had to take Edna on over material for front covers. Hitherto these had been supplied by New York, and Audrey had been able to choose which ones best suited *Brogue*. She wrote:

> Your series of summer covers was of course specially unsuitable for *Brogue* in wartime, and therefore it was not until your September 1st issue that we could get a cover that looked right for us. All kinds of small points now are apt to make your covers seem unsuitable to our eyes; for instance, your charming August 15th one which we should have loved to have, had to be ruled out on account of that full dirndl skirt which looks quite impossible to people who now must think in the skimpy terms of coupons. Again, sometimes coiffure or accessories are over-elaborate for England's present life, and we feel we must be most careful to avoid striking false notes.

While the bombs continued to fall on London, Liverpool, Plymouth and other cities, a group of statisticians at the Board of Trade, who had been safely evacuated to three large hotels in Bournemouth, licked their pencils and tried to work out what the clothing needs of the British population would be that year, next year and beyond. The cost of living had risen by over 25 per cent since the start of the war and the price of clothes had been a major part of that.

One of the reasons for this rise had been the switch of factory space from the manufacture of civilian clothing to military and other uniforms. Before the war many factories that produced clothes were tiny cottage industries with tens of workers at most. It made sense to combine forces, and consolidation happened over the autumn and spring of 1940–41.

Although the government was concerned with the safety and well-being of the civilian population, it was far more focused on the successful prosecution of the war, and when it came to it, the war took precedence over everything. The clothing situation in Britain had become a major concern for the Board of Trade, but that did not interest the prime minister and the war cabinet, even though it was set to have an impact on every man, woman and child in the country.

By summer, half of all clothing manufacture was for the military, which meant just half of the pre-war capacity was designated to make clothing for two thirds of the population. Added to that was the problem of acquiring raw materials. When it came to uniforms, the government had planned well. At the outbreak of war, the Wool Control was formed, requisitioning the home wool clip as well as purchasing the entire clip from Australia, New Zealand and South Africa.

Over the next few years there were shortages of other vital materials such as metal, rubber and cotton – three components of corsets, which were widely worn and advertised in *Vogue* and other women's magazines – but there was never a shortage of wool.

By the spring of 1941, the Board of Trade was sufficiently concerned about the clothing situation that it recommended limiting the supply on a rationing scheme. The introduction of clothes rationing was kept almost entirely secret until the day it was announced. The board was desperate to avoid panic buying, which would naturally favour the wealthy. At first, in order to preserve the secrecy, clothing coupons were simply the margarine coupons from the ordinary food ration book.

Clothes rationing came into force formally on Sunday 1 June

1941. It was announced on the radio by the president of the board, Oliver Lyttelton, later Lord Chandos. He spoke to the nation that morning telling people that to be badly dressed was to be considered patriotic:

> In war, the term 'battle-stained' is an honourable one. We must learn as civilians to be seen in clothes that are not so smart because we are bearing . . . yet another share in the war. When you feel tired of your old clothes, remember that by making them do you are contributing some part of an aeroplane, a gun or a tank.

For the overwhelming majority of the public, it was a complete surprise. Audrey was pleased by the idea of the democratisation of clothing, though she did not subscribe to the idea of women being badly dressed. In her July editorial, the first edition to appear after the announcement, she was typically upbeat, reminding her readers that *Vogue*'s policy for a quarter of a century had been to 'put your money into one good outfit and vary it with accessories'. This had been reinforced by the president of the Board of Trade, she went on:

> His rationing scheme drives home our message, inescapably; establishes our principle of 'quality rather than quantity'; leaves hats and accessory odds and ends unrationed as a loophole to let in light-heartedness in the way we have always advocated.

She admitted it was drastic but also that it was 'less alarming if viewed as the extension of a sound dress principle, proved by long use'. And anyway, she added, 'You can depend on *Vogue*. Where we once picked for style and price value, we shall now pick for coupon value, too.' In the back of the magazine, she listed the number of coupons needed to buy clothes for women and girls: fourteen for a coat, eleven for a dress or jacket made of wool and five for a blouse or cardigan. Undergarments and corsets would need three coupons and handkerchiefs in pairs, ties and collars one.

The Board of Trade had calculated sixty-six coupons represented about two thirds the pre-war level of clothing an average person might buy in a year. How did they come to that figure? Strangely, one of Lyttelton's colleagues at the Board of Trade had been working for the past eleven years with a statistician in the Bank of England compiling and sharing statistics on the subject of clothing. Lyttelton used their research as the basis for calculating the points required for clothes. Later, the statistician would claim their estimate had proved to be about 90 per cent accurate, which was adequate in the circumstances.

All through the 1930s, *Vogue* had been advocating ingenuity for readers on tight budgets. Articles on knitting hats, bed jackets and even swimming costumes had appeared in the latter part of the magazine after the dazzling spreads of Paris and New York fashions, so this new state of affairs was within the bounds of experience of *Vogue* readers.

Audrey told them that the Board of Trade did not expect people to go naked. 'They allow us ample material for our ingenuity and style and you cannot ration style. We must cut our cloth according to our coupon, but we can still snip as we please.' That message continued to be emphasised in *Vogue* throughout the next six months, but behind the scenes Audrey had begun to see how people were able to fiddle the system. She sent a long memo to Edna in December accompanying a feature on how four society women in London were surviving on sixty-six clothing coupons a year:

> I am afraid it has not got a very exciting appearance nor can clothes seem to have anything outstanding about them. What strength it has springs from the fact that the four women are well-known, well-dressed, and have been perfectly honest about their coupon spending. Please do not, in any editorial reference you make to the English coupon system, imply that smart women are not honest with their coupons, as I think it would have a very bad effect, but for your private information there is, of course, every kind of wangling going on made possible by the fact that there is no means of checking on any individual's coupon spending.

She went on to say that to her distress some of the worst offenders were women who *Vogue* would be interested in appealing to through the fashion pages. She had good grounds to know that many women were buying quantities of clothes, which their own and even their family's coupons could not possibly cover. Some women were buying coupons from their servants and others were asking relatives for favours: 'The shops themselves protest to us in confidence at the sort of behaviour they find, but they are helpless to prevent any except the really flagrant breaking of the law, such as handing loose coupons over the counter.'

Audrey disliked any form of cheating. She approved of the

fact that rationing of fuel, food and clothes had been brought in to see that everyone had as fair a share of commodities as possible. She told an interviewer years later that nothing made her more furious than cheats. Once, she had been standing in a queue at the off-licence trying to buy a bottle of sherry. Only one bottle per customer was permitted, but some would try to bribe the shopkeepers: 'I used to get so angry when I saw people in front of me openly slipping something to the man behind the counter to get two or three bottles. It went against the grain.'

Audrey explained to Edna how complex the coupon system was and how the Board of Trade had been fine-tuning it over the first six months of its existence. 'You may be amused to know that a kilt has till today been pointed at eight coupons, only one more than for an ordinary skirt, although it takes at least 8 yards of material. This has now been discovered, and a kilt from today costs sixteen coupons for a man, fourteen for a woman.'

The introduction of clothes rationing provided Audrey and other editors with an opportunity to refocus their editorial attention on issues of the day that affected women's lives in so many ways. The first eighteen months of the war for the civilian population had been unsettling (during the Phoney War) and then devastating and dramatic (during the Blitz). Civilian deaths outnumbered military deaths in Britain until September 1942. Thousands had died during the Blitz and many tens of thousands more had been made homeless and lost some or all of their possessions. She strove to maintain a balance in the magazine between fashion and beauty advice on the one hand and current affairs and wider political issues on the other.

Despite her best efforts, Audrey knew *Vogue* had its

detractors. A year after clothes rationing was introduced, the Welsh Labour MP Jim Griffiths expressed outrage that *Vogue* was being published on heavy, superior-quality paper, while it contained thirty, forty or more pages of luxury advertisements. He asked Oliver Lyttelton to stop paper supplies to magazines of this type.

Lyttelton replied that *Vogue*, like other magazines, was limited to 19.5 per cent of its pre-war usage, 'with a small addition in respect of export, and its advertisements are restricted to the same proportion of its space as pre-war'. Griffiths was not mollified. He described *Vogue* as a useless paper and was indignant that the Ministry of Information and the British Council bought large numbers of copies each month for distribution in neutral countries. He spoke of a widespread sentiment throughout the country that publishing luxury magazines was pernicious and damaging to the types of appeal for restrictions that the government was trying to instil in the public. Lyttelton fudged the answer and the questions moved on.

If she was piqued by the criticism, Audrey never shared it in correspondence, but she appealed to her readership to be generous with their copies since the wartime allowance was restricted to 80,000 per month and available only to subscribers. It was already widely known at *Vogue* through correspondence with readers that many subscribers shared the magazine with other women. A survey by Hulton in 1946 produced the stunning figure of an average of fourteen readers per copy, or over 1 million per month. It is quite likely that this figure was even higher during the war when *Vogue* was limited to subscribers and so much in demand that second-hand copies changed hands for three times the cover price.

It is easy to see why the government was so keen to see editors get behind the clothes rationing scheme, but the drive to encourage women to modify their behaviour beyond clothes also increased. Hair styling was another issue that the Ministry of Information wanted Audrey and other editors to address. Although the tradition for many women was the permanent wave, younger women looked to Hollywood for their inspiration. Few could fail to be dazzled by the screen idol Veronica Lake, who was famed for her 'Peek-a-Boo' hairstyle that seductively covered her right eye.

It was a stunning look, but hopeless for women who were operating machinery, and inevitably there were accidents. In Croydon, an incident in a factory was recorded in the diary of one of the female workers:

One of our new turners, going behind one of the lathes, got her hair entangled with a revolving rod of metal which was sticking out of Laurie Charman's lathe. Laurie on hearing her shriek turned off the machine at once and Rapley who was fortunately nearby, rushed up and cut her hair free of the rod. But it had taken the greater part of the hair off one side of her head and also left a completely bald patch about the size of a 5/- piece just above her forehead . . . actually we are not very surprised there has been an accident as Rachel obstinately refused to tie her hair up in a scarf and only wore a stupid little chenille fishnet which was no protection at all. She has now caused retribution to fall on all the machine operators as the decree has gone forth that we are all to wear the hateful khaki convict caps with a peak.

This and other well-publicised scalpings resulted in government propaganda posters encouraging women to protect their hair. Audrey ran a feature on short hair, showing how it could be chic, with photographs of the actresses Deborah Kerr and Coral Browne, as well as Elizabeth Cowell, of the Digby Morton photo shoot by Beaton, and Lesley Blanch. The caption read: 'Neat Heads. War work, whether in the services or factories, has always brought a wave of shorter hair – for neatness, easy cleanliness and good looks. The busy women opposite say it's easier, prove it's attractive.'

In order to make the pictures stand out, Lee Miller used her trademark solarising technique so that the overall effect is dramatic and memorable as well as beautiful. Audrey also ran a feature in that edition of *Vogue* on hats and turbans, so that every possible form of hair covering was addressed.

Throughout that year Audrey had almost full access to her star photographer, Cecil Beaton, and she made the most of him. His work appeared in every issue up to October, including September, when *Fashion is Indestructible* was published for the first time. In July, Audrey was able to secure a long, illustrated article by him called 'Winged Squadrons', which he produced having been embedded with the RAF.

The article is moving for Beaton's honesty about the trials of recording the war in photographs and the very deep emotions he felt:

No sooner was I beginning to get hardened to the wretched spectacle of bombed civilians, their cottages demolished, the prematurely aged children in the hospitals, or the awful overcrowding in the Underground shelters, than some different aspects of the war twisted a bit more the screw on my emotions.

Nothing had stirred him as much as spending time on air bases and observing the Royal Air Force at work and play. A casual visitor might conclude from a visit to an RAF station that the spirit was one of flippancy and lack of feeling, but

in a community where the presence of death is never far away, where the law of averages against survival is not kind, and so frequently from one day to another, from one hour to another, a friend may 'fail to return' (ignoble phrase with its note of censure), these subjects are avoided by tacit consent. If the emotional elements were allowed free play, the shocks would be harder to bear.

This was exactly what Audrey wanted for *Vogue*. Grit and glamour set side by side and in equal measure. The RAF pilots, the Knights of the Sky, were part of the most glamorous arm of the services, but their role was also among the most dangerous. A fighter pilot's life expectancy was measured in weeks, not months.

Beaton's writing was respectful, insightful and took Audrey's readers right into the heart of an RAF station. He described the 24-hour nature of the work, but also conveyed the way time itself had taken on a new dimension: 'The aeroplane travelling at such speed covers distance in almost miraculous time, so that history may have been made between drafts of beer.'

He contrasted the bravery of the Air Force crews with

the hysteria of the First World War, as he had witnessed it as a boy:

> the macabre recruiting scenes, the fanfares of trumpets and drums that heated the blood, and the military marches calculated to bring about wild deeds of bravery. In contrast . . . the new type of hero is one whose bravery needs no aids. He has a cool, calculated courage.

She was delighted. It made the men Beaton was writing about seem at once exceptional yet recognisable.

A follow-up article by Beaton on the ATS Brains Trust in September gave readers a glimpse of the development of secret weapons, 'the vanguard of the front-line' in the war, guarding secrets that had yet to be revealed to the prime minister. Lesley Blanch's article on the WAAF was illustrated by Beaton in October, as was her piece on the WRNS in November, but by then he had left London, sucked away by the Ministry of Information and told he would be sent to Cairo.

Just before he signed off, temporarily, from *Vogue*, Beaton told Audrey that he was keen for an enormous collection of his old photographs to be pulped for the war effort. Prior to the war wood pulp had come mainly from Canada, but once the Battle for the Atlantic had started, that had dwindled to a fraction of its previous supply. The war's appetite for paper was immense. Government departments such as the War Office, the Ministry of Information and the Ministry of Food consumed huge quantities of the precious material for advertising, propaganda and the inevitable bureaucracy.

Some of the most esoteric uses of paper were listed in a

Ministry of Supply report: corsets, no longer able to have metal stays (metal was required for aircraft), had cardboard stays that quickly went limp. Paper was used for everything from the obvious train tickets and food coupons to condenser tissue for wireless sets, the manufacture of concrete blocks and aeroplane runways. It is little wonder that the drive to save paper was stepped up as the U-boat war claimed an ever-greater tonnage of shipping.

Audrey answered Beaton's insistence on patriotic paper salvage by ordering all *Vogue* files to be pulped. In one massive purge and with the best of possible intentions, Audrey Withers and Cecil Beaton destroyed the entire pre-1942 archive of British *Vogue*. In March, Audrey reproduced a full-page black-and-white photograph of the destruction: print upon print of Beaton's photographs and drawings all scuffled together and ready for the salvage collector:

> This pile of pictures – treasure-trove for the waste-paper collector – is, in a double sense, the stuff of *Vogue*. These photographs of great ladies, of great beauties, of fashion and fashionables, were taken for *Vogue*: they have been published in *Vogue*; they are the essence of *Vogue*. Now they go to swell that flood of pulp, the merest particle of which flows back to *Vogue* as printing paper for our future issues.

She told her readers that this was just the beginning of *Vogue*'s drive to support the war effort in this practical way. 'This flood must be kept in spate, for paper is precious as a munition of war and as an essential implement of civilisation.' The image represented just a fraction of what Beaton had offered, she assured her readers, and urged them to dig out their squirrel hoards and send them for salvage and victory. From today's perspective, it is agonising to think how much material was lost in this and subsequent clear-outs, but at the time it was critical. It was another example of Audrey's inclination to look forward and not to cling to the past.

In her spare time, and when the bombing permitted, Audrey continued going to concerts with Jock and at the weekends they would go walking on the Downs or in the city's parks. London Zoo was still open and although there were fewer attractions than before the war, it still housed camels, zebras and bears. One Sunday morning Audrey and Jock joined Barbara Castle and her husband on a visit to the zoo.

Audrey was fascinated by a scene in the brown bears' enclosure. One of the keepers had a long handle with a wooden spoon on the end, which he dipped into a large tin of golden syrup and offered it to one of the bears, who stood up on its hind legs and licked the syrup off the spoon with great care. The other bears stood watching patiently until it was their turn to have a spoonful of syrup.

The reason this made such a deep impression on Audrey was not just the behaviour of the bears, but because she had never witnessed such extravagance with a precious sugary commodity on ration points. He must have been a bachelor, Audrey concluded. 'Barbara Castle and I, as housewives, could appreciate the extent of his devotion.' It is hard not to smile at the thought of Audrey considering herself a housewife.

~

In the early morning of 7 December 1941, the Japanese Navy Air Service attacked the American fleet at Pearl Harbor. It caught America by surprise and came as a profound shock. Edna and her husband had had guests to lunch that fateful day and had not turned on the news until the evening. They were in the car when she switched on the radio and heard the dreadful news.

> It seemed unbelievable, but of course we knew it had to come. How impossible though to imagine that we could have been caught like this. If there is any good side to it at all, I suppose it is that such a disaster as this has really gotten us awake at last.

Her next concern, of course, was for *Vogue*. Advertising would be adversely affected by the entry of America into the war, but sales of the magazine had never been higher. Like Britain, they saw a large uptake in the pattern book, which they believed would carry them through the difficult weeks and months until things settled down. Edna took great reassurance from London's experience of publishing *Vogue* during the war. She signed off the letter in an optimistic frame of mind: 'We all keep well in spite of everything. We know that we are going to win. The only question is how long will it take us?'

Condé Nast looked to Britain for guidance. The British, with their experience of the Blitz and a constant diet of war regulations, offered condolence, warmth and advice. Now in the third year of her war Britain had lived through many of the trials that were bound to confront America over the next weeks and months. It made sense to 'take many leaves out of her book of experience', he told Edna, and commended a five-page letter that Harry had prepared for Patcévitch, which contained a great deal of good sense, specifically in relation to the business aspect of Condé Nast publications in the near future. 'I cannot over-emphasize the need for you to read this letter with the greatest of care and thought. There is not an editor or department manager who cannot reap great benefit from it.'

The main thrust of Harry's long document was to reassure the Americans that *Vogue* would go on being relevant and that advertising losses would be offset against fewer returns as overprinting would be avoided. A second point was the way governments needed to catch the attention of the nation's women. He explained how the British government had learned very quickly that mass media and men's papers were not the way to do this. He predicted the American government would follow suit and urged the New York office to be on the front foot and push home the point that experience in London had shown that 'style percolating downwards is relevant . . . if the government can get *Vogue* readers to conform to the desired patterns of behaviour and thought, their influence will extend to other women.'

Condé Nast was very pleased with the advice. This would give him an early advantage against his rivals, but it would also fulfil his own belief that *Vogue* could and should lead on everything that influenced women's thinking. Nothing could be more important, especially as it was generally accepted that women in America had a bigger share in the control over family behaviour and expenditure than in England.

That same week, Edna sent Condé Nast an office memorandum asking him if he did not think it would be a good idea 'if we started to conserve writing paper by having our letters typed on both sides of the sheet? They have been doing it in England for a long time, and it seems to me that we ought to begin it now – before we are forced to it.' He agreed.

Where once Audrey had felt she was treated as a junior partner in the overall *Vogue* experience, she now provided a guiding and steadying hand as *Vogue* in America set out to find its way in the new environment of wartime publishing. The tables had turned in quite an unexpected manner. London could lead New York and Audrey lost no opportunity to remind her readers of the cosmopolitan nature of Britain's capital city in these changing times and its claim to be at the centre of the Allied war effort.

In the March edition, Lesley Blanch described the 'continentalisation' of London 'with new *boîtes* and *bistros* springing up overnight. *Plus Slaves que les Slaves,* we now boast *Sadko* at the Coliseum, *Sorochinsky Fair* and *The Great Gate of Kiev* from "Pictures at an Exhibition" at the Adelphi. There is the Anglo-Polish Ballet, Lydia Kysasht's Ballet, and Anglo-Soviet newsreels and films at the Tatler.' Audrey's editorial that month placed the Allies firmly in London and in a bold political statement she laid out her stall. 'We have great allies,' she wrote, describing China as a heroic veteran, Russia as a many-sided genius and America 'long generous in civilian aid and military equipment who, in December, took one quick stride from supply base to front line . . .' But London and Britain were at the centre of the action as the Allies worked to defeat Nazi Germany:

That part of our population which looked askance at 'foreigners' has grown used to the strange uniforms and strange speech. The Poles in Scotland; the Czechs in the Midlands; the Free French fishermen in Cornwall; the Dutch and Norwegian sailors in the ports, have become an established part of the landscape. A generation is growing up here of European citizens whose sympathies it would be impossible to blunt with the phrase 'a far-off country of which we know nothing'. And that surely may be accounted progress . . .

The formalities of diplomacy are being replaced by personal contact, direct and simple. Crowned heads and ministers meet without ceremony in the ordinary course of their business and social lives. They are finding fresh grounds for understanding and respect. They are hammering out strong bonds of unity. The foundations of the united states of Europe are being laid in England now.

6

AUSTERITY WITHERS

'. . . And for England with all its faults I love thee still, read
Audrey . . .'

— PAUL NASH TO AUDREY, 1928

When Audrey became engaged to Jock, Paul Nash disappeared
out of her life. The flow of witty, provocative letters that had
been a great source of joy to Audrey had dried up overnight. It
was probably not surprising given the change in her status, but
the sudden absence of a constant presence in the background
had been upsetting. In 1935, Nash started a love affair with the
British Surrealist painter Eileen Agar. His letters and postcards
to her during this period have none of the wit and delight of
those he wrote to Audrey in the late 1920s, but his relationship
with Agar went beyond infatuation and had a real influence
on his work.

He corresponded once or twice in the late 1930s with Percy
Withers, but it was not until late 1941 that Nash and Audrey
bumped into one another again, when she was thirty-six and
he fifty-two. By this time Audrey was a high-powered and

highly respected editor but Nash was delighted to see that she had lost none of her sense of fun. They were both ecstatic and immediately hatched a plan for Nash to write for *Vogue*. 'What fun it will be if you and I can produce an article,' he wrote to Audrey in late November. 'I think the proper procedure would be lunch together, on *Vogue* (or on me if that is not on).' They met up and she commissioned a piece from him called 'The Personality of Planes'.

Paul Nash had become an official war artist once again, one of only five to share that distinction in both world wars. He had developed a passion for aircraft and thought of them as central characters in the Second World War. He was no plane spotter, but rather an appreciative witness to their power. He wrote about the alarming and beautiful monsters that appeared in this world war: the tank, the torpedo, the submarine and the aeroplane.

> All had individual beauty in terms of colour, form and line, but beyond, or was it *behind* that actual appearance, these things possessed each a personality, difficult to define and yet undeniable. It was not wholly a matter of mechanistic character. There seemed to be involved some *other* animation, a 'life of their own' is the nearest expression I can think of, which often gave them the suggestion of human or animal features.

Kenneth Clark, who was chairman of the advisory committee on war artists, offered Nash the post of official war artist to the Air Ministry. Nash told Audrey that it was an opportunity that seemed almost miraculously providential. He photographed, sketched and painted the beautiful monsters – and not only British planes, but also German wrecks that were salvaged and taken to Cowley dump near Oxford. One of his most famous paintings from the war was of wrecked German aircraft entitled *Totes Meer* ('Dead Sea').

He submitted his article to Audrey in mid-December and received the edited version with suggestions of cuts a few days later. His letter acknowledging her proofs was full of the old affection and enthusiasm of his earlier correspondence:

> I am so very glad you enjoy this unexpected adventure. I welcome it warmly and am charmed by your own happy fusion of intelligent sympathy and practical sense. They are not so often found together, when they are wanted.

He went on to say that he would try to get the article back to her by New Year's Eve and that he had a

> childish desire to muscle in on some party. It is ages since I went to a New Year's Eve party which was a party in the right sense. Have you any ideas yourself? Something must be happening on the brink, as it were . . .

It was Paul Nash who broke the news of the aeroplane article in *Vogue* to Mamie and Percy, not Audrey. He wrote to them just before Christmas to share his delight that he and Audrey had managed to collaborate on the project. Mamie replied by return that Audrey had been to lunch with Jock and the whole article had 'been enveloped in mystery. She had not spoken of it. I'm so very glad that all is fixed up and that the fee will follow – it is so good that you have got together again after all these years.'

The article went back and forth between them for the next few weeks and his letters always started 'My Dear Audrey'. In them, there is a combination of his enduring teasing affection overlaced with a new respect for her role as *Vogue*'s editor. In the last letter before the article appeared, he wrote that he would like to think he could produce more articles for *Vogue* under her editorship:

> Why shouldn't I write at fairly regular intervals, I think I can find you some ideas. It's probably my turn to write for *Vogue*, damn well everyone else has had a shot. My word what an innings Bloomsbury had under Todd . . .

'The Personality of Planes' was published in March 1942 and ran to 1,700 words with illustrations in colour. It was an eccentric piece of anthropomorphism combining his passion for the artistic process of portraying their characters pictorially and his own expression in writing. Audrey was delighted, but Edna was not. She sent a memo to Audrey leaving no room for doubt that this was not the kind of feature she wanted for *Vogue*.

It was not the only article that was rejected during the war, but the manner of the rejection was harsh and it must have stung: 'We do not like the Paul Nash feature and we do not intend to use it,' she wrote. She then went on to say she was unwilling to share the cost of the engravings, 'which we do not feel are worth the expense.' As put-downs go it was firm and final, though she did acknowledge that Audrey would be disappointed on a personal level given her attachment to the artist. Edna was shrewd and she must have known that this piece had been born out of a friendship rather than a professional relationship.

Edna's reaction stopped the idea of further Paul Nash articles in its tracks, but it did at least open up the friendship between Audrey and him once again. He invited her to have a drink with him when he was up in London and she was expected at his exhibition at the Leicester Galleries that summer, signing off his letter to her 'your ageing devoted friend'. After the article appeared in *Vogue*, he gave her a drawing as a souvenir of their collaboration. It is a watercolour sketch of a tree in a winter landscape. On the back, the inscription reads: 'Souvenir for Audrey, intended for Christmas, missed New Year and nearly hit Easter, from Paul.' It is the only example of Audrey allowing a personal friendship to cloud her editorial judgement.

~

According to people who met him, Jock Stewart could walk into a room or a bar and women would immediately and discreetly check their hair or lipstick or straighten their skirts as he walked past them. At a little over 6ft, he cut an appealing figure, and it was not long before he began to seek pleasure and female company away from home. It suited him that his mother kept house for them and Audrey's long hours at *Vogue* meant that he had the excuse to take off in the evenings.

Audrey always maintained that none of her friends knew that she and Jock were living almost separate lives. 'We always remained great friends,' she wrote towards the end of her life, but people who knew her at work were aware of the almost irreconcilable clash between the tidily dressed, highly intelligent and motivated Audrey and the handsome, devil-may-care Jock Stewart who would turn up to *Vogue* parties always on the lookout for an attractive girl to flirt with.

He had left his job as assistant manager at Bumpus and was working as a salesman for a company called Cefoil that later became Alginate Industries Ltd. It used chromium alginate, harvested from seaweed, in camouflage netting as a replacement for Indian hemp, which was hard to acquire after the outbreak of war. The factories, four in total, were based in Argyllshire and Ayrshire, with the main alginate works at Barcaldine near Oban on Loch Creran and funded by government money, though it is unlikely that Jock ever got further north than Paddington Basin. His offices were at 22 Henrietta Street in Covent Garden, close to plenty of entertainment, even in wartime.

The staff in the *Vogue* photographic studio used to laugh about Jock's role, asking if 'Mr Stewart had picked up any more seaweed?', and it was always a joke that if you ever went to get anything to eat with Audrey it would be a seaweed sandwich. The change in job seemed to give Jock some satisfaction, and he appeared more settled and confident than he had pre-war. It would last only for the war years, however, when the challenge of providing raw material for the camouflage industry had an edge to it.

While Audrey kept her private life as far away from her office as she could, she was unable to hide an attack of chickenpox that developed into shingles in the summer of 1942. She was away from the office for three weeks and spent some of that time recuperating at Epwell Mill. It was not a happy stay.

Audrey was in great discomfort with shingles and Percy Withers was growing increasingly infirm. He had spent several weeks the year before in Acland House in Oxford being treated for the side effects of his diabetes, but there was nothing the doctors could do for him other than order him to rest. He returned home, weaker and more dependent on Mamie than ever.

Petrol rationing meant that they could seldom venture further than Banbury and their social life had almost come to a halt as a result of the war and Percy's ill health. He spent most of his time in his study reading or writing letters. His hand was now so frail that his letters were almost indecipherable, and short.

He wrote to Paul Nash:

> I am now becoming the merest wreckage. I cannot climb the stairs or safely walk on the level without Mamie's help. She waits on me hand and foot, and the only sound part of me is my heart – my memory gone, my wits gone . . .

Mamie in turn had written to Nash to warn him of Percy's declining health – 'He fails rather quickly: don't mention it!' she warned him.

The weeks she spent at Epwell depressed Audrey. Souldern Court had been the house full of sunshine and poetry, happiness and laughter. Epwell Mill was a sadder place and home to an ageing couple and their difficult son. Mamie struggled to maintain the peace between Percy and Michael, who were intolerant of each other and had nothing in common. Dinner times were either silent or passed in stilted conversation, neither of which made for a happy atmosphere.

Michael had been working at a local kennel for the past few years and on account of his unspecified condition had been deemed unsuitable for war work, though he had joined the Home Guard. He was now in his early thirties and towered over his ailing father. Audrey felt sorry for Percy in his ill-health, but even more sorry for her mother, though Mamie's dislike of any sort of sympathy or affection meant that she kept Audrey at arm's length and Audrey was in no position to fight. She was exhausted and needed to rest.

In keeping with her decision to hold the two parts of her life separate, she seldom shared any of her ideas and plans with Mamie or Percy. Mamie received a copy of *Vogue* from Audrey every month but it arrived without ceremony or explanation. That she was proud of her daughter there can be no doubt, but she could never tell Audrey anything as personal as that. She merely admired from the sidelines and made reference to the articles in *Vogue* that she particularly liked in letters to friends and family.

While Audrey was away from London, *Vogue* featured a new variation on the most recent clothing initiative introduced by the Board of Trade earlier that year: Utility and Austerity. This would affect fashion in a more dramatic way than rationing ever had. The board realised not long after clothes rationing was introduced that it did not go far enough. Even reducing the number of clothing coupons issued to the public, which the board proceeded to do year on year, would not be sufficient to guarantee an adequate supply of clothing for the civilian population.

There were several reasons behind the board's thinking, the major issue being the concentration of labour in factories. Fewer factories were devoted to making civilian clothing as more capacity was required for uniforms for the armed services. Another was shipping. The war in the Atlantic, which had begun in September 1939, was now in its third year, and the shipping losses that resulted from increased U-boat activity were double what they had been six months earlier. This resulted in a dwindling of supplies of raw materials as well as clothes.

A poor harvest the previous year and a reduction in clothing coupons had had a bad effect on civilian and forces morale. The Japanese had captured the impregnable fortress of Singapore and now the so-called Greater Co-Prosperity Sphere extended to cover almost the entire East Asia-Pacific region, cutting off the West's supply of rubber. And finally, closer to home, there were Hitler's 'Baedeker' raids on the historic cities of Bath, Exeter, Norwich, Canterbury and York in revenge for RAF attacks on Lübeck and Rostock, and increased food rationing.

The Board of Trade had debated reducing the number of coupons for women entering the services. That was voted down, but the maximum number of coupons for uniforms for what the board termed 'fancy dress' women was reduced from thirty-six to sixteen. Audrey must have bristled with indignation when she read that. The so-called fancy-dress women were members of the voluntary services of the women's armed forces, such as the WVS and the Mechanised Transport Service, both of which had proved vital to the war effort, especially the former during the Blitz. To label 1 million volunteers in such a manner was an insult.

Audrey was invited to confidential meetings at the Board of Trade where she and other senior figures in the fashion industry met the new president, the energetic Labour MP Hugh Dalton. There they discussed the best possible way to convince

Percy Withers at Souldern Court.

Mamie Withers with Oscar.

Audrey aged seventeen in *Quality Street*, a comedy by J. M. Barrie.

Paul Nash drew Audrey in her new dress and wrote: 'Bless your mischievous eyes.'

Audrey (centre, middle row) at Somerville College, Oxford, 1927.

Front cover of *Vogue*, 9 June 1937.

Beaton's portraits of the Duchess of Windsor at Château de Candé.

Designs by Lanvin and Molyneux captured by André Durst in *Vogue*, 9 June 1937.

Harry Yoxall and secretary, Vera Selfe, in the director's office, One New Bond Street, after a bomb blast, October 1940.

Audrey and colleagues put *Vogue* to bed in the bomb cellar of One New Bond Street.

The 'stuff of *Vogue*' is pulped for paper salvage.

Audrey was keen to show how her American colleagues supported Britain long before the US entered the war. *Vogue*, January 1941.

Date 3rd July, 1941.   No.

3-10/39-8000

JUL 14 REC'D

Subject   ELIZABETH COWELL IN DIGY MORTON SUIT.

We are sending you a series of poses of a Digby Morton suit, photographed in the ruins of the Temple, because the background is of such historic interest, and I wanted you to have a wide choice.

I expect your papers will already have reported the terrible destruction to the Temple which has been heavily bombed on several occasions and which has had much of its superb architectural architecture reduced to rubble.

I had long wanted to get Cecil Beaton to do a photograph of a smart girl against some such background, as I felt this would show so dramatically how it is possible for Vogue's entire world to carry on even amid such wreckage. In this case, the model is Miss Elizabeth Cowell, who was one of the first two television announcers, and the first woman announcer at the B.C.C. Besides having a lovely voice, she is a very good-looking girl.

The suit is by Digby Morton, in black and white lightweight herringbone tweed with black velvet collar. The jacket fastens to the neck with silver studs instead of buttons. The skirt is straight and narrow, as we feel all skirts will be in future owing to the rationing of materials. Hat by Hugh Beresford.

This photograph will appear prominently in the August Wool Fashions Export Supplement, and ixxx also probably as a frontispiece to Vogue's September issue.

B.E.3339-3344. Elizabeth Cowell among the ruins of the Temple wearing Digby Morton's suit.

V 4171

air mailed 7/5
rec'd 7/14

Memo 632, discovered in October 2018 in the Condé Nast archive, New York, showing that Audrey commissioned Beaton's *Fashion is Indestructible*.

Fashion is Indestructible by Cecil Beaton, 1941.

Fall of the Citadel, aerial bombardment, St Malo, France 1944 by Lee Miller.

Lee Miller with the essentials of life – a cigarette, wine and petrol, Germany, 1945, by David E. Scherman.

Infantry Waiting for Attack by Lee Miller, Alsace, 1945. She wrote, 'I'll never see acid yellow and gray again like where shells burst near snow without seeing also the pale quivering faces of replacements, gray and yellow with apprehension.'

Audrey (second from left) and Anne Scott-James (centre) study a design by Henry Moore for the 'Britain Can Make It' exhibition at the Victoria & Albert Museum in 1946.

'Everything you wear is only as smart as the way you wear it.' *Vogue*, June 1957.

Summer Life by Antony Armstrong Jones (Lord Snowdon), *Vogue*, June 1957.

Everyone who met Audrey commented on her eyes that sparkled with
enthusiasm even when she was well into her nineties.

the general public that more restrictions on clothing would be necessary.

Audrey advised the civil servants drawing up the scheme on the detail of austerity design restrictions. She had always approved of the idea as she felt it was right that design should be simplified and constrained in wartime. Her experience of the *Vogue* patterns over the past two years had convinced her that the public was ready for clothes with less yardage of material and thus greater simplicity.

Austerity dictated design specifics: the length of skirts and the number of pleats; the number of buttons to be used on coats and jackets; the length of men's socks and tails on shirts. It also forbade certain details, such as turn-ups on men's trousers, which was extremely unpopular, as was the restriction on the length of men's socks; double-breasted suits were replaced with single-breasted ones and large pockets were out of favour. Elastic waistbands and zip fasteners were ruled out, elastic was banned on almost all products with the exception of women's knickers, and designs for those were also limited by austerity. Even high heels faced a ban.

When utility was due to be introduced, the government was against the idea of publicising it, but the Board of Trade, led by the fashion editors, persuaded them that it would be popular – and they were right. The press was supportive, though the name drew criticism from all quarters. When the austerity rules on design were announced, Audrey applauded them publicly, as did Hardy Amies and Digby Morton, who joked that they had been making designs that would conform to the new restrictions for years. Chic, in their minds, had been pared-back British design at its best. It was then that Harry

Yoxall christened Audrey 'Austerity Withers' because of her enthusiastic espousal of the new fashion limitations.

The Board of Trade introduced the utility scheme in February 1942, the month that soap rationing was introduced. Utility was brought in to limit the amount of material and labour used in the manufacture of civilian clothing. Austerity restrictions on clothing design followed a few months later.

Concentrating production on a limited number of fabrics with much longer runs was both practical and sensible. It also had the effect of increasing the quality of material used to make clothing. Utility clothing was slow to catch on, despite the fact it was cheaper and often of better quality than non-utility garments. The government needed to do something to bring it to the public's attention.

To their credit, they allowed the Board of Trade to take the bold and imaginative step that Audrey had proposed of hiring top couturiers to produce designs for the mass production of clothes. She was pleased, as was her fashion team. This would prove their point that if the top women in society, such as the readers of *Vogue*, embraced a new style – even a government initiative – the rest of the female population would follow suit.

The board invited members of IncSoc to produce designs for outerwear that kept to the austerity guidelines. Edward Molyneux, Charles Creed, Hardy Amies, Digby Morton, Victor Stiebel, Elspeth Champcommunal, Bianca Mosca and Peter Russell each designed four garments: a top coat, a dress, a blouse and a skirt, which would be suitable for mass production. They had been briefed in March and the clothes were due to be shown to the public in September.

Audrey persuaded Digby Morton, Bianca Mosca and Peter Russell to allow *Vogue* to publish their designs for the Couture 'Austerity' in the July edition to show how full of interest the prospect of utility clothing would be. This was a full-bodied pitch to the *Vogue* reader, who, after three years of war, seemingly endless bad news and ever more restrictions, needed something to pick her up at a low point in fashion's history:

> Fashion is undergoing a compulsory course of slimming and simplification . . . It is a great opportunity for the couture. They, by sheer skill of cut, sheer interest of fabric, can turn negative restrictions into positive triumphs.

The double-page spread of austerity sketches was followed up by page after page of encouraging and uplifting fashion editorial about renovation, use of colour and rehashing last year's prints. It was hardly the stuff that dreams are made of, but it was the best the fashion staff could do in the context of ever more severe restrictions.

Such was the paucity of new fashion on offer that Audrey decided to focus individual issues of *Vogue* on aspects of wartime life. In August, the magazine turned its attention to 'Beauty and the Younger Generation', while in September the focus was on food production and cookery, with practical tips about bottling, pickling, pulping and preservation.

October's edition was almost ready to go to print when Audrey returned to the office. She was still weak after the shingles, but relieved to be back in London and away from the tense atmosphere of Epwell Mill. This was an important issue, as it featured, for the first time, the actual models designed by the IncSoc couturiers for the Board of Trade. She gave them ample space: six pages of photographs and a long, informative text by the fashion editor.

'Fashionable Intelligence' flew the flag for British fashion designers with energy, relating how the couturiers 'were passionately anxious to show themselves worthy of the place offered them in a grim and greying world . . . embracing a wider, more democratic field than has ever been covered before'. While it was a crucial message to get across to *Vogue*'s readers, it did not entirely reflect opinions behind the scenes. Molyneux was not the only designer who expressed his discontent with utility, but whatever their private thoughts, the designers kept them to themselves and the launch was a triumph. Audrey believed the utility scheme did a great service to British fashion in the way it dispensed with elaborate and over-fussy detail and focused on simplicity and clean lines.

The popular press, as well as *Vogue* and other magazines, was delighted, telling readers that the woman on the street could now wear a dress designed by the couturiers for the wealthy but for a fraction of the cost. Initially the only people deeply sceptical about the involvement of IncSoc couturiers were the trade designers, who complained that the Mayfair houses had been brought in to show industry its job. But soon enough the patterns from Molyneux, Stiebel and the others were in high demand by those very critics, and within weeks 'the society woman who pays 30 guineas for a frock will share her dress designer with the factory girl who pays 30s'.

October's issue of *Vogue* was barely on the newsstands when devastating news arrived from New York. Condé Nast, the greatest magazine publisher of his generation and champion of women's fashion and beauty, had suffered a fatal heart attack on 19 September. He had been unwell for some time, but the staff in the London office had no idea that his health was in such a parlous state and his death came as an enormous shock.

Although she had not known Nast on a personal level like Harry had, Audrey had formed a working relationship with him, especially during the Blitz, when his support, both moral and financial, for the staff of *Vogue* had been exceptionally generous. She also knew him to have been a man of exceptional judgement and rigour, something she as an editor greatly appreciated.

While Harry spent the next two days preparing obituaries for the trade press, Audrey planned her own tribute for the November issue of *Vogue*. In a 200-word article, she managed to condense her thoughts on Nast's vast contribution to the world of fashion publishing while bringing her own personal touch to the piece. She paid tribute to him as a man who always originated, never copied, who lifted the standards of fashion illustration and photography to the highest level and who put *Vogue* at the pinnacle of that achievement. She recognised his firm friendship to Britain and France in both world wars, 'long before the United States officially joined us in the actual fighting', and ended:

To us, who have worked with him and who feel his loss most deeply, he was a human, humorous, kindly and understanding chief. We pledge ourselves, as our memorial to him, to strive to maintain the distinguished traditions which he established.

She would never forget that when it came to placing faith in her, it was Condé Nast, not Edna Woolman Chase, or Betty Penrose, or even Harry Yoxall who batted for her, but the chief himself. He recognised that her talent was as a solid, safe pair of editorial hands and that trust was something Audrey never forgot.

In his autobiography, Harry Yoxall described Audrey as being like the conductor of a great orchestra. Her job was to evoke and direct the talents of her artistes. It was an apt description, and she had to deal with some very tricky instrumentalists in the course of her music-making.

The trickiest of all was Cecil Beaton, but she needed him on so many levels. His work with the RAF in Egypt had given her some of his finest photographs. His brilliant eye, which for so long had been focused on every nuance and detail of the female figure in sumptuous settings, was now trained anew to pick out the symbolism of war. The abstract in the here and now brought his photographs to life and helped to stimulate readers to think about what he had seen.

He told Audrey that the extent of his brief had been to be as accurate as possible. He found he was not interested in capturing the action but the build up to it and its aftermath. He photographed men in lectures, carrying out repair work and at leisure. He was fascinated by the burned-out carcasses of planes, tanks and other equipment because they told a story of what had happened when they met the foe. The light in Egypt was so much brighter than anything he had ever encountered that he discovered the best time to take pictures was before sunset or just after dawn. The photographs often have an almost ethereal quality to them.

One of his most poignant images from the desert is a line of washing hanging out to dry, the arms and legs of the pyjamas swollen fat by the wind. Another, which Audrey reproduced in *Vogue*, shows the skeleton of an aeroplane tail, its fuselage buried in the sand. It looks for all the world like some gigantic beast has plunged to an agonising death with its brittle bones all that remained of a once great monster. The frailty of the metal structure of the plane standing upright against a clear sky is echoed in the shadows in the sand on the ground below.

When Audrey stood with John Parsons and his new assistant, Alex Kroll, looking at these powerful images laid out in the art department, she was thrilled. They had a poignancy, even beauty, in death beyond anything she had imagined Beaton would capture and she gave them prominence in the November issue. The Ministry of Information was delighted that Beaton's RAF photographs had appeared in *Vogue*.

As Audrey's confidence grew, she brought the war into *Vogue* in new ways. In that same November issue, she published a photograph of a child by the American photojournalist Thérèse Bonney, whose article on the plight of refugee children in France she had published earlier in the year. This image, a full page, is of a little boy sitting on a pile of sacks, his head bent forward onto his knees. It is not clear whether the child is dead or sleeping, but the caption is blunt: 'As the Germans swept through Europe they made thousands homeless. But there was worse to come: starvation, disease, supplies all drained away . . .' It is a powerful reminder to her readers that total war affects everyone – man, woman and child – and it was an image designed to shock.

Another of Audrey's star photographers was Norman Parkinson. He was unlike Beaton in almost every way, although he was as professional as his rival and equally driven by money, Audrey would point out later. Younger than Beaton by just nine years, he was nevertheless of a different generation in terms of his photography, taking it out of the carefully lit studio and into the town and countryside. He was fortunate that his father agreed to support him through a photographic apprenticeship with the court photographer Richard Speaight. He learned the arts of lighting, studio photography and what he later called 'dark room magic', but after two years he was sacked and then set up his own studio in Mayfair at the age of twenty-one. Five years later, he began to work for the fashion editor of *Harper's Bazaar*, who opened his mind to the idea of photographing out of doors, using natural light and urban backdrops for his pictures.

When the Second World War broke out, Parkinson rented a farm in Worcestershire. He contributed to the war effort by producing food and through his photography, working as a reconnaissance photographer over France with the RAF and documenting the Women's Emergency Land Corps (WELCS). He began working for Audrey in 1941 and was initially asked to do shoots for the column Smart Fashions for Limited Incomes as well as for Shop-hound.

In a photograph called *The Freedom of the Farm*, he captured a model, wearing a coupon-free bib-and-brace overall, watching a little boy using a stick to herd geese while a second little boy in a siren suit stands on the wall above them watching the scene. Everyone is smiling and this bucolic scene looks almost completely un-posed – until one analyses it more closely and sees how carefully the composition has been designed so that the placing of the humans gives the picture as much movement as the waddling geese. Anne Scott-James described him as 'the pioneer of the lively, caught-you-in-action fashion snapshots which makes posed photography look stiff and dead'.

Striking-looking with a giraffe-like figure and a distinctive moustache, Parkinson wore loud tweeds, pyjama tops instead of shirts and sometimes a Kashmiri wedding cap. Often he would put himself into his fashion shoots, even with famous models: he was a man who liked to be seen. Photo shoots with Norman Parkinson were usually great fun, and he had the ability to put any model at their ease. His images are vital and full of energy. He was also the master of the surprise shoot. For one spread for Audrey, he photographed models hanging upside down on a trellis structure with ladders. Naturally enough, he is to be found hanging upside down as well.

His photographs for *Vogue* during the war were mainly commissioned fashion shoots, but they are instantly recognisable for their settings. His farmyard featured regularly, with models sitting on tractors or stroking the faces of animals, always with a sense of movement, humour and the potential for a slip in the mud.

Parkinson adored women and they loved him back. He was married three times, the first two briefly and for the third time to Wenda, his model and muse. She said of her husband: 'Parks has got a little bit of hypnotism about him. Women will do anything for him and he loves their company, adores them . . .'

It was not just women that he loved, but their bodies. He was excited by the way they moved and how the muscles in their legs worked and how their shin bones were shaped. He described his ambition as a desire to take moving photographs with a still camera. The effect was images that look spontaneous, often fast-moving action frozen in time, but in fact they were meticulously planned and executed. His little bit of hypnotism was wasted on Audrey, but she loved his work and delighted in his exotic and at times far-fetched images.

Audrey was camera-shy and not photogenic, but Parkinson took a photograph of her at work in her office in 1944 that captured her energy and passion for her job. She is seen in three-quarter shot, perched on a sill in her office, the spreads of *Vogue* displayed behind her along with a large vase of flowers. Pen held loosely in hand, she is dressed in her customary navy blue with a modern brooch at her neck and a bright, confident smile. She was thirty-nine years old and looks every bit the editor in charge.

Taking *Vogue* models out of the studio and into the countryside offered Audrey an extra dimension. It gave her the opportunity to reflect every aspect of wartime life and ground the editorial in people's actual experiences rather than in the aspirational and idealised world that had been relevant in the 1930s but which, for now at least, needed to be removed from centre stage. It was never Audrey's intention to dumb down *Vogue*, merely to reflect the mood of Britain in total war and to remind her readers that whatever the war subjected the country to, they could find the ways and means to cope.

Norman Parkinson was a godsend to Audrey, but he was also a gamble. Unknown in America, there was no guarantee that his pictures would find approval with the discerning Edna. However, a handwritten note on the bottom of a Withers to Chase memo about the difficulty of photographing in wartime gives away her relief that Parkinson was acceptable in New York: 'I'm delighted you like his work,' she wrote.

Despite all his charm and bonhomie, Parkinson could also be difficult. Photographers were naturally jealous of one another, paranoid in some cases, and tantrums abounded. Parkinson would march up and down outside her office, determined to get his way. 'No cajolery of the editor can be too subtle, no scene too hysterical, if this end can be achieved,' wrote Harry Yoxall years later.

The most notorious example of Parkinson's temper was over the choice of an image to be used in *Vogue*. Audrey insisted these decisions were made by the art department in conjunction with the fashion editor and herself, as she was the final arbiter of what went into the magazine. On one occasion, he lost his temper with a choice of photographs selected by John Parsons, and it ended in a spectacular scene when he ripped up a transparency using his teeth in front of John and Audrey, flung it onto Audrey's desk and stormed out of the office.

Audrey was shocked. For a moment, she and John just stared at each other, then she reached for the phone and rang Harry Yoxall to explain what had just happened. He in turn left a message for Parkinson to call by his office when he had finished his photographic session. Parkinson described how this summons made him feel exactly like a naughty schoolboy, 'preparing myself for trousers down and four of the best'. In the event, Harry Yoxall employed a far more intelligent and disarming rebuke. He said:

Parkinson, you have done a very bad thing; you have shocked both Audrey and John because they are your good friends and you have no right to offend them. However the damage is done; please never do it again. You have made a serious mistake, your behaviour is unforgiveable, but please understand I cannot afford to employ people who don't make mistakes.

It was a brilliantly judged admonishment and Parkinson's respect for and loyalty to Harry Yoxall grew: 'There are few men in the magazine publishing business that I admire more than this very sane man,' he wrote thirty years later.

Audrey made no mention of this episode in her autobiography, but she did refer to photographers' brainwaves, many of which she had to head off on the grounds of expense, sheer impracticality or legality. In one case, a Parkinson brainwave breached all three. He announced that he planned to hire two helicopters, one for the model and one for himself with all his equipment. They would each lean out of their respective aircraft while hovering over the Houses of Parliament.

Audrey was torn between appearing unimaginative and mean by refusing the request on the grounds of cost alone, though it would have been prohibitive, and being practical. The practical side of her nature won. She made a phone call to air traffic control and learned that commercial aircraft were not allowed to fly in the restricted airspace above Westminster. The shoot did not take place but many other expensive and often hair-raising ones did, though the results did usually justify the means, particularly in the case of Parkinson.

The main problem Audrey had in the second half of the war was that Beaton was away for long periods of time. When he announced that the Ministry of Information was going to send him to India and China for nine months, Audrey was distraught. Edna sent a memo saying how delighted she was that they would be getting interesting photographs from a different theatre of war, and Audrey responded with: 'Poor us! How shall we do without Beaton for all that time?' She had Parkinson, and he proved to be invaluable on the home front, but he was more interested in the farm than he was in photo shoots and would often turn down work on the excuse that the harvest needed bringing in or the lambing season was about to begin. Audrey needed someone she could rely on, and she found this in one of the most brilliant and unpredictable characters she ever had to work with: Lee Miller.

When Lee Miller burst into Audrey's life in the summer of 1940, neither woman had any idea that their lives would become inextricably linked and that they would form one of the most powerful and creative publishing partnerships of the Second World War. At first glance, it seems unlikely that the two of them would have anything in common. Lee was everything Audrey was not: attractive, sexy, outspoken, she drank heavily, smoked prodigiously and swore like the proverbial trooper. She fizzed with energy, humour and artistic talent, but she was also vulnerable, a side that few who met her saw. Audrey saw it all – and she liked what she saw.

Although she could not match Lee on any level of her lifestyle, she was as passionate about her work, and the two of them wanted more than anything else to make an impact in wartime. The appreciation was reciprocated and over the years it would turn into a deep understanding and great affection for one another. Lee's son, Antony Penrose, believed they had coincidental characteristics.

They were both honest, intelligent, quick witted, erudite and literate. They believed passionately that the truth about the war should be told and Audrey's weapon was *Vogue*. I could not imagine anyone else in the universe could ever have worked with Lee as Audrey did. It was an associative relationship and although Audrey had great power as editor, she knew instinctively that Lee would not have liked to have had that wielded at her.

Audrey was thirty-five when she and Lee first met. Two years her junior, Lee was Audrey's senior in life experiences many times over. She had already lived enough to last the average person a lifetime, and was about to embark upon the most challenging of all her varied adventures.

Born Elizabeth Miller in Poughkeepsie in New York State in April 1907 into a middle-class family, Lee's early life was shaped by a distant mother and a very attentive, not to say overbearing, father, mirroring in many ways Audrey's own family situation. At the age of seven, Lee was raped by the son of a family friend and contracted gonorrhoea. This ghastly episode in her life was dealt with by her parents in a matter-of-fact manner.

Her mother handled the medical side of her condition, which required frequent bathing and douching in an era before antibiotics – a shocking and painful treatment for a young girl. Her father sent her to see a psychiatrist, who explained to her that there was a fundamental difference between love and sex and that the two should not be confused. It led to her developing a sexual freedom that was liberal even for the times, and in the context of Audrey's own life, so outside her experience as to be incomprehensible.

Lee's first experience with photography was through her father, Theodore, who indulged his secret passion for nudes by having her pose for him naked, sometimes with her friends. Her beauty was exceptional. She was tall, with a sylphlike figure and an air of detachment that men and women alike found bewitching. She was a photographer's dream: wonderfully photogenic and apparently sophisticated beyond her years.

When she was picked up by Condé Nast – purportedly he rescued her from being run down on a New York Street – he immediately offered her modelling work at *Vogue* and she appeared on the front cover of the March 1927 edition in a drawing by the French artist Georges Lepape. She was just nineteen years old and had already been described as one of the most beautiful women in the world.

Despite her success as a model – she was photographed by all the *Vogue* greats including Steichen and Hoyningen-Huene – she found the life unsatisfying and yearned to go back to Paris, which she had visited briefly when she was eighteen. She returned to live there, with an introduction from Steichen to the Paris *Vogue* studio and to the American surrealist photographer Man Ray, leaving behind a string of lovers.

Man Ray was regarded as the most exciting photographer working in Paris at the time, and Lee, who had originally thought of pursuing her modelling career, now decided she wanted to become a photographer and, moreover, she would become Man Ray's pupil, even though it was known that he did not take pupils. She persuaded him to take her on as an apprentice and she soon became his lover. It turned out to be a productive partnership, despite Man's initial misgivings.

Lee posed for him and in return he tutored her in the art of photography.

Together they experimented and made discoveries of different printing techniques, including one they called solarisation, which in Lee's case had resulted from a lucky accident when she exposed some negatives in the development tank to light. It became one of the hallmarks of their artistic partnership, and it was a technique she would use in *Vogue* during the war twenty years later. She left him after three years to return to New York where she worked as a photographer before moving to Egypt with her first husband, Aziz Eloui Bey. He once described her as a thoroughbred who had been kept in the stables for too long. In truth, it was change that intrigued Lee. Mastering new techniques and facing challenges excited her. Lee's life over the next decade and a half saw her making friends within the art world in Paris, including Picasso and Cocteau.

When the Second World War broke out, Lee was in Antibes with her lover Roland Penrose, Picasso and Dora Maar. As the news broke that Hitler had invaded Poland, Lee and Roland beat a retreat to the coast, abandoning their car in St Malo, and succeeded in catching a ferry to Southampton. From there, they made their way to Penrose's house in Downshire Hill in Hampstead, where Lee found a 'strongly worded letter from the US Embassy' telling her she had to board the next ship to the United States or they would not be able to guarantee her safety. She tore up the letter and began to plan what she would do next.

Her first stop was the *Vogue* studio. As she had not worked as a fashion photographer for five years, she was initially turned away. Beaton reigned supreme and dominated the studio. She persisted and hung around, making herself useful and working for no pay until a combination of increasing staff shortages and Lee's innate ability to make friends persuaded Sylvia Redding, the studio manager, to recommend her to Harry Yoxall.

Harry met her for the first time when he and Betty Penrose turned up at the studio to hand out the usual Boxing Day gifts to the staff. He described the scene: 'Lee Miller, the new photographer whom we are trying out, threw a round of sherry with an amusingly decorated bottle and corkscrew wrapped in beige lace for Xmas. She is gay – and talented.'

Six weeks later, he offered her a job as second photographer at £8 a week, but she refused, preferring to work as a freelance. They went out to lunch to discuss terms and he described her as an amusing and intelligent woman. Shortly after that, Condé Nast cabled to say he was glad Lee would be joining them and was sure her 'intelligence fundamental taste sensitiveness art values must ultimately make you good photographer', and told her he would be sending criticism of her work in due course. Sadly, Condé Nast died before he got to see Lee's finest wartime work, but he was right to praise her intelligent taste and her sensitivity.

Audrey's and Lee's ascendancy at *Vogue* marked a similar trajectory in terms of time, influence and development. Both were troubled at the outbreak of the war by what role they would get to play in a conflict that seemed to have no shape. The Phoney War saw Lee carrying out pedestrian shoots for Choice of the Month in *Vogue* or features on maternity wear. By the time the Blitz came, her pent-up energy burst out in an exclamation of artistic surprise and delight. She turned to Roland Penrose, whom she accompanied on air-raid warden duty early in the Blitz and gasped with excitement as she saw the bombs bursting over London. She grabbed his arm and, 'eyes blazing with ecstasy, she gasped, "Oh darling, aren't you excited?"'

As well as photo shoots commissioned by the studio for the fashion editors, Lee began to take photographs of London in the Blitz. She roamed the streets looking for images that would do more than simply record the damage. While Beaton sought elegant juxtapositions against architectural debris, Lee looked for the quirky as well as the dramatic. A photograph of a barrage balloon on the ground in a London park with two geese facing one another in front of it was entitled, *Eggceptional Achievement/War & Peace in a London Park*.

Some of these photographs were reproduced in *Vogue*, while others were collated in a book called *Grim Glory*, which was printed in 1941 for an American audience to show the impact of the Blitz on Britain. One of the most striking images from that collection is the door of a chapel in Camden, the entrance blocked by a cascade of bricks and fallen masonry.

Lee's personal idiosyncrasies were summed up for Audrey by two bracelets that she had had made, which Audrey had photographed by the studio. One bracelet had a barrage balloon-shaped identity disc with the 'rather gruesome message': "This is (or was . . .)". The second was a gold-studded, leather dog-collared bracelet with a dog head whistle to be used instead of shouting for help when buried under debris.

It was not just Lee who wore eccentric, war-inspired jewellery, though she did manage to create something that would have been considered on the edge. Lesley Blanch loathed the idea of identity discs and so wore two pigskin dog-collars buckled together as a belt with her two addresses on the nameplate. There was a rush of objets d'art designed to overcome the blackout, such as luminescent hat pins, brooches, bracelets and even feathers. Handbags were designed to carry a gasmask unobtrusively, though the finished objects were hardly elegant. All these were featured in *Vogue* with information about where they might be purchased.

Audrey was impressed by Lee's photography of London turned into a theatre of war, feeling she had really captured the essence of the city's heart as it lay ruined but undefeated. So, when she learned that New York had run a feature on its photographers in its 15 June 1941 edition and omitted Lee, she wrote a memo to Edna berating her for the omission. 'Fortunately she [Lee] does not know that her photograph appeared in the first set of engravers' proofs that reached me . . . it does seem a little strange that you decided to remove it.'

Audrey then went on to explain how significant Lee's contribution to *Vogue* had been since their main studio photographer, John Rawlings, had left a year earlier:

she has borne the whole weight of our studio production through the most difficult period in *Brogue*'s history; since also she is an American citizen who is doing all this when she could easily have got home to comfort and safety, I do think there is a case for doing a small story on her to make amends.

For the first time, Audrey made her case for Lee:

I am always impressed afresh, every time I see her with her strong journalistic sense and her quick appreciation of news in all *Vogue* fields. She lives a high-powered social life through every kind of blitz and black-out and has an enormous and very amusing circle of friends. Through Roland

Penrose she is in touch with the most modern school of art and sculpture in England, and she even adds to her talents a gift for extraordinarily fresh and vivid writing.

This was written three years before Audrey published any attributed copy by Lee in New York, though it is probable that Lee wrote captions for her own photographs for features she did with Lesley Blanch. She had also published a piece on Man Ray for the monthly magazine *Lilliput*, and it is likely that Audrey had read that, given her interest in modern art. It is interesting to see how she already appreciated Lee's talent and potential as a photojournalist. To point out further to Edna the extent of Lee's bravery and willingness to go to the extremes to capture her art, Audrey concluded the memo with a copy of a photograph of the smouldering ruins of Fetter Lane. She described again how Lee, with the help of the firemen, climbed up on to what was left of a six-storey building opposite, which was still burning, in order to get a better view.

Over the next year Lee continued to photograph for *Vogue*. Some shoots were memorably strange: a feature on furs, which now attracted a 100 per cent purchase tax, was set in the studio where models interacted intimately with a large stuffed rearing bear and a kneeling giraffe, covered in a tiger skin. Audrey recognised Lee's frustration and paired her with Lesley Blanch, who had previously worked almost exclusively with Beaton. With the approval of the Ministry of Information, Lee and Lesley were briefed to produce articles on the women's services. They did features on the ATS girls operating the huge searchlights at night over London and the coast; they visited the WAAF, who put up the barrage balloons night after night; and they went further afield, to the countryside, to visit country houses set up as hospitals and to a naval dockyard in Scotland.

Lee had mixed feelings about America's entry into the war. It meant an influx of American photographers, journalists and war reporters as well as American service personnel. One commission excited her interest and admiration: she was asked to photograph the American photographer Margaret Bourke-White, 'accredited photographer to the US Army Air Force'. The article starts:

> No woman could have arrived at the peak of her career in a decade better calculated to exploit her inherent qualities than has Margaret Bourke-White. As a photographer and a reporter she has been able to fulfil an innate desire to travel.

Yet Lee was destined to remain in Britain photographing the Timber Girls of the Women's Land Army while Margaret Bourke-White was at large with the US Army Air Force. Cecil Beaton still got to have the pick of the most important society and political figures when he was around. General Charles de Gaulle and Sir William Beveridge were just two of his exceptional portraits in *Vogue* that winter.

Lee complained to Audrey. She moaned that she had not been given due credit for her photographs of Henry Moore in the underground, which she had taken for a film called *Out of Chaos*. She protested that they had been given too little space and that the text by Lesley Blanch was ineffectual:

> is it worth me spending five working days, to say nothing of travel, discomfort and material, the risk of having gangsters

do my jobs in London in my absence – and my pictures sent
to the engravers without my initials to have Mme X [Lesley
Blanch] report on a film? I'm all for group journalism if it is
group journalism – but not when I pay for it, *me*.

Audrey had to juggle everyone's assignments so that they were
fairly shared and that each played to their respective strengths.
Lee and Norman Parkinson had different areas of interest and
focus so there was no competition there, but when it came to
Cecil Beaton, there was always a tension. Beaton's work was
highly prized by both Audrey and Edna – Lee's less so by Edna,
but Audrey had a strong feeling that Lee had more to offer, and
she was sympathetic to her desire for more, interesting work.
Like Lee, she wanted to be closer to the war action. What had
been thrilling during the Blitz had died away, but now, with
London swarming with American press people, Audrey could
sense there was an opportunity.

One particular American was to become an influential and
critical person in Lee's life over the next few years. David 'Dave'
Scherman was a 25-year-old photojournalist on *Life* magazine.
She was fascinated by him and he by her. To him, she was
immeasurably sophisticated and had worldly experience beyond
his own. To her, he had the tools of the trade she needed to learn.
As Dave taught Lee the tricks of his trade, she taught him the
way of the world. Soon he moved into Lee and Roland's home in
Hampstead and the ménage-a-trois functioned happily enough,
except when Roland found Dave's silk pyjamas under his pillow.

Lee grew more and more frustrated by seeing the status of
American correspondents giving them access to exciting stories
as well as luxuries that were beyond the reach of most citizens

in the UK. Dave Scherman pointed out to her that as a citizen of the United States of America she was entitled to apply for accreditation. Lee jumped at this but she needed support and backing. Naturally enough this came from Audrey. She had already seen the strength and breadth of Lee's abilities, had understood the extent of her bravery and appreciated her desperation not to be left out of what might be the greatest story of her life.

Audrey had another motive. If she could manage Lee's future as a photojournalist in the thick of the action, then she could go beyond the confines of life in Britain with the odd report from foreign fields by Beaton and others and give *Vogue* a real investment in the war itself. Lee would be her war reporter in the field. With Audrey's backing, 'Mrs Elizabeth Miller Eloui' earned accreditation as British *Vogue*'s correspondent on 30 December 1942. Lee immediately went straight to Savile Row to order her uniform, something that flummoxed Dave Scherman but which Audrey took completely in her stride. After all, that was what all smart British women did on receiving their commission as far as she was concerned.

Not long after this, Harry Yoxall gave Lee lunch at a restaurant called the Aperitif. She arrived dressed in her uniform, with which she was very pleased. He also noted: 'She drank 5 gins at lunch.' Lee lived hard and fast but never more so than when she set off on the next leg of her extraordinary journey through life. As Audrey launched her in her new role as *Vogue*'s war correspondent on the ground, in what was still essentially Nazi-occupied Europe, Lee drew on all her inner resources and, when necessary, Audrey's too. It was to be a joint venture with Audrey in London and Lee in the rest of the world.

7

VOGUE AT WAR

'The proper business of a magazine is to reflect the life of its times. In a time of war, we needed to report war and Lee Miller might have been created for the purpose of doing just that for us.'

— AUDREY WITHERS, 1992

It took eighteen months to get Lee Miller into Europe. At that time, no female reporters were allowed on the front line, and with Europe still under Nazi control, there was nothing to be done other than to continue to work with Audrey on *Vogue* features, concentrating predominantly on women in positions of authority or in uniform.

Audrey was always keen to promote women, so she commissioned a piece from Lesley Blanch entitled 'Brains to Trust', which featured the novelist Rebecca West and the film critic Caroline Lejeune. She also ran a piece on 'News Makers and News Breakers', which focused on women in the media and journalism, including the director of the American WAAC (Women's Auxiliary Army Corps), Colonel Hobby, who was married with two children and who before the war had been a journalist and politician. She was always at pains to celebrate women with careers and families.

By the early summer of 1944, Britain was overrun with foreign servicemen and women. In addition to the Poles in Scotland and the Czechs in the Midlands, there were Canadians all over the South-East along with volunteers from the Empire, including Jamaica, India and African nations. And then there were the Americans who numbered 1.6 million by the time it came for the Allies to launch their offensive against the Germans. D-Day was in the planning for a year and the build-up of troops around the south coast of England in the spring and summer intensified as the secret date drew closer.

Audrey described Britain in her July editorial as one huge armed camp.

> Convoys pass in procession between high flowering hedges and through winding village streets. The sound of a plane is never out of the sky. Slow-paced market towns are bustled to life by our Allies' new ways and varied speech. American military police sort out the odd tangle of carts, cattle and jeeps.

Roger Descombes created a series of sketches to illustrate the country at war, including drawings of lorries on country-house lawns and American troops and tanks on village greens. Everyone was aware there was a build-up to some form of military intervention but no one knew what form it would take.

The Normandy landings took place on Tuesday 6 June 1944 and formed the largest seaborne invasion in history. Twenty-four thousand US, British and Canadian airborne troops landed in occupied France shortly after midnight, followed by infantry and armoured divisions who began landing on the coast in the early morning. The men met heavy resistance and the losses on the beaches were high, but the battle for France had begun and Audrey reminded her readers that all over Europe prisoners were waiting to be freed: 'Prisoners of war, prisoners of opinion, of race.'

She commissioned an article on France from Lesley Blanch, who wrote how for eight centuries 'France has been the heart of Europe in all its phases. Her civilisation belongs to the world, and yet is wholly French.' It was into this exciting moment in history that Lee Miller was about to be thrown, and she could not have been more ready for the challenge. She wrote of her first glimpse of the country she had lived in and loved twenty years earlier:

> As we flew into sight of France I swallowed hard on what were trying to be tears and remembered a movie actress kissing a handful of earth. My self-conscious analysis was forgotten in greedily studying the soft, grey-skied panorama of nearly a thousand square miles of France ... of freed France. It was France. The trees were the same, with little pantaloons like eagles, and the wall farms, the austere Norman architecture ... I found that it was no longer France, but a vast military area of planes, soldiers, and gargantuan material.

Lee's first assignment was to photograph American field hospitals behind the lines and she sent back several thousand words of text and nearly ninety photographs. The focus was to have been on the nurses, but inevitably she was drawn to the GIs and their stories. 'The wounded are not "knights in shining armour" but dirty, dishevelled, stricken figures – uncomprehending.'

Here was something new, fresh and exciting, and it took Audrey and her readers right into the heart of the evacuation hospital with Lee. Her awe at the way the doctors treated the badly wounded, her anger at the Germans, her horror at the sights she saw are all raw and immediate. Audrey wrote later that it was always difficult to edit great copy, but everyone who has read Lee's original typescripts and Audrey's edited versions agree that the editorial pen could not have been more sympathetically and efficiently wielded. It was as if Audrey managed to get inside Lee's head and see what she was thinking, understanding what she was trying to convey.

By the time the partnership between Lee Miller and Audrey began its most productive period, Audrey knew Lee could write. She had already published a piece on the American radio presenter in London, Ed Morrow, which had impressed her. But nothing could have prepared her for what was to flow from Lee's nimble fingers onto the pages thrust into her Baby Hermes typewriter over the next few months. The piece from the Normandy hospitals was the first of many features and the quality of her writing never wavered. Audrey wrote to Edna: 'As you may not have yet received my earlier memo by Ferry Bomber, I would like to repeat that Dave Scherman, of *Life,* considers this the finest "single" story to come out of Normandy.'

Audrey gave Lee's 'Unarmed Warriors' four pages for text and thirteen photographs with two turns in the back of the magazine: over 3,000 words in total and a long article by any measure of *Vogue*'s normal features. The photographs were action shots from the hospital with scenes from an operating theatre, including a dying man being treated by a crash team of doctors and nurses, as well as photographs of the rubble that had once been a Normandy village.

In her memo to Edna accompanying Lee's text and photographs, Audrey urged her to use the material for a feature 'quickly and importantly'. Lee's future success was largely dependent on how her material was used.

We are making an important four-page feature, immediately following our lead in the September issue. I need not remind you how valuable it is that *Vogue* should have a photographer accredited with SHAEF [Supreme Headquarters Allied Expeditionary Force] and with the chance of getting to France on assignments which should become increasingly interesting to us.

Audrey was so delighted with Lee's piece that she sent her a cheque for £15 as a bonus and

tangible proof of our appreciation of your work as the SHAEF correspondent. We do realize all the dangers and discomforts involved and we thoroughly appreciate our good fortune in having a photographer who can also write so well.

Edna was equally pleased with Lee's Normandy feature and gave it six pages. Lee was complimented by Iva Patcévitch, now Condé Nast's managing director in New York, who wrote:

Hope our message through Yoxall about your special bonus has been a cheering one but it does not begin to pay for all the appreciation of your outstanding work for our magazines in these eventful times. I send you my heartfelt thanks and warmest wishes of the season.

New York's presentation of Lee's hospital material was more generous than Audrey's had been able to be and she wrote to Edna to say:

I was never more jealous of your space. To think that we had to cut her article in half and then give it two whole pages up front to accommodate it all, whereas you can hand her eight-and-a-half turns – more than we get for turn material for the whole issue.

It is easy to imagine how much that would have pained her when presented with such outstanding material, but Audrey still managed to give Lee more space than almost any other contributor to the wartime issues of *Brogue*.

Despite her obvious talent, Lee was not confident in her ability to write. Earlier that year, when she submitted her first written piece to Audrey, she was convinced it had all been a big mistake.

I've spent fifteen or so years of my life learning how to take a picture – you know, the thing that is worth ten thousand words, and here I am cutting my own throat and imitating those people, writers who I've been pretending are *démodé*.

Audrey did not agree. On the contrary, she fell on Lee's reporting with wild enthusiasm. Her instinct told her that this was
a big opportunity for *Vogue* and it was a major coup for her
personally. Articles always have more power when the photographer also writes the copy, she would explain later. That
had indeed been her experience with Cecil Beaton, but Lee's
work was of a different order. Her writing was immediate,
visceral and it pulled no punches. Audrey was possessive and
defensive of Lee. She would not allow anyone else to edit Lee's
articles and initially nothing unedited went to New York.

We were so short staffed that I was writing almost all the
unsigned copy in the magazine and I made myself solely
responsible for editing Lee's precious articles. I used to
begin by cutting whole paragraphs, then whole sentences,
finally individual words. One by one to get it down. Always
I tried to cut them in such a way that there would be the
least possible loss of their impact. It was a painful business
because it was all so good.

Sometimes the articles came in the form of letters to Audrey,
on other occasions they arrived as manuscripts without a covering note. Often Lee would include comments on her problems
or plans, all of which made Audrey realise just how immediate
the material was. Lee typed as she thought and the result was
extraordinary.

Lee must have asked innumerable intelligent questions and
recorded the answers, which she then translated into vivid
prose. When you think that every situation she covered was

completely outside her previous experience it makes the sheer professionalism of her text even more remarkable. The facts always crystal clear and the reader presented with them with her skilful choice of words.

While Lee was in France, Audrey was in conversation with designers Hardy Amies and Charles Creed and the fashion historians James Laver and Cecil Willett Cunnington about the future of fashion. Laver predicted it would follow the path taken by fashion after the First World War, with low waists, straight lines and simple flimsy materials in pale colours. Dr Willett Cunnington thought that women would be more likely to want bright colours but regretted that they would have to put up with poor-quality material for months or years to come. Charles Creed thought it would focus on tweeds and silks in well-cut suits.

It was Hardy Amies who correctly predicted the direction of travel for fashion, with the celebration of the female form with full bosom and curvaceous hips. He wrote that he felt in his bones there would be a sea change for women who had had to suffer the privations of rationing during the war:

> Her clothes will be rich and rather grand, but she won't be afraid to wear them; for she will feel confident that people will know that, like everyone else, she will have had to work hard to earn them.

As Hardy Amies was her favourite designer, Audrey inclined towards his view and was keen to give her readers a sense that there was a future beyond rationing and Make-Do and Mend.

It was hard to be upbeat, however, at a time when the number of clothing coupons had been cut to two thirds of the original number from three years earlier.

Lee Miller was back in London three weeks after going out to Normandy, and photographing fashion shoots for Audrey, but both of them were just waiting for the next opportunity for her to go back to the continent. It came soon enough with an assignment to report on how the American Civil Affairs team moved in after hostilities to get things on the ground running smoothly once again. She sailed from Southampton and hitched a lift to St Malo, which was reported to have been taken by the Americans. Except it had not.

The intelligence was wrong. Rather than arriving at a well-run Civil Affairs office, Lee found herself at the battalion headquarters of the American 83rd Infantry, which at that time was under fierce attack from the citadel, still in the hands of the Germans, who were holding on to the bitter end. By coincidence, Dave Scherman was with the navy some miles outside St Malo and met a very scruffy looking Lee with two equally scruffy GIs.

At this moment, and for months afterward, I chuckled to myself at a monstrous irony: not only had Steichen's former fashion model been a fastidious, obsessive clothes-horse (snappy dresser, she called it), but she was also a rabid food hypochondriac . . . Now, in the excitement – and joy – of battle, all this nonsense went out the window. For about a year, with occasional exceptions, she looked like an unmade, unwashed bed, dressed in o.d. [olive-drab] fatigues and dirty GI boots, and she wolfed down, without pill or

powder, whatever chow the current mess-sergeant saw fit
to shovel up.

Lee's article on the siege of St Malo was even longer than
'Unarmed Warriors', but Audrey published it in the October
issue of *Vogue* over six pages with the caption: 'St Malo . . .
the siege and the assault covered by Lee Miller of *Vogue* . . .
only photographer and reporter there, under fire, throughout.' Opposite the caption she used Scherman's photograph
of Lee with the two scruffy GIs, captioning it 'Lee Miller in
Battledress, with G.I.S.'

The article opens: 'I thumbed a ride to the Siege of St Malo.
I had brought my bed, I begged my board, and I was given a
grandstand view of fortress warfare reminiscent of Crusader
times.' St Malo offered Lee the vivid contrasts that war pro-
duces: a *patronne* of the hotel where she was holed up was
polishing glasses behind the bar, but 'instead of a chattering
crowd of brightly dressed aperitif-drinkers, there were a few
tired soldiers lying on a banquette.'

From the hotel, she had a spectacular view of the old city
burning and of the enemy's position from which they were
under attack. She organised to stay on in the city: 'I had the
clothes I was standing in, a couple of dozen films, and an
eiderdown blanket roll. I was the only photographer for miles
around and I now owned a private war.' During a truce one
evening, she met a long stream of people the Germans had
allowed to flee:

couples with babies, prams piled high with all they had saved
of their possessions, boys, men shambling from shock . . .

prim, snotty women, and nuns in immaculate white, and whores ... I was kept busy interpreting, consoling and calming people.

The truce over, the battle recommenced and Lee found a spot from where to photograph, positioned between a dead horse and some dead Germans, but she could only stand the smell for long enough to take three pictures. By this time, Lee had become involved with the battalion commander, Major Speedie, who had taken a shine to the fearless photographer. He drove her around in his jeep, showing her the various observation posts and describing an assault he was planning for the following day. At one moment, they came under attack:

> We jeeped down to a corner on the quai, walked quickly around a block and down a messy street. Then one at a time – Major Speedie's men, me, then the major – dashed across the street open to the Fort and fell into the door of the Hotel. It was a shambles. Pictures of Hitler shaking hands with various Huns lay around. German hand grenades still cluttered the floor, and bits of equipment and personal treasures were scattered about in the typical confusion of an abandoned army post.

That night she was shelled for the first time, bits of masonry and plaster falling onto the corner where she was lying, a vast hole in the floor above pierced by ordnance that had destroyed their jeep outside the hotel's front door. She barely had time to reflect that the last time she had been in St Malo was five years earlier when she and Roland Penrose had left for Britain at the outbreak of war. From her hotel room, she watched a company filing out of St Malo 'ready to go into action, grenades hanging on their lapels like Cartier clips, menacing bunches of death'. Minutes later, they were warned of an attack from the air:

We waited, then we heard them, swelling the air like I've heard them vibrating over England on some such mission. This time they were bringing their bombs to the crouching stonework 700 yards away. They were on time . . . bombs away . . . a sickly death rattle as they straightened themselves out and plunged into the citadel; then it was swallowed in smoke . . . belching, mushrooming and columning . . . towering up, black and white. Our house shuddered and stuff flew in the window . . . more bombs crashing, thundering, flashing, like Vesuvius, the smoke rolling away in a sloping trail.

In the artillery barrage that followed, she was surrounded by horror. She saw men, feet away from her, blown up by a shell burst, 'sweeping them away. A pity, a brave pity.' All around 'there were boots, munitions, debris . . . there was barbed wire with booby traps where the café tables used to be in front of the now burned out Hotel Chateaubriand . . . the dead smelled and the dust swirled.'

The Siege of St Malo was also infamous for another, ghastly weapon: napalm. First deployed in a raid on Berlin in March 1944 by the United States Army Air Force (USAAF), it had been used in May on Compiègne and now, in August, in St Malo. Lee photographed the impact of this still unknown weapon and when the photographs arrived at *Vogue* there was intense excitement.

Audrey had been to the Ministry of Information to collect Lee's material from the censors. 'We spread out the photos in the art department and marvelled at the strange shapes of the explosions in the sky.' As they were poring over the images, the telephone rang and an agitated voice at the other end told Audrey that the photographs should not have been released. All the images were taken back by the censor.

She resubmitted them several times but 'I fear they were stopped because of the use of some explosive still on the secret list.' What this was she had no idea, and it was only years later, when the Vietnam War was at its height, that she realised Lee had taken a photograph of a napalm attack. Eventually the censor gave in and granted permission for eighteen of Lee's St Malo pictures, including some of the bombardment, to be published.

It was too late for *Brogue*, but they would appear in *Vogue*, which ran Lee's piece later. 'It does represent a great achievement of Lee's,' Audrey wrote in a memo. 'I think too, it confers prestige on us to be represented by the only woman photographer under fire in this campaign.'

Lee's piece from St Malo was both shocking and thrilling for Audrey. Where the report from Normandy had brought the reader close to the hospital with its doctors and nurses working tirelessly to treat the wounded, this drew them straight into the noise, confusion and stink of war in a way that no other writing in *Vogue* had ever done.

Its very honesty and freshness, its first-hand, worm's eye view of the actuality of war, was something altogether new. It was vividly immersive war reporting, with no difference credited to civilian or military suffering. Audrey, with her long experience of editing other people's writing, knew she had something unique, and she treasured every communication with her roving reporter.

After the siege was over, Lee wrote her a long letter explaining that she had got into trouble for having scooped her battle. A few days earlier the US military had issued a memorandum stating that from now onwards no female correspondent was to be permitted to enter the forward area under any circumstances. The US Army Public Relations Officer put her under house arrest in Rennes, the first twenty-four hours of which she spent catching up on her sleep.

Once refreshed, she sat down and started to write her report. For three days, she typed non-stop, producing over 10,000 words for Audrey, accompanied by a letter giving details of her current whereabouts. In commending the article on St Malo to Audrey, she wrote:

> I hope you like it – it is very bitter to me to go to Paris now that I have a taste for gun powder. I wanted another battle before Paris – and I've just sat on my tail here in Rennes writing for a week, when I could have been at the wars.

It was in Rennes that she saw her first collaborators. She was judgemental: 'stupid little girls – not intelligent enough to feel ashamed.' She sent Audrey photographs of girls with their heads shaved, a sign that they had been involved with German soldiers. As she photographed them, people in the crowds hissed and spat at the girls, but they kissed Lee, a '*femme soldat*'.

She ended the letter asking Audrey to arrange for Roland

Penrose to read her piece on St Malo as she had not written to him or anyone else since the final assault. Audrey was the conduit through which Lee liaised with the outside world and it was Audrey who had to listen to Lee's anger, frustration and hurt as well as her delights and triumphs. When she read the St Malo piece, she was over the moon and sent Lee a telegram: 'Good girl great adventure wonderful story.'

Sylvia Redding, head of the *Vogue* photographic studio, sent Lee a longer note:

> Lee darling, we are all sick with excitement at your letter to Audrey and the pictures which are through [the censor]. What a hell of an experience and now I'll lay odds that you are paddling off on your way to Paris. Every scrap of news of you I pass to Roland immediately, as so far, he hasn't heard from you. We were both damn glad to hear you had joined up with Davey . . .

On the ground, Dave Scherman was Lee's confidant, support, lover and companion. Writing the articles for Audrey was painful for Lee. She struggled to concentrate and relied on Dave to cajole, bully and coax her into sitting down at her typewriter and bashing out the copy. She wrote to Audrey in December:

> Every word I write is as difficult as 'tears wrung from stone'. I lose my friends and complexion in my devotion to the rites of flagellating a typewriter – and although the use of everything I send is madly satisfactory in the end, I've had time to be depressed to unproductivity, near suicide, or a change in career.

Audrey sent back a letter of encouragement, praising her again for her St Malo piece and telling her how valuable it was for *Vogue* to have her there in France, on the ground, reporting day by day, sometimes hour by hour, on the events that unfolded.

Lee managed to slip away from Rennes and by hitchhiking and 'bluffing her way' she arrived in Paris via Versailles two days after the liberation.

Lee's seven-page letter to Audrey from Paris is one long stream of consciousness, giving vivid impressions of the city she was so excited to see and capturing the mixture of sheer joy and bitter sadness in equal measure:

> The girls are fantastically pretty in their full short skirts of imprimé and blouse, nearly always white . . . they ride bicycles everywhere . . . [From the] Champs Elysees to the Bantignolles, the streets are devoured by hordes of locusts of bicyclists . . . tandem, with trailers . . . with musette bags like saddle bags, a baby popping out his head like a papoose or a house puppy, in a bag tied to the bars, quite happy. The short billowing skirts and bare legs of the girls are the dream come true of pin-up fans among our boys . . . who find the beautifully made-up, soignée Parisians very much to their awe-struck taste.

She told Audrey how the Parisians had flaunted their creativity in front of the Germans. If a rule came out limiting the amount of material allowed for a dress to 4 metres, they would immediately go and buy material on the black market and use 10 metres for a skirt alone. If the Germans forbade hats, the women would create enormous edifices, 'which stood out like traffic stops', she wrote with glee.

Michel de Brunhoff, the editor of Paris *Vogue*, was ecstatic to see Lee again, so very glad to be free from occupation, and yet his joy was embittered by a personal tragedy. His 19-year-old son had been murdered by the Germans sometime before the liberation while trying to join the Americans.

When she arrived at the offices at the Place de Palais-Bourbon, she met many of the people she had known before the war and gave Audrey a full account of everyone and how they had fared. To many, Lee was the first soldier they had seen, and those who remembered Lee as a thin, elegant model were amazed at the change in her. She told Audrey she had taken a lot of pictures and drunk copious quantities of champagne, 'so don't pay too much attention to the negs I'm sending you . . . and wait for the others. Paris looks like it was cleaning up after a gigantic binge . . . and it is.'

Whereas St Malo had been an adventure, Paris was a return home, and it was the visit that was most eagerly awaited in London. How had Paris coped? What were their women wearing? What was the mood like in the city of fashion? October 1944 was a bumper issue for Lee. With the cover announcing '*Vogue*'s first report from Paris', Audrey had devoted more than a dozen pages of the magazine to her writing and photographs. Except that there had been heartbreak for Lee. Her rolls of film from liberated Paris had gone missing. Her coat had been stolen and with it the precious film that had been in her pockets. Lee was bitterly disappointed, writing to Audrey: 'As you can imagine, I am pretty bitter about having been here and then to have pix by other people appear instead of mine: in fact, I am sick with rage and ill with jealousy about the whole thing.'

Audrey understood Lee's fragility, despite her brilliant and commanding presence, and this led her to warn Edna to use the French pictures in a minor capacity in order to avoid them overshadowing Lee.

Almost everything with Lee depends on how she is feeling and the kind of support she is getting and I feel that as our only representative there at the moment it is absolutely essential that she should be kept in good heart and with the feeling that she is being most thoroughly appreciated by you and by us.

I would like to emphasise once more my own conviction that she is a first-class journalist quite apart from her photographic ability: . . . she has a keen nose for news, quick summing-up of the possibilities of a situation and a vivid turn of phrase.

~

Although Audrey was almost completely consumed by her job at *Vogue*, and Lee's reportage in particular, she made time the following spring to work with a group of sixty women journalists to set up the Women's Press Club. The greatest surprise to them all on gathering at the Falstaff, a pub on Fleet Street, was that so few of them knew one another.

Nearly every woman there was conjecturing the name and the job of the woman sitting next to her – which in fact put up at once the most powerful claim for the need of a Club of their own.

Their first meeting took place in April and the aim was to provide a club in London where women could go at any time and be sure of accommodation, conveniences and basic kitchen facilities. Beyond that its aim was to 'enhance the status of women in the journalistic profession, by sharing social and working interests ... and to promote international understanding and goodwill among journalists.'

One of the worries was money. How could they possibly find the funding at such an unpropitious time? However, their chairman elect, Phyllis Deakin of *The Times*, announced that it should be funded by the press lords who had benefited from the hard work of their female journalists. 'Glasses clinked, sandwiches disappeared and sixty-two women dashed off to assignments and desks.'

Audrey was voted chairman of the Establishment Committee, which would be responsible for inspecting the newly found premises on Carey Street and advising how it could be turned in the shortest amount of time into a habitable space. The building had once been a Lyon's corner shop but had been badly damaged during the spring bombing raids two years earlier. It had no windows, the walls were festooned with strips of torn and flapping paper and the whole place gave off the miserable impression of a derelict hulk, the dingy ghost of a once inhabited house.

On her first visit, Audrey sustained a severe bruise to her right shin as she stumbled about the first floor of the derelict building with a torch. She and her team set about trying to render the place inhabitable. It was an endlessly frustrating process that took up far more of her time than she thought it would initially. Not only was there the problem of finding plumbers, glaziers, carpenters and fixtures, but the issue of permits took her by surprise. Only then did the full meaning of wartime restrictions and regulations and the manner of their administration become a reality 'to that dazed but valiantly determined Establishment Committee'.

Audrey discovered to her frustration that there were permits within permits and even something as simple as buying cutlery threw up all sorts of questions, including how much hard steel was contained in each knife. Most devastating of all was when they had managed to secure the services of a glazier who had replaced all the boarded-up windows with glass, and the following morning all the windows were found to be shattered after a flying bomb landed in the street. This happened not once not twice but on three occasions.

It must have been a most trying time, but, as the minutes of the launch event recorded, by July the premises at 52 Carey Street had been miraculously transformed 'by the genius of Audrey Withers'. She had given £100 of her own money towards the refurbishment of the building and others had shown equal generosity. She had even managed to get the Manchester Cotton Board to supply cheerful patterned curtains for each room and heaters from a company in Ascot.

The house on the corner of Carey Street and Serle Street behind the Royal Courts of Justice is a handsome Georgian three-storey building with decorative carved panels below the first-floor windows and a statue of Thomas More in an alcove above the front door. This featured on the front cover of the club's newsletter, with a caption telling members to look up and remember that he was the first great Englishman to give his daughters the same education as his son – 'A fitting patron saint for the Women's Press Club of London.'

Even after the Establishment Committee had delivered the refurbished building to the members, there were endless niggling problems with the heating. Audrey and the woman responsible for the day-to-day running of the Press Club, Miss Jean Moneypenny, set about getting that fixed, although there were fierce arguments about what sort of heating was possible. At that time, it was not permitted to leave a stove on overnight, and one minute reveals the extraordinary detail that the building was without a power point.

After the first full year, Audrey stepped back and allowed others to deal with the organisation of the committees, but it was a matter of great satisfaction and pride to her that a club for women journalists existed in the centre of London and that she had been a founder member.

The Women's Press Club was not just a place for journalists and their friends to meet up or stay the night if they were caught in London in the blackout. It had a wider welfare purpose, which was to help members in all aspects of their work, including securing employee rights, pensions and other work-related questions. This sat well with Audrey, who believed that every woman should be entitled to the same opportunities as a man in an equivalent position. How proud she must have felt when Brendan Bracken, the Minister of Information, who was a guest of honour at the founding dinner, said that the setting up of the club was 'the equivalent of running up the flag and announcing that there is nothing women cannot do'.

In her speech at the same launch, Audrey spoke as Periodical Press representative. Harry Yoxall and Lord Camrose were there as guests and heard her expound her views on the role of magazines in wartime and of *Vogue* in particular. Magazines were up against every kind of competition and had to seek new angles and new methods of presentation to remain fresh and at the forefront, she said:

> There can be no comparison between magazine and newspaper production. The time factor prevents that. A newspaper is produced against time with little opportunity to alter and improve. With a magazine, there is always time to change one's mind, to juggle, to alter, to improve.
>
> A magazine is able to select subject matter rather than have it forced upon one as in a newspaper, where the reporting of the news is the main object. At the same time, there is a certain amount of gamble in the selection. One has an ever-present worry that one's competitors may have hit upon one's cherished idea.

She told them how vital artists and illustrators were to a magazine like *Vogue*, and how it had a very strong character that had to be cherished and kept in the back of the editor's mind at all times:

> The idea for such a magazine as mine is that each time you turn a page you should be led up to and not jumped into the next feature . . . It must be designed, too, with the knowledge that it will remain in the home for a very long time so that many features can be of an almost permanent nature.

Little did she know that the wartime issues of *Vogue* are regarded as precious collectors' items eight decades on and counting.

That busy autumn American *Vogue* ran a feature by Lesley

Blanch on how the British editors were living, dressing and working in 'robot-bombed' London. This was a reference to the unmanned German rockets that were launched on London in 1944. Jessica Daves reminded her readership that British staff had had to do their clothes planning under paralysing restrictions and in the face of insurmountable shortages. However, it is the war-weariness that seeps out of Lesley Blanch's introduction:

> We don't so much live as manage. It's one long battle against lapsing into dullness and discomfort. Of course, we are frightened by the buzz bombs. Of course, they play havoc with our sleep, our nerves. But still, we are agreed, it's the little things that are the most trying in the long run. Imagine trundling every sort of parcel with you, always, everywhere. A string bag is as much a part of our equipment as a powder compact.

She told readers about the limitations and restrictions but then painted an upbeat portrait of how Audrey, Gertrude Pidoux, Lady Stanley and other editors were coping. Audrey was, in her opinion, 'a woman of really phenomenal drive and method. Always, she copes. And keeps au courant with all the new books, reviews, plays, and concerts. And buys modern pictures.'

> She wears suits almost all the time. The best possible ones. A black whipcord topcoat from Creed; a mannish grey tailored suit from Goodbrook, topped in winter by a boxy skunk jacket, or a wonderful reversible topcoat, grey-green and scarlet, from Bradleys. A severely impeccable navy wool dress, with tiny black tassels from Angele Delanghe. A dark

green suit worn with a pale blue blouse. A grey man's suiting dress and jacket, with grey shirting dickey, from Rahvis. She loves pigskin accessories, big bags; and always wears hats, usually little, off-the-face ones. At home, she likes to wear trousers cut as wide as a dirndl skirt with sweaters. For dining out, she wears a soft, sleeveless dress. She wears little jewellery, but clings to scarlet nail varnish, and will as long as supplies last.

In the accompanying photograph by Norman Parkinson, Audrey is dressed in the whipcord topcoat and wearing a dark hat with netting set at a jaunty angle. The overall impression she gives is one of complete confidence and control. Here is the editor of British *Vogue*, a woman 'upon whom executive and organizing work are piled. She must plan the issues far ahead, keep in touch with all the government departments, be ready to switch the pages round at the last minute, when, for example, the printers and engravers are bombed (as they were last week).'

Gertrude Pidoux is described as perfectly epitomising the elegant white-haired woman. 'She is small, miraculously groomed, with blue eyes, hair worn high, and has the figure, the feet and ankles that a college girl might envy.'

When Edna saw the images and Lesley's text, she wrote to Audrey to say that everyone was in awe of how well they looked. Little did she know that the office was at breaking point as the material from Paris piled up on their desks and caused havoc with the schedules.

Yet Lee Miller's work was of such significance to Audrey that she was prepared to tear apart planned issues and remake them at the last minute to include the photographs and reports. It put a heavy burden on the editorial staff and she asked Edna for patience when it came to getting pictures from Paris to New York with all possible haste:

> The fact is that we simply are not staffed to handle these rushed batches of pictures with the full efficiency and clerical completion we should wish. In fact, we are barely staffed to get our own publications to press.

For all her protesting, Audrey was in her element, fired up with enthusiasm for bringing such key material to her readers and, above all, for showing the world that, in her opinion, *Vogue* had the best war reporter in Europe on their books. Fiercely protective of Lee and Lee's work, she told Edna that there had been a question about *Life*'s London Office processing Lee's photographs. With Lee and Scherman in St Malo and then Paris together, the arrangement was first seen as a 'mere incidental act of kindness', but Audrey's antennae told her that the situation was not so straightforward.

> Lee and all the *Life* people are great buddies over here and maybe it was a simple act of kindness, but maybe on the other hand, Scherman, who is a clever young man, thought that in this simple way *Life* could get extra coverage of French subjects through Lee's work. Anyway, we did not think it was at all wise to let this tie-up continue.

Audrey's anxiety over the use of Lee's photographs only worsened when she realised that *Harper's* had got wise to the fact that Lee's pictures had to be fed into the Pool system, which had been designed to ensure that editors without a correspondent on the ground could have access to war images. As Lee was an accredited war photographer, any magazine or newspaper could use pictures from the Pool as they wished. Audrey described it as a blow that *Harper's* were now demanding Lee's non-combat photographs, as they had every legal right to do. It went against every fibre of her being to share Lee's images with them and she went through all possible variants on how she might protect *Vogue*'s exclusivity to them while abiding by the letter of the law.

In the end, she discovered a loophole: non-combat pictures were not time-sensitive, so she was able to hold them back from the Pool until they had been published in *Brogue*.

It seems a little hard that one's competitors should profit by one's own enterprise; but on the other hand, we must regard ourselves as so marvellously fortunate to have our own correspondent and the first use and choice of her pictures.

Audrey got her first Paris fashion photographs a week after the liberation. She reproduced the pictures in the October edition of *Vogue* but with a warning not to forget the photographs showing the battle for the liberation of Paris:

Remember them when you turn to the seeming normality of the following page. If it surprises you to see pretty girls in pretty dresses, to see the beautiful clothes which the fashion houses never ceased to make, reflect that the life of France and her civilian technique of resistance must necessarily have been the reverse of England's. Here, it showed patriotism to obey regulations, to do the work required of us, to take no more than our rations. There, it showed patriotism to flout regulations, to avoid work except where it would not benefit the Germans, to black-marketeer up to the hilt.

Over the page the reader is treated to double-page spreads of Lee's Paris photographs showing Picasso, Christian Bérard and Boris Kochno in their studios; girls on bicycles, one by the Eiffel Tower, or standing by tanks; skinny little boys in shorts smiling next to a pony and trap in which sits the wonderfully named Mme Beaurepaire 'in her high Legroux hat'. Next to this is a photograph of Paul Éluard, the poet and resistance writer, and his wife Nusch, who was 'so thin and delicate that her elbows were larger than her arms'. Lee told Audrey's readers that the Éluards had moved house eight times in six months to escape the attentions of the Gestapo, and even though their temporary home was hung with some of the most valuable paintings in Paris, they were starving.

London's relationship with the Paris office had generally been good, though the character of the magazines was different. Harry Yoxall spoke fluent French and was a regular cross-Channel visitor in the pre-war decades. Michel de Brunhoff, the long-time Paris editor, had once spent a year in London editing *Brogue* and Audrey had spent time in Paris doing the collections and getting to know the staff in Place du Palais-Bourbon. When she was able to re-establish contact with de Brunhoff and his team, she learned what they had done during the occupation to keep fashion alive while keeping French *Vogue* out of the hands of the occupiers.

Audrey's editorial introduced a series of images from the 1942 Paris collections:

Some of their triumphs over barbarism are preserved in *Album de la Mode*, a superbly produced magazine of the arts, the theatre and fashion, edited by Michel de Brunhoff in relation with *Figaro*, the famous Paris daily which has been allowed to republish.

It would be another four months until there was sufficient paper supply for *Vogue* to be published in France. The *Album de la Mode* was more or less an academic exercise, as no one in Paris dressed in evening clothes during the occupation. The women who would have worn the models were so undernourished that they could not have worn the luxuriant garments 'that bloomed strangely in that darkness'.

The drawings, covering six pages, showed the French designers' flights of fancy with towering, extravagant turban hats by Janette Colombier; dresses with cut-away bodices by Mad Carpentier, a fashion house that had been created in January 1940 by Mad Maltezos and Suzie Carpentier, and a loose-fitting coat 'very full in back and sleeves' by a designer at Lelong. By the 1944 season, the clothes were if anything more decorous, with ruffles, full-skirted jackets, deep pockets and a skirt by Worth 'with a deep basque flouncing over a slim skirt'.

Hats had been a key feature in Paris and Audrey was happy to give them a full page in this busy October edition, with an article by Carmel Benito, whose father was a Paris fashion artist and who was now working in the *Vogue* office there. Carmel wrote an uplifting article about how women had kept up their spirits during the occupation, how even when they were starving, and having to queue for hours just to buy a pound of onions from the grocer, they still did not give up.

Audrey was delighted to give readers a first-hand account from Paris by an insider. The Parisiennes had worn large hats to raise their morale, Carmel wrote, and when felt was no longer available they turned to chiffon, and when that ran out, straw. 'No more straw? Very well, braided paper.' Their hats signalled defiance against the occupiers, and a 'sort of contest between French imagination and German regulation'. When they were hungry, they made pastry-coloured hats and covered them with birds, fruits and berries.

Just as at the beginning of the war the British had been resolved to look smart and keep their morale high, so the French were determined to show their courage would not fail, despite everything.

> We were prepared to do without food, fuel, light, soap, servants: we were prepared to choke in over-crowded Metros and go everywhere else on foot: but we wouldn't look shabby and worn out. After all, we were Parisiennes.

With hunger came inertia, but that had its compensations too, she wrote, describing how they took to watching people going slowly about their daily lives. The pace slowed as the hunger bit but people kept going. The fastest things on the streets were

> goggle-eyed, dark-glassed girls whirling past on their bicycles, with their dirndls made of curtains floating out over the saddles. It is a wonder we weren't all turned out into a new kind of centaur – half human and half bicycles.

Next to the turn on this article is an advertisement for dried eggs and how to make a packet last a week, which makes a strange juxtaposition with an article that describes families coping with no gas, coal or wood, no electricity and no proper cooking facilities. Yet Carmel Benito's article ends on a note of optimism: 'women have shown they don't need a gun to fight. They have stood up for four years against the trials of war, and won. Perhaps because they kept smiling . . . and wore those hats.'

Audrey asked Lee to send her the fullest possible details about the designers working in Paris. After four years, London needed reminding who they were: 'Our office is completely out of touch with the Paris fashion situation, and in any case new members on our staff really need re-education in the whole business.' What she also needed was up-to-date information on

> their present standing and particular tendencies and all those things of which one used to have a body of knowledge kept fresh by the big Collection reports and by those gossipy memos they sent all the year round.

Audrey relished the reintroduction of Paris to the fashion scene and was excited by the prospect, but there was so much to learn about how things had developed under occupation. She and Harry had a long conference over a lunch at the Aperitif and they came to the joint conclusion that they would be guided by Michel de Brunhoff on which houses to support in the future.

The question of who had been judged to be collaborators and who had been given a clean bill of health was something that seemed to change daily, and Audrey was anxious not to make judgements without good evidence.

I feel it is only people on the spot and can sense these day to day changes of feeling from whom one can get rulings on this very delicate point. I am confident that Lee is fully alive to the situation and very rigorous in her attitude towards anybody who may be suspect.

At the end of October, Michel de Brunhoff submitted a confidential report to Audrey on the standing of various fashion houses and their couturiers. She asked that it be forwarded to all the New York editors in the Condé Nast stable to ensure they toed the line.

The communication back and forth between Audrey in London and Lee in Paris in September was almost daily. They discussed fashions, artists, friends, life under occupation, the future of French *Vogue* and Lee's articles. Audrey relied on Lee to write almost everything from Paris as the French authors took too long over their texts. Lee had told her that a piece by Mme Astruc could have been reduced by about ten days.

Audrey wrote to Edna:

I believe you are likely to agree with my view that one wants straight dope as fast as it can be turned out: enlivened, of course, with any picturesque turn of phrase but not, as it were, written up too much.

Despite her delight at having Lee on the ground, Audrey was worried about her. She felt she had taken on too much and was in need of practical help, but she did not know how this could be organised. She told Edna she had asked Lee to get secretarial help for herself, 'as my impression is that she types out every word of her own articles and captions and looks after the whole business of keeping us in touch with what is going on.'

This was fundamentally to misunderstand Lee's process of writing. She was not anything like as organised as Audrey and had no experience of dictating material to a secretary. Also, Lee was a fast typist and she wrote as much through her fingertips as she did through her brain, so dictation would have proved yet another hurdle to overcome.

It is unlikely that any secretary, however brilliant, would have been able to cope with Lee's chaos. She lived in room 412 in Hôtel Scribe, where the Allied press corps was based. She occupied the room on and off for eighteen months and it was more of a junkyard than a hotel suite. There was camera equipment cheek by jowl with guns, crates of cognac and other bits and bobs that she had picked up on her adventures. Her table on which she perched her typewriter was covered in half-filled glasses, bottles and ashtrays overflowing. Even her balcony was a makeshift store, with bottles of champagne and three jerrycans, one of which was filled with a cocktail of looted wines and liquors.

Scherman was a frequent presence there and later compared being in the room when Lee's creative process was in action to 'feeding his brain slowly through a meat grinder'. Antony Penrose wrote:

It was Dave who alternately comforted and badgered Lee through her worst moments of anguish. If they had not been bound by love as well as a passionate camaraderie, he could never have stood the torment.

The Hôtel Scribe had water and power, unlike most other businesses in Paris, as it had been used by the Germans as their press bureau up to the time of liberation. There was excellent communications equipment and the latest developments in radio technology were soon linked up to London rather than Berlin by engineers. It was from there that Lee was in constant touch with Audrey, sending her telegrams asking for everything from spare uniforms to guidebooks and Tampax. But she did not always appreciate being so easily reached by London and found her privacy compromised by the ease of communication with the hotel.

While Audrey was busy editing the October edition of *Vogue*, bursting as it was with reports from liberated France, Lee managed briefly to escape from Paris with a new permit from SHAEF. She told Audrey that waiting around for the Paris fashion houses to complete their autumn collections was boring and she wanted to go to war again. Not long after that she succeeded in linking up with the 83rd Division in the Loire, which is where they had gone after St Malo.

Lee was present at the 'surprise surrender' at Beaugency, near Orléans, when General Elster surrendered 19,500 men on 16 September 1944 to Lieutenant Sam Magill, of the 83rd Infantry Division, without permission from his superiors. Lee and a group of filmmakers witnessed columns of prisoners 10 miles long, 'mostly happy and all quiet', making their way to the official surrender point 90 miles away. The presence of Colonel Speedie and the delight at seeing so many Germans taken prisoner led her to tell Audrey it was duty mixed with pleasure. Lee told her that she was getting to be 'the surrender girl'.

What is clear from this memo and others is Lee's visceral

loathing of the Germans. She could barely look a German in the eye; even the German nurses in Normandy had been almost unbearable to her. Audrey did not share that hatred, but she did not edit it out of Lee's reports, although she only ever used the word Germans in her correspondence to refer to them, whereas Lee used the derogatory 'Hun' liberally. Audrey was pleased that Lee had had a few days away from Paris. She could remind people that Lee was still in the war and Lee had got her 'gunpowder fix'. It did her good. It needed to, as things were about to get more difficult for her and Audrey, though in very different ways.

Audrey was puzzled as to why the Americans were not more excited about the news from Paris than they appeared to be. 'Perhaps it is that we here are nearer the scene and feel a greater excitement about news from France.' Harry Yoxall was probably nearer the mark when he told Audrey he suspected the American fashion trade was concerned about the return of French competition. Edna was even clearer about it, writing:

There seems to be a very mixed feeling in the trade in regard to the opening up of French resources for models etc. Many people, especially the houses who cater to the private trade, express themselves as delighted and are eagerly awaiting their chance to return to Paris again. At the same time, there is a distinct undercurrent among a number of houses who wish to go on with the idea of developing their own talent free from influence. It makes a difficult situation for us and one we must handle fairly. My attitude about the whole thing is that a good design is a good design and that wherever the best fashions are created that is where the laurels will go.

Voices of discontent were also being heard in Britain, but it was the general public rather than the trade expressing opinions. There was criticism of pictures coming out of Paris showing women looking charming, 'when our women have spent the war in uniforms and factory overalls'. The situation continued to be difficult throughout the autumn and by the end of November Audrey was concerned enough to write a memo entitled 'Fashion Policy' in which she expressed her conviction that *Vogue* had an obligation in all three countries 'to get fashion onto an international basis as quickly as possible'. She was not talking about trade, which she realised was still some time off, but fashion models in the abstract.

> I think that now Paris fashions are being published in America and England, it is confusing for women to see absolutely different lines. I believe it is most important for the prestige, not only of *Vogue*, but of fashion in general, that it should speak as quickly as possible with a single voice.

She described the current situation as fashion anarchy and urged Edna to let her have New York's views so that they could co-ordinate an approach for the New Year.

While she clearly enjoyed being the middlewoman between Paris and New York, Audrey was often exhausted by the effort of keeping everyone informed of the other's thoughts and opinions. In November, she wrote a long letter to Edna talking about the wave of optimism that had led them in August and September to believe the war would be over before Christmas. She had been making efforts to prepare a Victory number to go to print in just such an event. As it happened, her optimism was premature, but she was nevertheless in high spirits when she wrote:

> The handling of the Paris material has, it is true, been a heavy chore, but it has given us a tremendous thrill to be in this key position at such an exciting time. Just to be in touch again with Paris and able to cable and write and get replies, has been like a release from the sort of imprisoned feeling which we all felt after these years of being cut off from the continent.

People in Paris were understandably nervous of starting up again on the international stage just weeks after liberation, and Michel de Brunhoff told Audrey that his staff felt as if they were working in a vacuum. 'I am sure they would find it very helpful to be told just where their stuff was hitting the mark and where falling wide,' she wrote to Edna at the end of September.

> I feel it is very important to build all the time a strong bridge between both our offices and Paris in order that they may feel they are part of an organisation whose wishes they understand and who appreciate their efforts.

At the time, de Brunhoff did not have the facilities to communicate directly with London and had to rely on Lee working in the press bureau at the Hôtel Scribe. It was not an ideal situation and hardly surprising that Lee felt overwhelmed by the pressure she was under. Once again Audrey told Edna that she could tell from Lee's typescripts that she was beating out every word of the thousands she was submitting herself and burning the candle at both ends.

Audrey gave Lee her personal backing, agreeing that speed was everything at the time and she would accept Lee's material in whatever form it arrived in London. She had told her she was contemplating sending someone from London to help her cope with the work, to which Lee replied: 'If you manage to send anyone else over here, please have it a whipdriver, not an artist!' This was a reference to Cecil Beaton, who had arrived in Paris thinking it was perfectly acceptable to use Lee as his office girl.

Given that Audrey had sent Edna thirty-seven memos in September alone, it is not surprising that some of the material got confused. Today the memos are all beautifully ordered in ring-bound folders in the Condé Nast archive in New York, but at that time, when the war was still being actively fought, it seems nothing short of extraordinary that anything got through at all. The memos were sent by one of three methods: by Army Courier, by Ferry Bomber or by Air Mail. Audrey preferred the Ferry Bomber method as it was the most reliable, but it only worked in one direction. It was a joint Anglo-Canadian venture, which was taken over in Britain by the RAF from the Ministry of Aircraft Production and flew out of White Waltham airfield in Berkshire. According to 'received stamps' on Audrey's memos, this service usually took five days after the memo had been passed by the censor. The USA had to rely on Air Mail to get things to London, which seemed to be more erratic.

~

In October, Paris launched the first fashions since the spring of 1940. Michel de Brunhoff told Audrey and Harry that it was an exhibition and a celebration of French talent rather than a full fashion show. No one in France had the money to spend on clothes, and it was no longer patriotic to flaunt new outfits as it had been under the occupation, but these shows were a statement about the future.

The first event, a hat show, was described in an enthusiastic letter to Audrey as

a real field day – there were at least three times as many invitees as gold chairs . . . A hat show is just as always, a mad house and after the show the favourite clients and friends of the house stayed on trying on hats and gurgling.

Despite the return to something resembling familiar shows, Lee told Audrey everyone had neuralgia from going about with wet hair because there was no means to dry it. Only one salon in Paris had hair dryers that functioned. She explained how Monsieur Gervais had

rigged his dryers to stove pipes which pass through a furnace heated by wood debris. The air is blown by fans turned by relay teams of boys riding a stationary tandem bicycle in the basement. They cover 320 kilometres a day and dry half as many heads.

Michel de Brunhoff took Lee with him to all the shows, starting with Piguet, who gave them a preview and got them off to a flying start. Lee found she was at home and comfortable writing about the fashion as much as she was about the couturiers themselves. In early October, she and de Brunhoff were invited to a party to welcome Molyneux back to Paris.

Lelong and Mme Lanvin – 'the Doyen of the Couture' – received him, she told Audrey, and everyone in the Gown Workers Union was there to see him. He arrived in time to see his models shown next to Lelong, Schiaparelli, Bruyère, Worth and Paquin, something he found deeply affecting. Clothes were simpler than those made under the occupation, the emphasis being on practicality rather than frivolity. Bosoms were still emphasised, hips accentuated by sashes, flares and basques, and wasp-waisted suits with a backward look to the 1930s were a feature of Lelong's offering.

Schiaparelli's black wool fur-lined coat with a stand-up neckline caught Lee's eye as she photographed the mannequin outside on the street. Edna sent Audrey a telegram complaining about the quality of the French mannequins, which Audrey forwarded to Lee, knowing that it would infuriate her:

> Edna critical snapshot fashion reportage and especially cheap mannequins urges more elegance by studio photographs and well-bred women and excellent drawings. Edna says 'can't believe pictures typical high-class French fashion but if really typical then will show them as they are.'

Lee fought back immediately, telling Audrey to remind Edna there was a war on: 'I find Edna very unfair – these snapshots have been taken under the most difficult and depressing conditions.' The models had just twenty minutes for their lunch hour and were giving up their time, while the photography was done without light as there was no electricity. Given the restrictions on so many levels, Lee's photographs from Paris are remarkable. Her unerring eye for detail and her understanding of texture and light combined with her exceptional grasp of the essence of what her photographs could say make her work unique. She conveyed the joy and relief of the liberation but she also captured its impact with clever juxtapositions. In one photograph, a law student sits in a bar resting her elbows on a table, a half-finished beer in front of her and behind her half a dozen bullet holes spread like a spiderweb on the window. In another, a girl sits on her bicycle in front of the Eiffel Tower as an army jeep thunders past in the background.

After the fashion shows were over, Lee begged Audrey to allow her to write a piece on the German occupation of France. 'The undercurrent of tragedy is appalling,' Audrey wrote to Edna,

and the surface gaiety of the French is merely a manifestation of their marvellous spirit . . . I fully agree with Lee that very little of the real truth of France is getting into the papers and so much that is grossly misleading. I have therefore told Lee to go ahead and do a story, as I know she burns to do.

Audrey asked her to focus on the intellectual and creative people in France when she wrote this piece, but she was also very keen to hear about women of the resistance and children who had grown up under the occupation. 'I get bits and pieces of these stories in from time to time in an occasional photograph mixed up with a fashion roll, but I am holding them till the stories form more thoroughly.'

In the end, this story was never written. Instead, Audrey asked Lee to write a piece for her January issue called 'The Pattern of Liberation'. Lee wriggled like a fish on a hook over this article but it turned out to be one of her most successful. 'This is a very difficult piece you have sent me,' she complained to Audrey in December, before coming back to London to spend Christmas with Roland Penrose, '. . . the pattern of liberation isn't very decorative by itself and it's very monotonous to watch scene after scene disclosed, each a plagiarism on the last.'

She agreed to give it a go, although she found it harrowing:

I, myself, prefer describing the physical damage of destroyed towns and injured people to facing the shattered morale and blasted faith of those who thought 'things are going to be like they were' and of our armies' disillusionment as they question 'is Europe worth saving?'

In her letter, but not in her piece, she continued with her private thoughts about the impact of war, describing the mental malnutrition of four years that had sapped the strength of the occupied.

Audrey knew that Lee was eager to stay with the military rather than reporting on civilians. Her desire for gunpowder had returned with a vengeance as she watched the Americans attacking the Siegfried Line in Luxembourg. She knew that there was nothing she could say to stop Lee. Nor would she have wanted to. Lee was on her way to Germany to witness the final act in the drama of the Second World War, and Audrey would have a ringside seat for *Vogue*.

8

IN THE SHADOW OF DEATH

'Women in wartime have been marvellous. They have gone
everywhere, been an example of energy, enterprise and
courage, and I think higher offices should be extended to
them.'

— BRENDAN BRACKEN, MINISTER OF INFORMATION,
FEBRUARY 1944

For Audrey, the final months of the Second World War were
a test of her nerves and reserves. On a personal level, she was
exhausted – and it showed. Her hair was now completely
grey and she had lines around her eyes that had not been there
five years earlier. Like everyone else in London she had been
affected by constant rationing and she felt dusty and drab in
her well-worn suits. The weeks after the liberation of France
had been the most exhilarating of times for her, but also the
most challenging. Sandwiched between Edna in New York and
the emerging story in Paris meant that she was constantly in
demand to interpret, facilitate and modify demands, expecta-
tions and material.

The added pressure of managing Lee Miller's colossal output

from Paris, Luxembourg and Brussels was exciting but a constant task. No plans for an issue survived first contact with her material and nor did Audrey mind that, but she had to keep all the other aspects of *Vogue* going, with comments on Paris fashions, features on British designs for shoes, Shop-hound in the build-up to Christmas and at the same time keep Edna happy.

In November, there had been experiments between London and New York sending drawings by radio to increase speed and reduce cost. These had not been an unqualified success and Edna wanted Audrey to tweak the process at the London end, ensuring the background tones should be crisp white, with no signs of grey. The paper should be thin, high-quality photographic paper, not the thicker paper the studio had been using of late. How she would have time to deal with an experiment amid everything else that was going on around her is hard to imagine. And besides, in the wartime conditions of acute paper shortages, she had no idea where she could possibly obtain the high-quality thin paper the Americans requested. The subject was dropped and not picked up again in correspondence until two years later.

The year 1944 drew to a close under a blanket of cold, damp fog with temperatures hovering around freezing for the last two weeks of December. London and the surrounding counties were in the seventh month of the V-Bomb attacks, which would continue until March. Hitler's *Vergeltungswaffe*, literally translated 'retribution weapon', in the shape of the V1 flying bomb, was first launched in June in revenge for the attacks on the German forces at Normandy. Known as buzz bombs or doodlebugs, they were horrible missiles powered by pulse jets, which cut out before the bomb dropped. That silence was what everyone feared. Hundreds lost their lives in this last phase of attacks on London, though far fewer than had perished in the Blitz.

Later, the V2 rockets were launched at Britain with deadly effect. Over 2,500 Londoners were killed in the attacks and nearly 7,000 injured. The last sting in the tail from an implacable foe exploded for the final time on 27 March 1945. Despite the weather, the cold and V-bombs, Audrey's January editorial for the coming year began with a prediction that it would be 'the year of delivery, the year of peace . . . Hope dares to raise her voice'. But the blows of the war had struck at the heart of modern civilisation and she would continue to publish features that shone a light into the darkest shadows.

At One New Bond Street, there was excitement as Harry Yoxall planned his first post-war trip to Paris to help with the relaunching of French *Vogue* but there was also no central heating in the building and everyone was cold and weary. Weary of the war, weary of a long winter, weary of rationing – though none of that was anything to the suffering of the people of Poland and Greece, France and Belgium, Holland and Luxembourg. Audrey continued to run features that reminded her readers that while Britain had had its share of bombing, loss and deprivation, it was little in comparison to countries occupied by the Germans.

An article by Jane Stockwood drove this point home as she wrote of the moral wound, 'the unhealed cicatrice of humiliation, suspicion and fear – the cumulative mental fear of a people which has lived under the Gestapo'. She wrote of the privations suffered by French families, of the lack of food, heating, electricity and water. It might not have been what *Vogue* readers wanted to read, but it was what Audrey needed them to understand, and she did not let up. While this article had none of Lee's bile against the Germans, it pulled no punches, describing in detail the massacre at Oradour-sur-Glane, when SS troops shot 190 men of the village and burned 247 women and 205 children alive in the church. 'They chose their moment well: it was market day, and the eve of the First Communion.'

To balance the features on war-torn Europe and to prove that she was looking forward to the future, Audrey introduced a competition for readers under the age of twenty-five. It was a brand-new initiative that she would run into the late 1950s and its aim was to give young people who wanted to have a career in fashion a head start. First prize was £25, plus a job on *Vogue*'s London staff for a trial period of six months. Other prize winners and candidates submitting interesting entries would also be considered for positions on *Vogue*'s staff.

The questions had clearly been discussed with the fashion staff, but two of them had Audrey's handwriting all over them. The first, which was compulsory, asked the candidates to list ten features or articles they would like to see in *Vogue* and to suggest the style of writing, photography or drawing they felt would be appropriate. The second asked whether they drew a clear distinction between editorial and advertising pages in the magazine, and what they considered to be their respective values to a reader.

Other questions asked participants to list the contents of their ideal post-war wardrobe (without regard to coupons), and how they thought post-war beauty would develop. It was a clever idea to revitalise interest in *Vogue* at a time when fashion was limping along, restricted by everything from coupons to cotton. It was also a clarion call from Audrey to young women who might not have considered that the fashion world could offer them a career. She listed the various areas involved with fashion: design, manufacture, buying and selling, advertising and, her special interest of course, journalism.

> In the United States, these careers each year attract the brightest of the new crop of college graduates, to the great gain of the American fashion industry. Our English fashion industry, too, would benefit incalculably from similar lively, educated recruits.

The response to the talent contest was enormous, far greater than Audrey and her editors had imagined it would be. Over 700 young people entered, including a handful of men, and Audrey was delighted with the result. She wrote in her piece announcing the winners that the judges at *Vogue* had been impressed by the wide range of interests shown, by the serious desire for information 'coupled with a very proper instinct for frivolity', by sound dress philosophy, good common sense and 'shaky spelling'.

The first winner, who worked at *Vogue* for a few years, before going on to become an artist in her own right, was Lydia Kemeny. The runners-up included a young naval officer, Lieutenant The Hon Frederick Shore, later the 7th Baron Teignmouth, commander of a Motor Torpedo Boat and evidently an avid reader of *Vogue*.

A later winner was Penelope Gilliatt, who would go on to be a talented writer of film and television scripts, most famously *Sunday Bloody Sunday*, which appeared in 1971. She described the nerve-wracking event when the fifteen finalists met fifteen senior Condé Nast staff at a lunch, which in her day was held in the Hyde Park Hotel. 'The Condé Nast judges moved up two places at successive untouched courses so that everybody met everybody: the Mad Hatter's tea party with nary a dormouse for respite.' Gilliatt worked and, later, wrote for *Vogue* after winning the competition in the 1950s.

Early in February, Harry returned from Paris clutching two precious advance copies of French *Vogue*, the publication of which had been delayed due to frost, Audrey explained to Edna with her accompanying memo. 'We are rushing one off to you so that you may share as quickly as possible in this exciting moment of *Vogue*'s history.' Her excitement bubbled over in her memo, telling Edna that Harry's experience in Paris had been extraordinary: 'you can't get a cup of tea because there is no heat, but you can get champagne . . . with paté de-foie-gras, there is no bread to put it on.'

~

Two days later, Audrey took the train to Banbury and cycled to Epwell where she was welcomed by her mother. She spent the next five days looking after Percy while Mamie went into hospital to have her teeth extracted. Percy was thinner than ever and spent much of the day dozing in his study. Even reading a book was an effort and his handwriting had deteriorated so badly that it was nothing but a spidery scrawl. When he was awake, they spoke of the past and reminisced about swimming in Derwentwater, climbing trees in Broadway and his many friends and correspondents who had shared happy times at Souldern Court.

They discussed what would be done with his papers after his death, as well as his library and pictures. Audrey promised him that she and Monica would find a home for them where they would be accessible to serious scholars. She had talked to him many times about his autobiography, which he had been working on for several years. It was a document that said as much about her father for what it left out as for what it included. She realised that her father would die, as he had lived, a contradiction: an intensely private man with a vast number of friends. It was the last time Audrey would spend an extended period with Percy and she found his fading health heart-breaking. He would live to see the end of the war but barely notice it.

By the time she returned to London in mid-February, she was desperate to get back to work, far away from the stuffy atmosphere of her dying father's study. Her desk was piled high with envelopes of photographs from Lee, as she had hoped, and she was soon into the swing of editing Lee's next offerings from the war. The photographs were from Alsace, where Lee was embedded with the 83rd Division. She told Audrey the text would be arriving in instalments. For the first time, Audrey felt truly overwhelmed by the quantity of material her war reporter was providing. The first two instalments, of five in all, totalled some 8,000 words and she knew that would be more than she could possibly accommodate in *Brogue*.

Hearing that Lee was safely back in Paris after the dangerous assignment, she sent her a telegram telling her to have a rest and warning her that she would probably only be able to use 2,000 words but to write as much as she liked as America might be able to take more. Once she sat down to read Lee's report, however, she realised it was too good to cut as much as she had planned. She immediately cabled Lee: 'Delighted thanks magnificent Alsace story have cleared decks April *Brogue* include four pages four turns.'

The article told the story of the battle for Alsace, the last major German offensive of the war, which Hitler had heralded as the destruction of the enemy forces. It was fought between November 1944 and February 1945 in treacherous winter conditions with large losses on both sides. Lee joined the 83rd Division in January as Operation Nordwind was underway. She was confronted by temperatures of −22°C and a metre of snow underfoot. Undaunted, she photographed and described the humours, tragedies and triumphs of the campaign.

The writing was as lively as ever, but Lee was unable to hide her fury and disgust at the death, destruction and misery caused by the war:

> It was the women who spoke French, falteringly, the women without men, who evoked pity. Their men were gone. They were the ones who understood these final stages in the labor of liberation.

The ten photographs that accompanied the article show the magnitude of the destruction and the desolation of fighting in winter conditions. One shot is of a company, all dressed in white over their uniforms, leaving their position in a forest and walking past a soldier in a hole, head bowed, with the body of a dead comrade on the road under a blanket. It is captioned: 'Camouflaged in night-gowns, petticoats, hand-woven sheets from peasants' trousseau: the Moroccans wear them with the style of Roman senators.'

At the same time as Audrey was ploughing through Lee's powerful photographs and texts from Alsace, she was also dealing with spring hats from Paris; changes to the rules of bridge, which had excited the interest of Harry Yoxall, himself a keen bridge player; and a series of requests from New York for photographs from Buckingham Palace.

There was as usual keen interest in New York in images of members of the royal family and the British aristocracy. A planned feature on the 18-year-old Princess Elizabeth was causing particular tension in London. It was to be titled 'The World's Most Famous Bride to Be'. Betty Penrose had requested photographs of Lord Euston and Lord Uxbridge to feature alongside the princess, but Audrey had drawn a complete blank, having tried every agency and every society photographer without success. She was unwilling to press further for fear of causing embarrassment to the families: 'you will remember the retiring habits of the British aristocracy', she reminded Betty, adding: 'sorry to sound so stuffy. These aren't my personal reactions but "typical British" ones!' Betty wrote back assuring Audrey that she had no intention of causing any embarrassment to anyone in Britain but that this was a very interesting piece to the Americans. She signed off the memo with a PS: 'I really am warming up to a personal letter to you, Audrey dear, anytime now! EP'

A few weeks later, Audrey had lost all the stuffiness of that memo and wrote with enthusiasm about the proposed visit of President and Mrs Roosevelt to Britain in the early summer. She was excited at the prospect, telling Edna that she would very much like to have 'a really outstanding feature here ready to be published on that occasion'. She must have known that she was pressing a sore point with Edna, whose sympathies towards the Roosevelts were well known and antagonistic. Audrey explained how much admired the president was in the UK but acknowledged:

> I know it is always somewhat irritating to think that other countries should be almost unanimous over politicians about whom there is always much controversy in their own countries, but I think for an article to be published in England it is essential to take into account this marked British feeling for the President.

Three weeks later, Roosevelt died of a cerebral haemorrhage. It was a shock and caused grief throughout the Western world. Audrey was so moved she immediately suggested that they should feature the President on the front cover of *Brogue*. That was a step too far for New York. Condé Nast had always referred to Roosevelt as 'that man' and to Eleanor Roosevelt, emphatically, as 'that woman!' Edna said later that she was a little startled when she got word from Audrey that she was considering putting his picture on the cover of British *Vogue*.

> Audrey's political beliefs are strong and very much part of her daily life, but I could not help feeling that, deeply grieved though she might be, it was scarcely a good idea to depart from a format of twenty-nine years' standing for one issue and one man. And that man a Democrat!

Roosevelt did not appear on the front cover of *Brogue*, but he did feature in the Victory issue of June 1945 next to profiles of the other two Allied leaders of the moment, Churchill and Stalin.

Meanwhile, material from Lee in Germany was pouring onto Audrey's desk via the censor, and from Beaton in Paris. Memos, photographs, letters and manuscripts all went backwards and forwards across the Atlantic, with Edna concerned that she would never find the space in *Vogue* for all the Paris material that threatened to overwhelm even their more generous magazine space. The sense of urgency, optimism and at the same time anxiety that reigned in Audrey's office in April is evident from the exchanges with New York.

One issue that bothered Audrey was the British Army's attitude towards war correspondents. She wrote to Edna to say how pleased she was that Mary Jean Kempner would be *Vogue*'s war correspondent in the Pacific and how delighted they would be in London to have some really good stories from Australian forces but, she added,

> When it comes to reporting on the Services, I am afraid that Miss Kempner will be in the same position as Lee Miller, i.e. allowed to go where she pleases among the American Forces, but only allowed the most official and boring contacts with the British Forces.

This 'sex discrimination which possesses our War Office' drove Audrey to distraction and she could not understand why the British were not prepared to allow women to report from war zones when the Americans had. It was recognised that the female photographers and journalists were every bit as brave and capable as their male counterparts.

I am most anxious that we should do nothing to perpetu-
ate the idea that there are no British troops in the Pacific.
Our War Office's refusal to give facilities to women war
correspondents has forced us to publish Lee's whole series
of stories from the continent in which British troops are
only mentioned or shown on one occasion – i.e. on leave in
Brussels. Though actually I have had no readers' protest, I
do think it extremely unfortunate that a British magazine
should have so utterly to ignore the part played by the British
Forces in the war on Germany, and I do not want this to be
perpetuated in the Pacific.

Is it possible that Audrey was frustrated that none of her readers had picked up on the fact that all the war reports in *Vogue*
referred to American forces? She was certainly anxious to keep
her independence from New York and in this particular aspect
she was in danger of losing it.

Edna was sympathetic and promised Audrey she would make
sure Mary Jean Kempner got an excellent piece on Australia
especially for *Brogue*. She wondered whether Beaton could not be
sent as a British war correspondent. 'I am sure he would bring
a personal point of view to bear on many of these places which
would be different, and not necessarily interfere with Lee.'

That idea died a death before it hit Audrey's desk. That there
was no love lost between Lee Miller and Cecil Beaton was well
known, and Audrey knew that if she sent Beaton to Germany,
Lee would see it as a betrayal of trust, something Audrey was
not prepared to countenance. Beaton would remain in Britain
or Paris as far as the editor of *Brogue* was concerned.

On the morning of 25 April, Audrey got notice from the

Ministry of Information that photographs taken by Lee Miller in Germany had been released by the censor and she could collect them from their offices. She sent Alex Kroll, who had been responsible for sorting through the scores of Lee's images on contact sheets before getting them printed for Audrey and John Parsons.

Alex Kroll had joined *Vogue* in 1942. The son of a Lithuanian industrial chemist, he had been born in Moscow but the family moved to Berlin when he was seven to get him treatment for spinal TB. Kroll escaped from Germany in 1938 and joined his sister in London. His parents remained in Berlin and were interned in various prison and concentration camps but both survived the war. Kroll had worked closely with Lee since he first started at *Vogue* and his keen eye always sought out the most striking pictures, which he would use to create a powerful layout.

Edna had been complimentary about the improvement in the design of *Brogue* since the previous summer and Audrey had been anxious for her to know where the praise should be heard:

We have two young men who lay out *Vogue* practically without help. One is John Parsons, whom de Holden-Stone engaged as a junior and who, when de Holden-Stone and Young left us, took on his new responsibilities with most admirable success. He is only about twenty-six and I have the greatest hopes of him. The other man is Alex Kroll, who is even younger, and he only came as de Holden-Stone was leaving. He too, has made great strides. These two boys make an excellent team as they have very different taste, but such a great liking and respect for one another, that they are able to correct one another's errors to a great extent. I think in them we have two very valuable young men for the future.

That Audrey had to introduce these two men to Edna is a reminder of just how isolated London had become. Visits from the American office had stopped with the outbreak of war and the guiding hand that had been present in the 1930s had long ceased to lead the way.

It was always a moment of excitement at the office when material from Lee came in and these were images that she had heralded in a telegram. They were photographs she had taken in the Nazi concentration camp at Buchenwald. Audrey spoke of the moment when she, John Parsons and Alex Kroll spread out the photographs on tables in the art department, 'just as we were accustomed to spread out fashion photos or pictures of personalities'. Lee's cable read: 'I IMPLORE YOU TO BELIEVE THAT THIS IS TRUE.' Audrey described her horror when confronted with Lee's images:

There was no difficulty in believing. The difficulty was, and still is, in trying to understand how it was possible for such horrors to be perpetrated not just in a fit of rage but system- atically and carefully organised over years. To me, it was far more frightening than the existence of a Hitler or a Stalin and the fact that their crimes could not have been carried out without the willing cooperation of thousands who applied to work for the gulags and concentration camps just as if it was a job like any other.

Lee's first experience of a concentration camp had been at Ohrdruf, which had been liberated three weeks before she arrived. She was so shocked she put her camera down. 'I don't take pictures of these things usually,' she told Audrey, 'as I know you won't use them . . . I won't write about this now, just read the daily press and believe every word of it.'

From there, she went to Buchenwald, where she was shocked to the core by the scale and the ghastly stench that came from barracks that had held over 50,000 inmates. She picked up her camera and took photographs, some close up, and these were what Audrey, John Parsons and Alex Kroll were looking at that morning in One New Bond Street. 'Her photographs, which we could hardly bear to look at, showed piles of bodies – bodies reduced to hard-edged skeletons so that their entanglements gave an appalling effect of an abstract pattern.'

Audrey had to decide what to do with the images and whether to include them in the Victory edition of *Brogue*, as she knew she should. Lee, meanwhile, went further south in Germany and with Dave Scherman was one of the first reporters, and the first female photographer, to enter Dachau, outside Munich. They arrived at the camp as it was being liberated by the Americans:

In this case, the camp is so close to the town that there is no question about the inhabitants knowing what went on. The railway siding into the camp runs past quite a few swell villas and the last train of dead and semi-dead deportees was long enough to extend past them. The cars are still full of skeletal dead, and the path beside the trains are littered with the fleshless bodies of those who tried to get out and walk to their execution.

Lee walked around with her camera, focusing her attention on the human side, using the medics and GIs to frame her photographs, to show the shock they felt at bearing witness to such scenes of degradation. As such, we feel empathy with the young soldiers, and their horror communicates an immediacy that Lee grasped would work.

For once, Audrey's courage failed her, and she could not bring herself to run an entire feature on the atrocities that Lee had witnessed and photographed. The stories and ghastly images had already been shown in the London newspapers, so people knew of the camps. In the June edition of *Vogue*, there is a small picture by Lee of bodies piled up at Buchenwald. Still a remarkable photograph to see in a fashion magazine, but not the bold spread Audrey later wished she had had the courage to include. She spoke of her shame at this failure when she gave a lecture fifty years later:

But where were those pictures which have lived in my memory? I went through all the possible issues again and again and finally found one, only one and that not more than three inches square in that Victory number. I couldn't believe it and I was further mortified to find four pages of them displayed in the contemporary issue of American *Vogue*. I feel deeply ashamed and have tried to think how such a decision could have come about. All I can imagine is that we were at last celebrating victory after a war which had bereaved hundreds of thousands and exhausted millions. We must have felt the public wanted to rejoice and were in no mood for further suffering. They wanted to celebrate, not to be faced with horrors. In America, it was rather different.

They had not experienced the war in their daily life. They were able to stand shocks.

Edna had not published the photographs with the impunity Audrey credits her. In her autobiography, she described the anguish she and others felt at seeing the gruesome images and sensing Lee's unbridled rage at what she had witnessed. She wrote later:

> We hesitated a long time and held many conferences decid-
> ing whether or not to publish them. In the end, we did and
> it seemed right. In the world we were trying to reflect in
> our pages, the wealthy, the gently bred, the sophisticated
> were quite as dead and quite as bereft as the rest of mankind.
> Anguish knows no barriers.

Lee's war was not over, but Audrey's was. The 'Victory Number' of June 1945 had a defiant message, accompanied by Lee's photograph of the Figure of Justice still standing among the ruins of Frankfurt. Audrey wrote a powerful editorial:

> In Frankfurt, amid complete devastation, a figure stands
> inviolate: the figure of Justice with her sword and scales.
> Behind, the unscathed cathedral spire proclaims the
> Christian and cultural heritage which the Nazis aimed to
> destroy. Now, instead, they are themselves destroyed. But
> the statue and spire remain, symbols of justice and aspira-
> tion . . . The first phase of the struggle is over. We do right
> to rejoice, before we turn to complete the winning of a just
> war and the founding of a final peace.

On the following page is a portrait of Churchill with his famous victory sign and opposite that ten of his most famous quotes that had inspired Britain through the war. A few pages on, after profiles of Roosevelt and Stalin, is Lee's piece about Germany, its bitterness and anger barely restrained:

> My fine Baedecker tour of Germany includes many such places as Buchenwald which were not mentioned in my 1913 edition, and if there is a later one I doubt if they were mentioned there, either, because no one in Germany has ever heard of a concentration camp, and I guess they didn't want any tourist business either. Visitors took one-way tickets only.

Audrey may not have had the courage to show more than the one image from Buchenwald, but Lee's report is brutal. There is no escaping the horror of what she saw in the prison camps for *Vogue*'s readers:

> The 600 bodies stacked in the courtyard of the crematorium because they had run out of coal the last five days had been carted away until only a hundred were left; and the splotches of death from a wooden potato masher had been washed, because the place had to be disinfected; and the bodies on the whipping stalls were dummies instead of almost dead men who could feel but not react.

As Audrey was preparing that edition of *Vogue*, Lee's latest service message arrived on her desk. She wrote how she had long speculated where she would be and what it would be like and how they would celebrate 'for the end of the war or the death of Hitler or whatever it was'. She went on: 'I was living in Hitler's private apartment when his death was announced.'

Lee and Dave Scherman had driven from Dachau to Munich and were billeted in 27 Prinzregentenplatz. Antony Penrose described the building that he saw forty years later:

> It was in an old-fashioned building on a corner, which showed no outward signs that anybody more elevated than a merchant or retired clergyman lived there, so it seemed an unlikely setting for one of Lee and Dave's biggest scoops. The impression of ordinariness continued inside with furnishings and decor that could have belonged to anyone with a moderate income and no heirlooms. Only the swastika combined with the AH monogram on the silver gave it away as Hitler's house.

Lee stripped off her filthy, Dachau-infested clothes and stepped into Hitler's bathtub, where Scherman took a photograph of her that was to become world famous. Holding a flannel in her right hand, she rubs her shoulder and looks away from the camera. On the edge of the bath is a framed photograph of the Führer and on the pale primrose yellow bathmat her dirty army issue boots. In her letter to Audrey, she described how Hitler had become more alive for her than ever before, now faced as she was with the everyday paraphernalia of his apartment.

> He became less fabulous and therefore more terrible, along with a little evidence of his having some almost human habits; like an ape who embarrasses and humbles you with his gestures, mirroring yourself in caricature. There, but for the grace of God walk I.

She described Dachau as everything you'll ever hear or close your ears to about a concentration camp.

> Dave Scherman and I took off from Dachau to go look for the war front which seemed a mirage of cleanliness and humanity. The sight of the blue and white striped tatters shrouding the bestial death of hundreds of starved and maimed men and women had left us gulping for air and for violence, and if Munich, the birth place of this horror was falling, we'd like to help.

She signed her letter, 'Love and kisses Lee.'

Lee would not stop. She could not stop. Her experiences on the battlefield and in the concentration camps had taken their toll, as they did on everyone who witnessed them in the immediate aftermath of their liberation. She was a restless soul who could find no peace while her anger was still raging. From Munich, she went with Scherman to Berchtesgaden and saw Wachenfeld, Hitler's house, in flames.

Immediately after the war had been declared over, she drove across Germany to Denmark having accepted an assignment to photograph Danish fashion. From there, she came back to London and to a rapturous reception at *Vogue*. A lunch was given in her honour and Harry Yoxall made a speech praising her exceptional reporting.

Back in London, Lee was unsettled, and Audrey could sense that she needed to be back on the continent, fulfilling her promise to herself to witness the reconstruction of Europe. Over the next several months she travelled to Austria and beyond to Hungary and Romania. She sent back reports and photographs, which Audrey continued to publish in *Vogue*, and her article on Romania, written in a haze of self-doubt and whisky, appeared to acclaim in the May 1946 edition. Antony Penrose wrote: 'It was the swansong of Lee's days of high adventure.'

Audrey had been the grounding force in London for all the time Lee was away. Now that it was over, she too had to come to terms with the fact that her war reporter was a citizen of peacetime Britain. She knew it would not be easy for Lee to adapt, as indeed it proved, but she also knew that they had created something remarkable in their joint determination to bring the war into readers' lives. In a lecture given at the Institute of Contemporary Arts in 1992, on the occasion of the publication of *Lee Miller's War* and an exhibition of her photographs, Audrey paid this heartfelt tribute to her brilliant star contributor:

> Lee's courage was never in doubt. She drove herself unstintingly to the cause of presenting and interpreting the war to the British and American public. That was her life's work, packed into about eighteen hectic months. That is what she has left us, an explosion of creativity that can still illuminate an era half a century later. That was her finest hour.

While Lee Miller was working out what her post-war life would look like, Audrey was firmly focused on the future and *Vogue*'s role in a peaceful but shattered world. The end of the Second World War brought Audrey relief rather than joy. She was exhausted after carrying an enormous burden. Harry Yoxall told Edna he was worried about her weariness, but

Audrey herself did not let up. She had a Victory issue to publish and a magazine to rebuild for the new era. She and Harry had already discussed how they would expand *Vogue* when paper rationing was lifted and civilian goods once again became more readily available in the shops.

The end of the war brought with it a hangover of dislocation and bureaucracy. Four and a half million servicemen and women were repatriated over a period of eighteen months and they returned to families who had grown up, changed, been evacuated or bombed, or a combination of all this and more.

The disruption to family life was exacerbated by a severe lack of housing, a lack of building materials to repair houses that had been requisitioned, damaged or re-fashioned for wartime use. The country was criss-crossed by defence lines, Britain's shoreline was wired for repelling invasion and all over the country people were trying to find a way to carry on with life. None of this was a fraction of the situation on the continent, of course, where in Germany alone there were over 12 million refugees and whole cities in both Allied and Axis countries were demolition sites.

Nevertheless, Britain was in poor shape physically and the scars of war had cut deep psychological wounds in the minds of many who had witnessed terrible sights. One of the groups most badly affected were the men, women and children who had been prisoners of the Japanese in camps throughout South East Asia, the most infamous of which were along the trace of the Thailand–Burma Railway.

Audrey had not suffered the loss of any close family, but she had lived vicariously the experience of Lee Miller's adventures.

The impact of the images and reports describing the battle for Alsace and the horrors of the concentration camps had had a very profound effect on her. It had made her harder, on the one hand, and more distrustful of human beings on the other. She said later,

> Visiting Germany briefly after the war and Russia many times, I was haunted by the fact that unknowingly one might be meeting those who had done that work and who looked like ordinary, decent people. How was one to know?

If the war had changed Audrey internally, it had also changed her professionally. Five challenging, uncertain but extraordinarily exciting and creative years had given her confidence in her professional abilities that she had not had when she took the helm from Betty Penrose in 1940. Over the course of the war, particularly before America entered the fray, she had had the advantage over her New York colleagues, leading the way and placing *Vogue* in the right place for the time. This was also the case, later in the war, when it came to the liberation of France, where Audrey was the conduit between New York and Paris. She led the way on reporting the war in Europe and the unfolding liberation stories with confidence.

Harry was proud of her wartime work and told Edna that her record as editor during the war had given her a claim to recognition and security from *Vogue* as well as a significant increase in salary. 'I do not know exactly how you feel about Audrey's work now, but I believe I can assume that you are completely satisfied with it.' He praised her excellent professional editorial qualities and said that the critical judgement she had shown when fashion and features editors had brought her material was first-class.

This was praise indeed from Harry, who acknowledged that he had leaned on Audrey heavily during those years. He now wanted to put her on a three-year contract and pay her £2,000 a year, some of which would be a dress allowance to avoid income tax. It is extraordinary to think that although she had been made a director of Condé Nast Publications in 1942, she had not had the security of a formal contract as editor of *Vogue* for five years.

Betty Penrose had told Harry she longed to return to Britain, and this would have posed a serious threat to Audrey's position. Harry felt it would be grossly unfair to unseat Audrey given that her abilities were at least as professional and proficient as Betty's and that she was entitled to the editorship given the fact she had carried the role during the war years. Edna agreed, stating confidently that she thought Audrey was 'now an experienced editor and under peacetime conditions she will probably edit the magazine as ably as Betty would have done'. She said it would be a great injustice to unseat Audrey and she proposed an even more generous financial settlement for her over three years, rising, eventually, to £2,500 per annum.

All Audrey knew was that Edna was preparing to reinforce her influence on the London office now that the war was over and she had the opportunity to exercise full control. In March, she had written to Audrey in a blaze of fury over a caption she had included in a photographic profile piece on Cecil Beaton. She felt it was far too intimate for publication in *Vogue*.

How could you? How could you? I refer to the caption of

Dahl-Wolfe's photograph of Beaton in his own very unfortunate words, 'This is the midsummer way I'd like to look; the way I feel my skin is; the way I should smell.' I don't know how the British public will react to this but I could tell you in one word how the American public would react to these pages. I know of course you want to please Cecil but I really think you should have somehow or other wriggled out of this feature, or at any rate this caption with that Dahl-Wolfe photograph should never have gotten into print.

Audrey did not defend the Beaton article. She was too busy juggling material for the Victory issue planned for June and, in any case, the feature was sufficiently beautiful to carry a flamboyant caption.

Five days after the war ended, Edna fired off another salvo:

I haven't had time to make a considered judgment yet but I can say offhand that I think Lesley Blanch's article is very boring and completely out of the present mood. I am wondering if you were wise giving so much space to this article.

The following month she sent Audrey a cable admonishing her for an unnecessarily wordy telegram. Audrey wrote back apologising for having become slack, justifying it only by telling Edna that to send a message by telegram 'economically, yet with absolute clarity' took time. This change in mood between Edna and Audrey increased over the spring and summer as Audrey continued to pursue the same confident independence that she had during the war years.

It was something that Harry noticed as well. He always stood up for his editor in the face of Edna's criticism, but there were times when she felt under-appreciated and overworked, especially given the difficulties of post-war life. One of the greatest problems she faced was the continuation of wartime mentality among civil servants and government offices.

In a memo labelled 'Staple Gun, Staples & Film', she wrote asking New York not to send any goods or gifts without paperwork, however welcome and badly needed they were in Britain, because they did not have an import licence and were thus held up in customs. 'We are endeavouring to clear them as unsolicited gifts,' she wrote. The only item in a shipment of office materials that had got through unchallenged was a steam iron.

In June, the British general election returned a Labour government with a large majority, removing Churchill, the great war hero. It was a result that made Audrey happy, but she knew enough about Edna's politics to guess at her thoughts. Edna wrote:

> You are right about the American reactions to your elections. All my friends (dyed-in-the-wool conservatives, of course) practically expired with froth on their lips. There was an awful outcry; and pained surprise that the British could be so ungrateful.

Audrey wrote a long and beautifully argued letter laying out before Edna all the reasons she thought the electorate had rejected the Conservatives and explaining how she personally felt Roosevelt's death had had a bearing on the result. She believed that had he not died, some people in Britain might have hesitated to break the triumvirate that had been successful in bringing the war to its end.

> And hereby hangs what is in my opinion another contributing factor, namely the deep-rooted antagonism to the supposition that any one man is essential to a country's future. Must one not admit that this is of the essence of democracy, and that to believe that the future of the world is in the hands of a few elderly statesmen is a most precarious position to take up?

This letter was designed to give Edna the clearest possible picture of the country's thinking. Why was that important? Audrey answered her own question:

> I am telling you all this because our two countries must understand one another, and that can partly come about through those of us who are fortunate enough to have friends in our respective countries.

It was a theme that she would return to in the 1950s.

~

In June, Audrey's beloved father went into heart failure. She was called to his bedside but he no longer recognised her as he slipped in and out of consciousness. He died on a rainy day at the end of June with Mamie and his two daughters at his side. His funeral service was held at Epwell on a beautiful warm day in July. Jock held Audrey's arm as she listened to the vicar speaking of Percy's life. She mused that Percy would not have been concerned about the afterlife. He had no belief in it, but Mamie had and this service was about her trust in the existence of life after death.

Audrey looked at her mother and for the first time saw how frail she was. Her cloud of thin, wispy white hair was tucked under her black hat, her shoulders were hunched forward and her face lined with sadness and a sorrow that Audrey came to realise was not just about Percy's death but about her own life. Mamie Withers would outlive her husband by just over two years. She died in November 1947 at the age of seventy-seven.

Audrey and Monica had been comforted by the thought that after Percy's death Mamie and Michael would be able to live together happily, Mamie no longer torn between her husband and her son. Tragically, as they were to learn only after Mamie's death, that had been a vain hope. It turned out that Michael had so disliked feeling her presence anywhere in the house that she had been forced to walk the lanes or spend hours in the garden in all weathers. Audrey wrote:

My mother was the kindest and most unselfish of women; but she had never opened out to me – or I think, to anyone – so I never got near her and never helped her. And how much she needed it was revealed when, after her death, I found in her jacket pockets scraps of paper on which she had scribbled, over and over again, 'Lord Jesus help me!' I can think of my father with a happy gratitude, because he gave me so much that has been the foundation of my life, and because he knew my love for him; but the knowledge that I failed my mother haunts me.

After Mamie's death Audrey and Monica sold Epwell Mill and with that their ties to Oxfordshire were cut. Michael moved into a cottage in a nearby village where the neighbours looked out for him and became fond of this gentle, eccentric character. He was always happier with animals for company than people and he never visited Audrey or Monica in London, nor did he expect them to come to see him. At first, they made an effort, but Michael was not pleased to have his routine interrupted. He died of a cerebral haemorrhage in his sleep ten years after the end of the war. He was forty-five. No one ever explained to Audrey or Monica what had been wrong with him and it is likely that his condition remained undiagnosed, which seems sad given that his father had such close links to the medical profession.

Audrey's personal life had survived the war because both she and Jock had been fully occupied by their work. Their home in Blomfield Road had been untouched by enemy bombing but it was looking tatty and unloved after six years of neglect by the council. Building materials were scarce and expensive and local authorities had far greater housing problems to worry about than tidying up council properties in Little Venice.

Inside the flat was in better shape, but it had become over-crowded. Audrey had inherited a collection of her father's prints and after the sale of Epwell Mill she brought them to London and rehung the sitting room and hall with his pictures. One of them was a portrait of her by Paul Nash, which he had given her when she was sixteen. She believed it was the only portrait he had done of anyone outside his family. He too was no longer alive, having died in his sleep of heart failure as a result of his asthma.

Audrey attended his funeral in July 1946 and mourned his passing. He had been a lynchpin in her youth and she felt a great void in her life. After the funeral she wrote to his widow, Margaret, asking her if Paul had by any chance kept the letters she had written him from school and university. He had. She was overjoyed and asked Margaret whether one day she would be able to have copies of them to remind her of the happy days in the house of sunshine and poetry.

In response, Margaret Nash asked Audrey to become a trustee of the foundation she had set up in his name. She said she needed her to join the board and then gradually take over the secretarial side and be a general manager of the men. She appealed to her by saying:

> I want you because, Audrey, you really loved Paul and he so admired your achievements in life and what you made of it. He often spoke of you with admiration and with great affection. I always respected and loved your devotion to him and indeed how could anyone help loving him.

Audrey never took up the offer to become a trustee of the Nash collection. The excuse she gave was that Margaret Nash wanted to influence which of his works were chosen for exhibitions and publications, rather than allowing the curators and editors to choose, something that would have grated on Audrey's editorial nerves. However, it was the offer of being secretary to the trust and managing 'all those men' that Audrey took exception to and so she refused. It took Margaret four years to get around to having the letters transcribed. Eventually she sent Audrey transcripts that ran to 13,000 words. Sadly, those transcripts no longer appear to exist. Audrey must have destroyed them.

In the autumn after the end of the war, Audrey went to Paris. It was her first trip to the French capital since her visit to the fashion shows the summer before the war and she was enchanted. She was installed in unprecedented splendour in the Ritz Hotel but there was almost no food available in the restaurant and hot water and electricity were haphazard. Transport was difficult as so many Métro stations were closed and she had to walk almost everywhere on foot:

> Yet all these minor trials counted for nothing against the mere fact of being in Paris – and a Paris more beautiful than I shall ever see again. Just imagine the city with practically no traffic, only a few bicycles and an occasional army truck. One could cross the Champs-Elysées without bothering to look either way. The September days were cloudless and still. When one walked along the Seine, the only movement one could see was that of a leaf dropping into the water.

For the next fourteen years, Audrey would visit Paris twice a year for the fashion shows and every time she was delighted anew by the great city, but never was she as moved by it as she was that week in the aftermath of the war.

One of Audrey's great personal strengths was her ability to look forward and to leave the past behind. In her private life, Audrey and her sister Monica were close, and that familial link provided her with as much security as she needed to carry on after the loss of Percy, Mamie and Paul Nash. Her life with

Jock was not happy but she was so good at compartmentalising her private and professional lives that few of her friends or colleagues ever knew that things were not going well. Audrey continued to work long hours at *Vogue* and Jock spent longer hours in the company of other women.

Only Monica truly knew how unsatisfactory Audrey's marriage had turned out to be. Jock's relationships with other women had become ever more open and Audrey found being with him wearisome, especially when they went away on holiday and he was on the lookout for someone interesting to seduce. She maintained later that she and Jock had always remained good friends, but she felt betrayed by his serial affairs and humiliated as a woman no longer attractive to her husband.

Monica had inherited her father's abhorrence of all things intimate, so discussing anything of a very personal nature was impossible. She told Audrey that she had once been in love with a man but it was not reciprocated and the rejection led her to live, as Audrey put it, 'an entirely sexless life'. She could not read novels nor could she watch films that had love scenes, however discreet, and when it came to shows of affection between men and women, she could not bear to see that either. She certainly could not discuss Audrey's marriage or Jock's infidelities in any detail.

Harry Yoxall had a strong hunch that things were not all rosy for Audrey, and he and Edna arranged for Audrey to spend Christmas 1945 in New York, without Jock. He wrote a confidential letter to Edna who replied, after the visit, that she had made a point of

exposing Audrey to a great deal of entertaining and, in fact,
I think she had quite a whirl. She seemed to be very much
impressed with the social atmosphere of our office, both
internally and externally. In fact, she talked to me about it
and said she realized that this had been very much lacking in
her own sphere and that she felt very strongly that she must
make a great effort to change her attitude.

Audrey arrived in New York two days before Christmas
having travelled by flying boat via Portugal, Africa, Latin
America, the Caribbean and into Boston. From there, she
took a train to New York and was welcomed at the *Vogue*
office with open arms. Having left in 1938 as a fresh-faced
managing editor, she returned seven years later quite the
veteran and heroine of the moment. The Allies had been
victorious, Britons were popular and for a brief moment she
found herself in the limelight, representing not only London
Vogue, but Britain itself.

She was congratulated by Edna, Jessica Daves, Betty
Penrose, Dr Agha and Iva Patcévitch for the excellent job she
had done keeping *Vogue* going during the dark days of the Blitz,
the years of rationing and austerity. Most of all they praised
her for the astonishing reporting and photography she had
used from Cecil Beaton in the Middle and Far East and, without doubt the high point, Lee Miller's photojournalism from
the European continent. She in return was keen to relay the
heartfelt thanks of all the London staff for the generous food
parcels that had been sent from New York. 'So it was a happy
atmosphere,' she concluded.

After the drab grey streets of London and the unimpressive

window displays in the department stores, she found New York thrilling, 'as splendid and unreal as a pantomime'. She marvelled at the huge, brightly lit Christmas trees running the entire length of Park Avenue and goggled at the jewellery counters that seemed to be hundreds of yards long.

Edna and Pat entertained her lavishly, introducing her at one lunch party to Marlene Dietrich and the Surrealist artist Salvador Dalí who had spent the war in the USA. She went to concerts at the City Centre but she had limited success with getting tickets to the theatre as productions were sold out weeks in advance. What she noticed was a more relaxed frankness between employers and employees, which she found refreshing. There was no fear of showing ignorance and British reticence was disliked intensely by Americans, 'who approved of genuineness above everything'. She found that uplifting and wanted to bring a dose of it back to her office.

Audrey spent Christmas with Edna and her husband, Dick Newton, who spoiled her with as much as they could muster in the way of kindness and treats. Edna gave her a magnificent triple string of pearls as a Christmas present and as a thank-you for everything she had done during the war. Audrey was overwhelmed by their hospitality, though she was amazed by some of the shortages, which she had not expected to find in New York. Sugar had been rationed and was rarely available, so that even the smartest hotels in the city served saccharine. She was astonished to discover that nylon stockings were unobtainable: these treasured articles had been the envy of the British when the GIs descended on Britain in the later years of the war armed with nylons by the bagful.

Even lingerie was in short supply and in limited colours and sizes, she told an eager audience at the Women's Press Club two months after her return. However, she did notice a marked shift in Americans' interest in politics and international affairs. They were obsessed by the atom bomb and within minutes of any gathering, be it a party or a serious business meeting, the subject would turn to the bomb. The other thing that she found herself quizzed on was Britain's general election, when Churchill had been roundly defeated and Labour had swept to victory.

She returned to Britain in early January, rested, refreshed and reinvigorated. Edna told Harry she thought Audrey had had a very happy visit and she had made friends of all the staff in the New York office as well as many people on the outside. Harry agreed and said that Audrey had returned entranced by the reception she had received in New York and had come back to London in splendid form. The visit to New York was a reward to Audrey for the work she had done at *Vogue* during the war, but it was also an opportunity for her to get away from London and achieve some perspective after five long years of attrition. Audrey's thank-you letter to Edna, written 'between Bermuda and Lisbon' on New Year's Day, is one of her most bubbly and effusive:

A visit to America is an exciting enough experience at any time; but coming from England, it seems a New World indeed, and a wonderful one. But far more than all that was the warmth of the welcome which you and everyone gave me. I have never experienced anything like it in my life – and hardly expect to again, for I realise very well that I was just the lucky representative of my office – and perhaps even of my country – and that the kindness shown to me was the means of your generous appreciation of them.

She went on to thank Edna and Pat for their confidence in her, 'knowing so little of me', and promised that she would do everything she possibly could to deserve and maintain that respect.

> It was very encouraging to find that though physically separated for so long, our minds seemed to be moving along similar lines and that there was no real gulf of taste or outlook between us. I feel confident that, with improving conditions, *Brogue* can go right ahead and establish itself in a position of authority comparable to *Vogue*'s.

This is a theme that she would return to in the autumn of that year, because cracks did begin to show as Edna began to flex her editorial muscles once again. But for now Audrey was riding on a major high: 'I do thank you for it with all my heart, and also for the kind things you said, which warmed and encouraged me more than I can say.'

9

FIGHTING FOR FREEDOM

'*Vogue* stands in all fields for all that is most advanced. We
support everything that is new, challenging, revolutionary . . .
We stand for opportunity for women.'

— AUDREY WITHERS TO EDNA WOOLMAN CHASE,
17 OCTOBER 1946

The exhaustion after the war and the drudge of day-to-day life
under rationing, which now included bread for the first time,
was a subject that Audrey decided to tackle in her own way. She
commissioned an article from the writer Daphne du Maurier.
It took weeks of negotiating, but by March 1946 Audrey had
landed her catch. Du Maurier was at the height of her fame,
having learned recently that the millionth copy of one of her
books had been printed in America and that the royalties from
the French translation of another had paid out what a French
family might have expected to earn in a year.

In an article called 'Just Idling Along', she wrote:

I do nothing. I delight in doing nothing. I hope I shall continue to do nothing to the end of my days . . . Few people

will admit to being dull. It is the ultimate deadly sin, which
I glory in with complacency.

She then summed up the world-weariness felt by many people
in Britain after the long war that had changed the lives of so
many and in myriad ways. In the piece, she mused on the
destruction caused by the Blitz, on churches empty of worship-
pers, 'because, with modern warfare, hell-fire holds no terror
for us', and on the food – or lack of it:

> On what shall I feed my husband when he returns from
> Singapore? He tells me he has a dinner party every night.
> The problem of our time. The soldier husband who returns,
> not to an empty house but to an empty larder.

She concluded with shoulder-sagging relief:

> I switch on the news. No longer 'Three hundred Lancasters
> of Bomber Command today attacked the targets of . . .'
> That, thank God, is over. Over for how long? We, of the
> middle years, have no illusion.

Edna was delighted with the article and begged Audrey to send
her photographs of the author at her house in Cornwall or with
her children. She was anxious that the question of payment
should be discussed quickly. Audrey wrote back to say that Miss
du Maurier had written: 'Instead of payment direct I think it
would be much more fun for me if you would let me have –
say – a two year subscription to *Vogue*.' Audrey pointed out that
with taxation at record levels and Daphne du Maurier 'making

a mint of money', most of what they would pay her by direct fee would be swallowed up in her tax bill. Seven Withers to Chase memos give a glimpse of the negotiations that had to be undertaken to get a photograph of the famous author to illustrate the piece. In the end, a portrait by American photographer Clifford Coffin appeared opposite the article, and Daphne du Maurier was rewarded with a two-year subscription to *Vogue* and *Brogue*.

The personal relationship between Edna and Audrey was always warm and affectionate, but their professional relationship after the war was difficult. The two women had so much in common, both having an eagle eye for detail but a decidedly stubborn streak in their natures. Audrey's manifested itself through quiet but determined argument; Edna's through more stormy interventions. Now Edna wanted to take back control of British *Vogue* and Audrey was equally determined not to let that happen, having gained autonomy and authority through hard work in difficult times. Things reached a crunch point in the autumn of 1946.

Audrey had been asked by Condé Nast a few months before he died to give her opinion on the scope of British *Vogue* and its outlook and attitude to life. In August, Edna invited her to readdress the issue but the response was silence. Telegrams demanding an answer were met with more silence and private letters to Harry had no discernible effect. What she did not know was that Audrey was up to her eyes at work and on an exciting exhibition project that would come to fruition in September.

When Audrey did eventually respond, Edna was in a state of extreme high dudgeon with her British editor. She was rewarded with a ten-page memorandum, which is the closest

thing to a manifesto that Audrey ever wrote. She told Edna that
the topic had occupied her mind constantly

> since the days I first began to have responsibility for *Vogue*
> policy. I was in the process of trying to put my views on
> paper for Mr. Nast at the time of his death; but that event
> decided me to drop it for the time being, and the war years
> brought a unity of purpose under which differences of opin-
> ion sank into the background. Now here is peace, and with
> it the differences return.

Audrey gave Edna three headings on which she enlarged her
ideas. The first was the breadth of *Vogue*'s subject matter, the
second was the argument that *Vogue* could not be non-political
and the third was the statement that '*Vogue*'s politics must
be progressive.' Audrey knew that much of what she was
expounding would not find a willing ear or eye in Edna, but
she felt passionately about the future of *Vogue* and, above all,
about its place in London publishing now that *Harper's Bazaar*
had an able new editor, Anne Scott-James, who was poaching
talent for her magazine.

She wrote of how the demise of *Vanity Fair*, also of the Condé
Nast stable, in the late 1930s had been the best possible thing
for *Vogue*,

> for with the 'incorporation of Vanity Fair' *Vogue* grew up,
> and became like an adult, intelligent, modern woman.
> We, here, find an almost universal admiration for *Vogue*'s
> increased scope and breadth of interest. I think *Vogue*
> should never again be simply a 'fashion paper', but should

be the best kind of magazine – mainly for women, but with sufficient in it to interest men also; covering fashion very professionally, beautifully and importantly, because fashion is one of women's great interests, but also covering every subject in which the intelligent, sophisticated woman is currently interested.

She went on:

I think *Vogue* should be like the complete woman, with beauty, brains, personality and an intelligent interest in everything that goes on in the world around her. Just as the intelligent woman no longer travels from one luxury hotel to another without touching the life of the country she visits – but walks in the streets, asks questions, notices the appearance of the people, and the way they eat – so *Vogue* must do also. It simply is not modern to be unaware of, or uninterested in, what is going on all round you; and the great appetite for personality profiles and for the Miller-Mannes type of travel article that digs down into the countries they visit, shows how very far from superficial are people's tastes today . . . There is no question of fashion being crowded out; there is room for both; and I think it would be nothing short of a tragedy to throw away for nothing the position we have gained.

Where Audrey had the greatest difference with Edna was over politics. She believed it was in their best interest to take note of the politics that touched every aspect of their lives. In her '*Vogue* cannot be non-political' point, she reminded Edna that politics affected everything from education and health to freedom to travel and the cost of goods. What was the good of shying away from dealing with questions that affected everyone, she wanted to know?

She used as an example a feature she was about to publish on the future of the English country house. It could have taken the line that deplored the tax and death duty situation so swingeing that it was almost impossible for an individual family to keep up a large country house. An alternative view might have been that the situation was part of a change of attitude and could devote itself to exploring ways in which the great houses could be preserved and used to the advantage of the community.

It is not difficult to see which side Audrey would have come down on in this argument and the point was well made. Being non-political was not an option in her opinion:

> One is being every whit as political, for instance, in giving one's tacit approval to things as they are, as in pressing for change. It is an old right-wing trick to sit tight and say nothing (because that's the best way of keeping things as they are) and to accuse the left-wing of being 'political' – because it is forced to be vocal in advocating anything new. Actually, both sides are being equally 'political'; and so it must be with *Vogue*.

Where Audrey got most excited was when she talked about *Vogue*'s attitude towards women. She told Edna that the status of women and the attitude towards them was

> one of the clearest indexes to the political complexion of a society. I think I am correct in saying that it has always

improved in politically progressive countries; remained bad in 'traditional' countries; deteriorated when a 'right' succeeded a 'left' government.

She went on to describe a strong right-wing movement that had emerged in Britain in the middle of the war and advocated the return of women to the home. It concluded that they did not need education but should rely on their intuition and that their influence should not be exerted directly but only through men. This had horrified her, and she put that notion firmly where it belonged: in the garbage.

Vogue, in addressing women, constantly emphasises intelligence, personality, ability; tells them to make up their own minds; blows up the notion of the appealing brainless beauty. *Vogue*'s whole attitude to women is of the most progressive.

She concluded that *Vogue*'s philosophy was anti-snob and profoundly democratic. She believed that it had done more than any other force to push up the standard of living for women from the lower end of the income scale by constant reiteration of its philosophy that taste is more important than money and that one good dress is more important than a wardrobe full of mediocrities.

Our emphasis on dual purpose and interchangeable clothes reflects our acceptance of the fact that the great majority of our readers have a limited amount of money to spend. And *Vogue* never suggests any regret at this state of affairs. It never sighs for the spacious days.

She felt that *Vogue* had to be bolder in future and not sit on the middle-of-the-road plank as it had done in the past:

> Courage almost always pays. I think *Vogue* should always help towards understanding, open-mindedness, tolerance, generosity, fairness; that it should constantly support the conception of opportunity and good living standards for everyone – and present that ideal as perfectly compatible with the culture and elegance for which we stand.

Once she had given Edna the full benefit of her views, Audrey came to a summary of her own role in the magazine, and it gives the most valuable insight into where she was in her own professional development at the time:

> I have always realised that in some important respects I am not a 'natural' *Vogue* editor. I have tried hard to alter or suppress certain attitudes and qualities which I realized were not in the picture, and to cultivate others which were; and I think through experience and a true devotion to the magazine I have become more *Vogue*-minded than at one time seemed possible. Only you and Harry and Pat can judge whether I have succeeded well enough. But there is a point beyond which one cannot alter or suppress parts of one's character without becoming a less effective person – and that would be doing the magazine no service in the end. I don't want to burden an office memo with a personal creed and I think you know mine well enough. I have tried as honestly as possible to judge my own motives, and I do not think I am guilty of using the magazine as a

personal platform. I think the outlook of an editor cannot help but be reflected in a magazine, but I make bold to say that my outlook (which would not have been rightly the magazine's outlook fifteen or twenty years ago, and may not be right in the future – unless I and the times can change along together) was right in the war years and is right now.

Audrey's memo caused her editor-in-chief many headaches, especially when she expanded her ideas about *Vogue*'s philosophy. Edna scribbled exasperated notes in the margins of the pages and wrote Audrey a long letter abhorring the idea that *Vogue* should develop a political voice. She told Audrey she asked too much of one magazine:

> This is a day of specialization and no one will deny, I think, that *Vogue* is the leading subject specialist in its chosen field. The support of the new, the challenges of the revolutionary is fine in its place, but it seems to me our role should be a more discriminating one. We should present rather than support, everything we feel to be worthwhile within our scope and not be obliged to sponsor the new and revolutionary if we may consider it to be tasteless and false. As I see it, *Vogue*'s job is to direct and develop the taste and manners of its readers and let them set the pattern of their political thinking themselves.

Harry intervened, telling Edna that Audrey had no malice in her, 'it is just to her, socialist theory is self-evident truth, and she is surprised that everyone doesn't agree'. In an attempt to bridge the gap between Edna and Audrey, he wrote a long letter putting down his own thoughts on Audrey's memo. He was clearly closer to Edna in his thinking than he was to Audrey's progressive politics and he too abhorred the idea of publishing political articles in *Vogue*.

Audrey was not cowed by the reaction to her letter. She knew that she had been provocative but she also knew that she had to make a mark in her role as *Brogue*'s post-war editor. And she understood as well that *Vogue* had to keep up with the changing times. Edna was not happy. She wanted Audrey to reply to her response line by line but Audrey was absorbed by work and had no time to focus on policy when the day-to-day aspect of her working life was so all-consuming.

Her managing editor and fashion editor had been off ill and since June she had been serving on the committee for the 'Britain Can Make It' exhibition, which had opened at the Victoria & Albert Museum in September. This was Audrey's first major public role after the war and it was to propel her to the highest level within design circles and ultimately lead to two national honours. It was not only a feather in Audrey's cap to be invited to take part in the exhibition, it was also regarded as a major tribute to *Vogue*'s status as the pre-eminent fashion magazine in London. Audrey's standing with the Board of Trade was without doubt the main driver behind the decision to include her.

This exhibition was the brainchild of Sir Stafford Cripps, the president of the Board of Trade. Two years earlier, the board had set up the Council for Industrial Design in order to support Britain's economic recovery after the war and to promote 'by all practicable means the improvement of design in the products of British industry'. The emphasis of 'Britain Can Make It' was to be on good, new design, but it was not to ignore the best pre-war designs if there was the possibility they would go back into production. It was also colourful and optimistic, something that bombed-out, rationed, austerity-weary Britons were only too delighted to see. One of the designers, Dorothy Braddell, wrote later: 'The psychological effect, just after the war, of the gay and enchanting settings was, in itself, valuable.'

Audrey had been asked to sit on the committee that selected all the fashion merchandise, fabrics and accessories for the exhibition. It had taken hours of work with long meetings with the fashion committee, which comprised her former colleague and now rival editor of *Harper's Bazaar*, Anne Scott-James; *Vogue*'s former fashion editor, Madge Garland; Daisy Fellowes, who was President of IncSoc and once described as the most wicked woman in high society; and Phyllis Panting, the editor of *Women and Beauty*. It was a formidable line-up but a critical one, because fashion occupied a quarter of the entire exhibition space of BCMI.

Audrey contributed the catalogue essay that tackled the issues facing design in the post-war world. She had always had an excellent eye for good design and was a passionate believer in its importance, exchanging long letters on the subject with the writer Marghanita Laski. In the essay for the exhibition catalogue, she explored the question of clothes design:

Design in clothes has all the elements of design in other fields. It is composed of balance, proportion, line, detail, colour. But it has a distinctive character derived from the fact that it is concentrated not with inanimate matter, but with flesh and blood. True, the design is executed in material, but it is a limp, insubstantial thing which only comes to life when it is worn. The dress and the body beneath it lend their qualities to one another; the body brings out the design of the dress and the dress imposes a design on the body . . . It follows, then, that the two main requisites of a dress designer are sensitivity to fashion trends and the gift of expressing that sensitivity in terms which relate to human anatomy.

She described the importance of good-quality fabrics and how critical it was to match the design to the right material: 'How often one sees a nondescript dress that would derive line from the substance of satin; or a clumsy dress that would find grace in the fragility of chiffon.' Design was both an art and a craft, she told the reader:

an art resembling painting, in that it demands powers of composition and colour sense; a craft resembling cabinet making, in that it calls for precision cut, snug fit, fine finish and a loving appreciation of the medium.

She praised British manufacturers for embracing new ideas and creating new and innovative fabrics out of familiar material. She particularly singled out the wool trade, which for so long had produced heavy tweed but now offered superfine wool crepon and *velours de laine*, both weighing a fraction of what tweed had traditionally weighed. She also mentioned the British textile industry, celebrating the fact they had used artists and designers of the first order including

Henry Moore, Graham Sutherland, Felix Topolski and Cecil Beaton, all regularly featured in *Vogue*.

This was Audrey showcasing her own thoughts on design and fashion. It placed her firmly alongside the leading opinions and opinion-makers of the time. She relished the move away from austerity restrictions but warned that it would be sad if four years of clean, uncluttered clothes were to be replaced by design that was 'all bits and pieces' as it had been pre-war.

She rejoiced in detail such as wrap-over skirts, double hems, double pockets and double sleeves; black velvet used for trimmings on black garments for collars, buttons and pockets, and for the return of fur trimming. She was also pleased that the new London season models were

exceptionally wearable and becoming – adjectives most gratefully used by women to describe clothes which look as if they had been designed with them in mind, and not merely as show-pieces for display by show-girls. It is indeed the real woman – with a figure and skin, not perfect, but responsive to flatter, whom the couturiers seem for once content to clothe; and since the world is peopled with such, these Collections should have a special success at home and abroad.

She concluded that all designers, in whatever field, had to be aware of changing tastes and needs and be mixing constantly with their potential customers:

But the fashion designer needs to be up and about earlier than the designer in other fields; for fashion is so responsive (being quickly produced, and representing an immediate personal reaction) that he and his colleagues are actually creating those trends which others will follow.

Over 1.5 million people visited 'Britain Can Make It' in its six-week run and it was judged to have been a phenomenal success. It showcased the best of British design to an excited audience who queued around the block to get to see what the future might hold. In addition to the clothes, fabrics and accessories, there were new, practical ideas for kitchens and bathrooms as well as a few outlandish designs that the BBC announcer was sceptical would ever take off: 'There is even a plan, perhaps a little nebulous, for travelling to the moon by what they call a space ship. No bookings can be made yet, at any rate, no return tickets.' The future of yachting was represented by a catamaran that could sail closer to the wind than any other vessel, and there was an air-conditioned bed for hot summers.

The public was warned that they would have to exercise patience while manufacturing caught up with demand and that export would have to take precedence over the home market as Britain would not survive without foreign sales. It led some to quip that the message of the exhibition had been 'Britain can make it but Britain can't have it'.

The exhibition was of great personal interest to Audrey and she gave it more space in *Vogue* than any of the other magazine editors. That December she was elected to the Council for Industrial Design and served on it for the next fifteen years. Marghanita Laski wrote her a letter on hearing the news:

I want to congratulate you most sincerely. It's most encouraging to know they've had the sense to do so, and every sign of things moving in a good and proper direction is most exciting. I suppose you'll have all the fun of planning for the 1951 Exhibition.

Meanwhile, Edna was awaiting a response to her latest letter. Audrey, fresh with ideas from the exhibition, wrote to her from home one Sunday afternoon underlining her belief that *Vogue* had to be able to reflect the new world order.

I think that famous tenet of 'gracious living', for which *Vogue* stands, is only established safely when it is established broadly on good living standards throughout the community; and that an attempt to preserve it by putting a wall round it and ignoring what went on outside would be as unrealistic, and as ineffectual, as (to use a thoroughly melodramatic analogy) the attempts of noble households in the Middle Ages to keep out the plague by shutting themselves up within their castle gates.

Although Edna wanted her to toe the line, Audrey knew that things had to evolve in London. Her determination to keep *Vogue* at the forefront of British fashion publishing, and ahead of their rivals, was sincere, and Harry backed her. He knew that above all else she had the best interests of her magazine at heart and she would never put that in jeopardy.

She had ended her long letter to Edna: 'I have tried to put down everything that is in my mind and (since *Vogue* is a large part of my life) in my heart also.' In a later, personal letter to Edna, Harry wrote:

I want to say what a joy it is to have such an intelligent, competent, loyal and hardworking colleague as Audrey. Of course she has her faults but they are so small in comparison with her virtues.

He urged Edna to drop the subject of Audrey's memo as lessons had been learned on both sides and Audrey must be free to get on with planning *Vogue* for the future.

So much had changed since the last time Edna had been in London. The office had moved from New Bond Street to 37 Golden Square that spring and Condé Nast Publications Ltd was about to launch *House & Garden* on the world. That had given everyone a sense of a new start in whatever direction times would take them.

One of Audrey's greatest concerns in the late 1940s was the role of women. She asked her readers how women would fare and what their position would be now the war was over. This was a far bigger question that merely wondering how women would adjust to peacetime and the inevitable return of men to take the jobs they had been occupying during the war. It was a question about the fundamental place of women in society and of their future.

And where do they go from here – the Servicewomen and all the others who, without the glamour of uniform, have queued and contrived and queued, and kept factories, homes and offices going? Their value is more than proven: their toughness where endurance was needed, their taciturnity where silence was demanded, their tact, good humour and public conscience; their continuity of purpose, their

submission to discipline, their power over machines . . . all
the things men like to think women couldn't be or do . . .
How long before a grateful nation (or anyhow, the men of
the nation) forget what women accomplished when their
country needed them? It is up to all women to see to it that
there is no regression – that they go right on from here.

She had always believed there should be no bar to a woman
working in a job for which she was qualified and when the
question arose of employing married women, even women
with a family, she was completely open-minded about it. This
was at a time when women who were qualified teachers had to
give up work when they got married.

Her beauty editor, Evelyn Forbes, was a mother of four who
had always worked because her husband had never had a job,
and so she had carried the whole family for the majority of her
married life. Audrey admired her and was amazed that she
could be 'such a good mother while having as heavy a burden
of office work as anybody in the organisation'. She encouraged
Evelyn to increase the size of her team and was proud that the
two assistants she had working for her had made their way up
through the ranks at *Vogue*, having joined as secretaries.

Evelyn Forbes had started as managing editor at *Vogue* but
had not been happy on 'an inside job' as Audrey termed it.
They had discussed her thoughts and worries and between
them had come to the conclusion that she would be far better
suited to a job that took her out and about. In addition to the
Beauty column, Evelyn Forbes worked on Shop-hound, one
of the most successful of all the *Vogue* features, which sought
out good-value purchases for readers. It is typical of Audrey's

management style that she looked to ensure that the people who worked for her played to their strengths rather than being pigeon-holed regardless of aptitude and ability.

Evelyn Forbes became a close friend and the two of them shared the same sense of humour. Audrey loved hearing her stories about her travels around the country giving talks on various matters concerning beauty. When she was in the West Midlands speaking to an audience of women about face creams, a woman who had been too shy to ask a question at the talk came up to her and said: 'Mrs Forbes, you said quite a lot about nourishing creams. You seem to think that they are very important.' She replied, 'Yes, I do think so.' The woman then responded; 'Well, I really have tried, but I simply can't like the taste.' Evelyn Forbes, with enormous presence of mind, pulled herself together, and said: 'Actually some people do find them very helpful applied to the skin.' The woman said: 'Thanks, I will go back and try again.' This story made Audrey laugh years after she first heard it. She loved nothing more than to hear about the impact of *Vogue* in all its guises on her readership and the postbag was something she looked forward to after every issue was published.

Eighteen months after the end of the war, Gertrude Pidoux, who had been the fashion editor at *Vogue* for six years, stepped aside from her post to begin a partial retirement while overseeing the incoming fashion editor, the Vicomtesse d'Orthez. Isobel d'Orthez was much younger than her experienced predecessor but she was highly intelligent, had a good eye and had been working in the fashion editorial office since the middle of the war. British by birth, American by education and French by adoption, Isobel was in many ways an ideal choice. She had been married to the Vicomte d'Orthez and had lived in Paris for six years before the war. Yet Lesley Blanch had described her as unmistakably English, being tall, fair and the 'candy-pink-and-white' type who knew how to handle wearing pastel shades to their best effect. She favoured Molyneux as a designer because his suits did not date, she claimed, and loved good quality tweed. At first, Audrey was delighted with her new fashion editor. For one, she was very happy to adopt and adapt fashion to fit in with the newest technology like television.

In November 1946, *Vogue* became the first magazine to get involved in televising fashion. Audrey did the commentary for *Editor's Choice*, described in *Vogue* as a new television series. The subject she and Isobel chose was a simple, basic wardrobe, 'a challenge in these rationed days', which they decided to meet realistically by building up each outfit, whether for town, country or evenings, starting with a basic skirt and a variety of different tops. The photographs were by Lee Miller and Audrey told viewers where each model could be acquired in London: 'Handsome red leather jacket to take the skirt to race meetings and other country occasions. As tough as it is charming and it does not spot . . . from Leathercraft.'

Two years later, *Vogue* was back on the BBC, this time in a half-hour documentary presented by Isobel d'Orthez in which she told viewers that being well dressed depended not only on the clothes you wore but how you wore them. It was an excellent opportunity to showcase *Vogue*'s strengths and Audrey was always delighted by endorsement for her magazine.

~

As Audrey was forging ahead exploiting new media, the world of fashion was about to receive one of its biggest and most powerful shocks in decades. Paris had been rebuilding its reputation and confidence in the years since Audrey had first reported on the liberation. Now, just weeks after she had written in her essay of how fashion was so responsive, Christian Dior launched his first haute couture collection in Paris to a worldwide gasp of astonishment.

At 10.30 a.m. on Wednesday 12 February 1947, fashion journalists and couturiers got their first glimpse of what would come to be known as the New Look. Audrey was sitting in the front row, next to Isobel d'Orthez, wearing her trademark dark suit and trimmed hat, with a string of pearls around her neck. In walked girls wearing his radical new designs, and the atmosphere in the room became electric. The editor-in-chief of *Harper's Bazaar*, Carmel Snow, exclaimed: 'It's quite a revolution, dear Christian! Your dresses have such a new look!' With its emphasis on beauty, seductiveness and light-heartedness, the New Look mapped out a fresh chapter in the history of fashion: 'femininity had been recaptured: tiny waists, full skirts and "devilishly sexy" busts'.

Audrey, Isobel d'Orthez and the fashion editors at *Vogue* were thrilled. In March, they ran two pages on his show, and Isobel wrote how, with his first collection, Dior had not only shot to fame, but

retrieved the general situation by reviving interest in a somewhat uninspired season . . . his ideas were fresh and put over with great authority, his clothes were beautifully made, essentially Parisian, deeply feminine.

Whereas other Parisian designers that season had opted for big, rippling collars on jackets and fussy embroidery on summer dresses, Dior's new look was clean, simple and avowedly feminine. He explained what he had wanted to achieve:

I wanted my dresses to be 'constructed', moulded on the curves of the female body whose contours they would stylise. I accentuated the waist, the volume of the hips, I emphasised the bust. In order to give my designs more hold, I had nearly all the fabrics lined with percale or taffeta, renewing a tradition that had long been abandoned.

The signature' piece from the collection was the 'bar jacket', a cream shantung coat that had rounded tails closely following the curves of the bust. Contrasted with that was a large, black pleated skirt that flared out and gave the gait a never-before-seen elegant swing.

For many in London, the New Look was too much of a shock, and at first it was condemned by the general press. It accused Paris of launching designs on the world that did not have the material to copy them, nor the money to buy them, nor, indeed, the leisure time to enjoy wearing them. But even the austerity-struck British could not resist the gorgeous designs and the following year the tide changed. New Look models poured into London shops to be relished by a beauty-starved generation of young women who had grown up wearing utility clothes and sensible shoes.

By the end of the decade, there was trouble in the fashion department in Golden Square. Problems arose when Isobel's health began to deteriorate and Audrey discovered that her editor had a serious drinking problem. It was not the first time she had been confronted by alcoholism in the *Vogue* family, nor would it be the last, but it was distressing and she had many heart-to-heart conversations with Harry about Isobel as well as letter exchanges with Edna.

The kindness and concern that had been extended towards Audrey at the end of the war was now focused on helping Isobel to get better. She was given three months' leave to go to Scotland and have a break. On her return Audrey was pleased to see that she looked calm, rested and 'years younger', so it was with distress that she learned just weeks later that she had been seen at a dress show obviously suffering from a hangover.

Isobel left *Vogue* soon after this, having agreed to cite grounds of ill health, 'the evidences of which were visible enough', and she would receive six months' salary tax free, which was the equivalent of a whole year's pay. Harry and Audrey agreed this ought to give her time and funding to get better and secure a job. They tried to help her to find a new position but it had not been possible as others were aware of her reputation. Audrey was sad because she liked Isobel personally and had valued her contribution to *Vogue*.

The Condé Nast generosity towards staff who had been part of the *Vogue* family was one of the defining features of the organisation. 'These human situations that must arise in such large organizations are always hard to face but I am sure you and Audrey have handled the situation with the utmost sympathy and fairness,' Edna wrote to Harry.

Soon after Isobel left, Audrey wrote to Edna to say that Miss Powell, whom she had replaced in 1935, had suffered a serious setback that had required further surgery from which she was never to recover. It became clear, when reading through this correspondence, that Condé Nast Publications continued to pay Miss Powell a small retainer up until her death, as well as covering her medical expenses until the formation of the National Health Service in 1948. She received regular visits from her old colleagues, including Audrey and Vera Selfe, who had been to see her the week before she died.

In March 1949, the president of the Board of Trade, Harold Wilson, announced the Consumer Rationing (Revocation) Order, which 'brings to an end the rationing of cloth, clothing and household textiles'. He described it as a 'relic of war'. That clothes rationing had continued for four years after the end of the war had been a point of contention that often boiled over into anger in the general public.

Two years earlier, Ernest Bevin had written to Wilson to complain about the 'irksome' restrictions and urged him to reduce the number of coupons required for men's socks and women's underwear if he could not remove them altogether. This request was met with the excuse that the returning armed forces had put a lot of pressure on the clothing system and thus restrictions had to remain in place. A few items were taken off the ration in January 1949, including furs, handkerchiefs, towels, knitting wool and pyjamas, but not nightdresses.

The truth came out in Wilson's report to a government advisory committee in which he wrote:

> It would have been easy for us to abolish rationing at any time in the last three years by retarding the export drive and putting the home market first, but I need hardly say that this

course has never been a starter. As it is the export drive in textiles will continue to be pressed with the utmost vigour.

Publicly the Board of Trade took a carefully judged line that was a good example of spin:

Rationing has never been the means by which we diverted goods to export but has simply distributed equitably what supplies could be made available to the home market. These points should be emphasised.

The end of clothes rationing and the end of a decade gave Audrey the opportunity to take stock. The 1950s would be in some ways even more important for her than the previous ten years. With the end of paper rationing, there was the opportunity to spread her wings and she did – not only at work, but abroad in every sphere. On the other hand, the world was still recovering from the devastation of two world wars in half a century and with strides in scientific and technological progress. In her editorial for the new decade, she reflected on the changes wrought in the first fifty years of the twentieth century. Entitled '*Vogue*'s Eye View of a Long Journey', it begins:

The road runs from the black-plumed funeral of Queen Victoria to the exile of most of the monarchies of Europe; from the discovery of radium to atomic warfare; from bicycles ridden by courageous and knickerbockered young women to Globemaster aircraft; from the daring of Zola's novels and Shaw's theatrical bombshells to *The Naked and the Dead* and *A Streetcar Named Desire*; from the Empire of

Rudyard Kipling to world politics waged behind iron fron-
tiers; from the tweeny in the basement to the owner of a
National Health Insurance Card.

She was of course describing everything that had happened
within her own lifetime. She wrote of how the mood of the
nation had been one of pride at the turn of the century, but
now, fifty years on, science and technology had advanced at
such a rate that people could no longer keep up with the speed
of change:

Exhaustion, bewilderment, loneliness follow in their wake . . .
Man, once the heir of the ages, now carries a burden of knowledge a million times the size of the Original Apple, and feels
himself 'most infinitely disinherited'; anger and fear merge
into disgust.

There was only one defence against this, she told her readers,
and that was to embrace and move with the times and to believe
that there was great hope in the future. 'We who live in the
open will welcome 1950, and the year after, and the year after
that. Count no man happy, not until he is dead, but until he
has lived . . .' What readers made of Audrey's philosophising
is not recorded, but she showed them time and again that the
future held promise and that *Vogue* would help them to get to
grips with that future.

Isobel d'Orthez's departure in 1951 left Audrey without a
fashion editor, though her absences through ill health during
the last year of her time at *Vogue* had meant the department
had suffered considerably. She and Harry decided to give a

member of the fashion staff, Patricia 'Pat' Cunningham, a trial of three months.

She turned out to be the most successful fashion editor Audrey ever worked with, but she was also difficult, and there was some doubt as to whether her ambitious drive would make her a good manager of her fashion staff. Audrey overruled Harry and Edna, whose misgivings were expressed openly in an exchange of letters:

> She has the taste, intelligence and ambition. I wish I admired her character more; it tends towards the bitchy. Audrey hopes, however, that with authority and responsibility Pat Cunningham will develop a more generous personality.

Pat Cunningham had had a successful war working as a codebreaker in the Wrens, having proved her intelligence by learning Japanese in less than three months while still in her teens. She ended the war as personal secretary to Lord Mountbatten. When she returned to London in 1945, she had nowhere to live so moved into a women's hostel and 'fell in with a bohemian crowd that congregated around Notting Hill'.

Through this milieu she met fashion photographers and became the house model for several British couturiers including Hardy Amies. A year later, she was a model at *Vogue*, doing photo shoots with Norman Parkinson, Cecil Beaton and Clifford Coffin. By the time she was under consideration for the role of fashion editor, Pat was married to the designer Charles Creed, and Harry was concerned that this might put *Vogue* in a difficult position. As there was no other obvious candidate available, he and Audrey concluded they would have to take the risk. Initially she was appointed for a three-month trial and was told that Isobel would be coming back, which was never the intention, but Audrey did not want her to assume she had the job on a long-term basis:

> My one real doubt is as to whether she can show the loyalty to the company that one must expect from the head of an important department. Unfortunately, through her marriage to Creed, she mixes with people in the fashion business to a pretty considerable extent in private life. She has a very definite and very critical personality, and so far I have reason to know that she has not minced her words on such occasions, in discussing her colleagues and the management. In telling her that we were making her acting fashion editor, I warned against the dangers of getting business mixed up with private life, and advised her to make a practice of discussing office affairs as little as possible. I cannot but think that she is sufficiently intelligent and sufficiently ambitious to watch her step in this respect.

Pat proved herself exactly as Audrey hoped she would and was given the role on a permanent basis in the autumn. This appointment ushered in a new era for Audrey and one that she would ultimately find satisfying and creative. Under Pat's leadership, the fashion pages of *Vogue* were transformed, and she championed some of the most talented photographers of the 1950s, including Henry Clarke and William Klein. Robin Muir observed that 'colleagues and collaborators valued her judgment and her forthright opinions, less so their brusque delivery.' She had a mean streak when it came to promoting the younger, talented girls who worked in the fashion room, denying them opportunities that might have helped their progress. One of the young staff of the time explained that, in her opinion, while Pat Cunningham was extremely tricky, she was also a sad person. 'Highly intelligent but unfulfilled. She put all her life into her own ego and tried to retain power.' Pat's fashion colleague Clare Rendlesham was equally difficult.

Pam Makin remembered Miss Cunningham, as she always was at *Vogue*, as ruthless, and the bitchiness in the fashion room being legendary,

> but Audrey didn't want anything to do with that. She only saw what she wanted to see and she had no interest in gossip, nor did she ever take sides. *Vogue* was her priority and she was prepared to use the talent around her in whatever form it came.

Yet Audrey's management standards were way ahead of the era. Not only did she make every effort to encourage her junior staff to seize opportunities within the magazine, but she was always on the lookout for their welfare and would intervene if she could. Pam had been working as a runner in the photographic studio, but when the new studio manager replaced Sylvia Redding, Pam found herself under a new regime that endorsed sexist and snobbish views.

Pam Makin came from a middle-class background and was surrounded by girls in the office who had been debutantes and were often titled. Colonel Patrick Matthews, her new boss, was the son of the Bishop of Leicester and was infuriated that Pam had managed to ingratiate herself with Lee Miller. On one occasion, Audrey had asked Pam to entertain a visitor from the New York office and Pat Matthews had given her a piece of his mind the following day. Pam went to Audrey and told her the whole sorry story. She was rehoused in Golden Square with a new position as merchandising manager. It was a role she was to hold for several years and it is a tribute to Audrey's light touch and kindness that Pam stayed at *Vogue* for as long as she did.

One thing that Audrey would not tolerate was sexual harassment. She took a very dim view of it, her secretary, Lillie Davies, remembered, and was clear about the rights of women in the workplace. When one of her female staff complained to her about the managing director of an important advertising account, she called him into her office and gave him a serious dressing down. She lost the account, but as far as she was concerned it was principle before profit and if she had had to take the matter further, she would have had no compunction about doing so.

The next ten years of Audrey's working life were packed with a large amount of activity, travel, excitement and recognition. In the early years of the decade, she continued to forge ahead with *Vogue*, bringing in new ideas, writers, photographers and features. The magazine could only thrive and remain at the peak of fashion publishing if it continued to offer excellence but also look forward. A flick through the issues for those years show how full of energy and enthusiasm she was. There is animation and humour, sometimes even a hint of the risqué, which predictably brought a squeal of indignation from 73-year-old Edna.

When the editor-in-chief first saw the June 1950 edition with its gloriously sexy and defiant cover and the brilliant

Irving Penn photographs of the 'inflated skirt' from Paris, she upbraided Audrey with a rebuke:

> Of course we are all eternally striving for a fresh attack and something which will be memorable, but I still feel that if we must choose between banality and vulgarity, I would vote for the banal . . . I should infinitely prefer that *Vogue* should be described as ladylike rather than sexy.

Audrey clearly did not agree with Edna. She responded that the last thing any of her younger models would like to be described as was 'ladylike'. With affectionate respect, she ignored some of Edna's more conservative views and continued to allow Pat to encourage flamboyance and sexiness in the fashion shoots. She told Edna that it was vitality that brought fashion to life:

> I think all of us here who work on the magazine feel very strongly indeed the need for boldness, strength, a feeling of liveliness, high spirits, and, complementary to this, a real dislike of the flat, conventional, dead-pan type of fashion picture. We long for models who look like "real people". We would rather they looked as if they had personality, humour, brains, mischief, than that they should be simply pretty, or even beautiful. We would rather have character and emotion in a face than emptiness.

One of the features of Audrey's editorship were the Critical Conferences that she held after every issue of the magazine had appeared. She valued her colleagues' opinions as much as she did that of the readers. A full post-bag was always of interest to her, but even more so the thoughts of people from all the different departments, even those who did not work directly on the magazine.

There are usually some features which everybody likes, some features which everybody dislikes and despises, and there are usually some features which a section of the Conference loudly praises and another section loudly condemns. Now, I think it is not in the nature of things that one can always produce features which everybody likes. We produce far too many features which nobody likes. But I have never worried much about the features on which there is a marked cleavage of opinion, so long as a proportion of those in favour of them are people whose judgment I normally respect. When I first succeeded Betty, one of the things which worried me most was that, when choosing photographs with two or three colleagues, each of us might strongly favour a different pose. How was I to reconcile these opposing views and how was I to know which of us was right? I took this problem, like so many, to Harry, and he said that "if our staff are rightly chosen, probably any of these four pictures would be perfectly publishable. Perhaps not any of them is positively the best. There may be things to be said for all of them and the varying views are questions of personal opinion." I have always remembered this, and I think it is true; so when we have controversial features or pictures on which the staff itself is divided, I imagine that one's readership is likely to be divided too, and I do not think this a bad thing, for controversial features are important to a magazine.

She concluded her letter:

> I cannot stress too much my main anxiety lest *Brogue*
> becomes flat, conventional and mediocre. Of course, the
> magazine must always have plenty of good bread and butter
> in it, though even that should be able to have vitality without
> in any way obscuring its fashion value; but especially in the
> high fashion pages one longs for excitement and strength and
> the creation of something memorable.

That autumn she visited New York for the first time in five
years. Once again, the personal warmth between Edna and
Audrey was evident in her letter after the visit. She had brought
back with her not only fresh ideas for problems that had been
worrying her but also an endorsement of Edna's and Pat's confidence in her abilities, which was a reward she prized and one
she hoped to continue to deserve. As Audrey was leaving, Edna
gave her a personal gift of an antique brooch, which she said she
would treasure. 'I shall wear it constantly and with pleasure –
as I still wear the pearls you gave me on my last visit.'

In February, Audrey published the first Britannica issue of
Brogue. It was 20 per cent larger than the normal issues and
focused entirely on British culture and fashion at a time when
the country was in the lead-up to the Festival of Britain, which
opened three months later. She justified this by telling readers
that an annual focus on the British scene, covering fashion,
arts, landscape, architecture and the beauty of the countryside would 'dramatize, for our home and overseas readers, the
varied contribution which Britain makes to civilization'.

It was an enormous success on both sides of the Atlantic,

with plaudits coming in from every corner. It sold 186,000 copies, almost double monthly sales. One of the most beautiful yet unexpected features was one Audrey had commissioned from the American photographer Irving Penn. He took a series of stunning portrait photographs of men and women in traditional blue-collar jobs, such as chimney sweeps, cobblers, butchers and fishmongers, but also some in roles that no longer exist: two lorry washers standing proud with long-handled mops and one pail between two; a park gate keeper smart in his long coated uniform; a rag-and-bone man with a sack over his back; and a trounce, who, the caption explains, 'is a dray-man's workaday mate, fitted with leather apron for unloading the heavy beer barrels from the dray'.

Penn was one of *Vogue*'s star photographers, working for all three editions of the magazine over the next fifteen years. Audrey admired him and occasionally would sit in on one of his photo shoots, something she did not do with other photographers. He told her he had been inspired by seeing traders on the streets of Paris and began photographing them in portrait style in their work clothing. Audrey managed to get three double-page spreads devoted to men and women from the working class in *Vogue*, something that surprised many of her readers. If she had been worried that Edna would object, she need not have. Edna was delighted with Britannica and praised her for an excellent issue. 'I liked especially the "small trades" feature, each person seemed so typically British, and I felt it was really quite an original idea.' In the same letter, she commented on a photograph by Norman Parkinson of a man and woman in a country pub.

From the title, one gathers that they are man and wife. She, however, looks like a well-dressed mannequin, while he seems to be the typical working man. Don't tell me that rural England has come to this or didn't I understand the caption?

The photograph was a Parkinson spoof: the woman was his wife and muse, Wenda. Edna was right to be confused.

Audrey's role on the Council for Industrial Design consumed all her spare time in the five years leading up to the 1951 Festival of Britain. Of the twenty-three members of the committee, she was one of just two women. Unlike the 'Britain Can Make It' exhibition, there was no fashion involved, but Audrey was committed to the notion of good design. She was pleased to see what was to be exhibited in the Dome of Discovery and the various pavilions that made up the South Bank Exhibition.

How proud John Summers would have been to know that his granddaughter was representing industrial design. How apt too, for it was at the Great Exhibition 100 years earlier that he had bought the nail-making machine which helped make his fortune and thus paid for her education.

The Festival of Britain was the most ambitious exhibition ever undertaken by a government. Millions of people visited the newly created South Bank and the twenty-seven acres of pavilions and displays. 'Conceived among the untidy ruins of a war and fashioned through days of harsh economy, this Festival is a challenge to the sloughs of the present and a shaft of confidence cast forth against the future.'

The organisers heralded it as the autobiography of a nation, celebrating its past achievements in the fields of agriculture, science, exploration, design, music, literature and the arts. It took place in cities throughout the whole of the United Kingdom with focus on different aspects of cultural life. York basked in choral music and medieval drama, while Glasgow celebrated industrial power with displays on the history of coal and water. Liverpool's maritime heritage was married with theatre and music events, while Brighton had an international puppet festival. Audrey's interest in the London-based festival focused on the arts and science. She was thrilled by the structure and layout of the South Bank and wrote: 'I do not think anyone who saw it doubted that it was one of the most important events in the world of design for a very long time, and that its impact would be felt for years to come.'

In 1952, Edna made what was to be her last official visit to London, though she came back privately for the coronation the following summer. She wrote to Audrey's secretary, Lillie Davies, to finalise arrangements. She hated the idea of flying, so she would travel by sea in a state room. The ship docked late at night at Southampton so on this occasion she decided to remain on board for the night and asked for a car to be sent down for her and her travelling companion.

For the occasion of our arrival at Southampton, I think that if we could be met with a big limousine it would be helpful since both Mrs Roulston and I are planning to bring only hand luggage. I shall probably have three large suit-cases (maybe four), a dressing bag and a hat box, and I hope to be able to bring a medium-sized carton with some tinned meat, sugar etc.

She added that Mrs Roulston would be travelling with the same amount of luggage, and then requested a visiting maid to come in each morning who should bring her own iron and ironing board.

A visit from Edna was a personal delight for Audrey, who wrote to say she was overjoyed at the prospect of seeing her in London. From a logistical point of view, however, these visits caused major upheaval both in the office and in the private lives of those who were expected to accompany her to the theatre, ballet, Ascot or wherever she decided she wanted to be seen.

In the past, she had taken over Harry's office at One New Bond Street, but the set-up at Golden Square was different and she would have to share a room with Audrey and her assistant, Patsy Hill. Audrey drove down to Southampton to collect Edna and Marjorie Hillis Roulston and drove them back to London where they were staying at the Connaught. There was a bit of friction on arrival because the rooms that had been booked were not large enough for Edna and she insisted on being upgraded to a suite. This settled, Audrey and Harry took them to the Albert Hall to hear Yehudi Menuhin and the London Symphony Orchestra play the Tchaikovsky and Mendelssohn violin concertos. Both of them felt that Edna had aged in the past two years, probably brought on by the death of her husband, but she was as keen to make her views known as she had always been.

In February 1952, the king died at Sandringham and the nation went into mourning. The news reached Golden Square at eleven o'clock, just as the board were assembling for their weekly meeting. They agreed to adjourn for half an hour while

Audrey raced off to make the necessary changes for the March issue. Harry Yoxall observed in his diary that

> from our selfish point of view, if it had to come it came at a pretty good time; only about 700 copies of the cover had been printed and we had a late form of sixteen pages to be done quickly by gravure of which four were set aside for the royal tour to Australia.

They dropped the royal tour, moved fashion back and introduced an opening about the late king and the new queen. The *Vogue* cover for March had no image. Instead, it was plain royal purple, as it had been fifteen years earlier on the death of George V. Inside, Audrey paid a moving tribute to the king, describing how he had 'put the demands of his country before everything in his heart, and kept the inner vision of his duty clear and true'.

She was given a press pass to the lying-in-state in Westminster Hall and to stand inside the walls of Windsor Castle, opposite one of the doors into St George's Chapel, for the funeral. She described the scenes as immensely impressive, though in typical Audrey style she had worried about 'the old boys who lined the streets for 4 miles in the cold wearing only their long black tights and silk coats'. She went on:

> We knew that the train had drawn in at Windsor station, because suddenly, from the castle tower, the half-mast Union Jack was hauled down and up went the Royal Standard to the top of the flagstaff. British ceremonies seem good at these small touches.

The death of the king meant a coronation in the offing – and of a young and beautiful queen at that. The ripples of excitement that flowed towards the coronation turned into waves of euphoria by the spring of the following year. Audrey had been selected to chair the committee to oversee coronation memorabilia. There had been a feeling within the design community that some of the items produced for the previous coronation were nothing short of tat, and there was consensus that things had to improve this time around. Unfortunately, the quality of the merchandise was still not of the standard that Audrey and her committee had hoped for. She complained privately that there were only a handful of things that she could be really proud of, despite the fact that they had given a great deal of time, thought and advice to the designs, seeing some of them twice or three times in the hope of improvement.

Audrey's role on the committee was recognised in the 1953 New Year's Honours list when it was announced that she had been awarded an OBE for this work and also for her contribution to the Council for Industrial Design. There was great excitement about this both in London and New York, which produced an unprecedented moment of recorded pride from her when she told Edna: 'I am delighted to find how pleased our friends in the fashion trade here seem to be with my New Year Honour.' She still could not bring herself to say how pleased she was as that might have sounded like boasting. It was mentioned in New York's round-up of what people were talking about in London and Harry Yoxall threw a cocktail party for her at his home in Richmond.

Success and stability at work was not matched by happiness at home. Audrey's marriage to Jock had finally fallen apart. His serial infidelity had reached breaking point for her when she was approached by a husband who was suing for divorce and was naming Jock in the proceedings. Audrey said Jock could have a divorce from her if he wanted one, but so far he had not asked for one. Then one day, out of the blue, she received a phone call from Victor Kennett, the man she had met thirteen years earlier on her way back from New York. He was coming to London and invited her for a drink at the India Tea Centre in the Haymarket. She accepted, intrigued to meet him again, but sure that there would be none of the old magic left. How wrong she was. The minute they met it was clear that their feelings for one another were at least as strong as they had been before, and this time Audrey felt certain that she should leave Jock and spend the rest of her life with Victor.

Harry Yoxall, with his antennae focused on his staff's well-being, had spotted that Audrey was unsettled and out of sorts. He took her out to lunch and she told him the whole story, including the fact that she had almost left Jock thirteen years earlier on her way back from America. When he was in New York a month later, he told Edna about Audrey and she, as a divorcee, was understanding. She wrote: 'Harry tells me you are not quite well. Do take care of yourself. I know how difficult it is to tear up roots no matter how much they may seem to have been loosened.'

If divorce had been a serious undertaking in 1938, it was only marginally less so in 1951. There had to be guilty and innocent parties so that one could sue the other for damages. Audrey and Victor needed to give their spouses grounds for divorce, so they named a hotel in Woodstock where they had spent a night. Jock threatened to sue Audrey but retreated from that position when she agreed to make a generous settlement on him. For weeks, she commuted between Blomfield Road and Victor's flat in Ennismore Gardens in Kensington. Finally, she and Victor decided they had to engineer a clean break: Audrey would leave Jock and move in with him.

But even this was complicated by Jock's relationships. Just days before Audrey was due to move out of Blomfield Road, a telegram arrived announcing the death of a woman in Switzerland. Letters with Swiss stamps had been arriving for weeks and she had guessed that this relationship was a serious one. When she saw Jock's reaction to the telegram, she realised she was right; he was devastated. The woman had died of tuberculosis in a Swiss sanatorium and they had been close for years.

Audrey told Victor that she could not possibly leave Jock in such a terrible state, so once again Victor had to wait. But this time it was not years. Audrey left Jock a few weeks later and moved in with Victor. She wrote that she was short of good-luck wishes from her closest friends, but was delighted that Victor's Irish housekeeper embraced her with warmth immediately: 'I'm so glad! Poor Mr Kennett! He's been so lonely.' This was another of Audrey's myths; in fact, everyone around her was delighted that she was so happy in her new relationship.

Jock Stewart disappeared out of Audrey's life after their divorce in 1952. His parents moved back to Brighton but he remained in London and eventually, in 1964, remarried. His second wife, Valerie Rogers, was twenty-eight years his junior. Jock died in Salisbury in April 1979 at the age of seventy-one. Audrey did not comment on his death. The only thing she ever mentioned was her regret at the loss of the lithograph by Renoir, which she had bought for him as a birthday present in the 1930s. He had sold it soon after their divorce for £4,000. 'I did not grudge him the money; but it was the most beautiful thing I have ever possessed, and the only one that I parted from with pain.'

Victor and Audrey married in a small ceremony in London at the beginning of February 1953, just weeks after she had been awarded the OBE. Harry threw a nuptial dinner two days before the wedding and wrote to his wife: 'Audrey is to be made an honest woman of on Wed., after the March issue has gone to bed she is to go there too. We had good food, good talk, good fun.' They enjoyed smoked trout with Pouilly-sur-Loire, beef with fresh vegetables and peaches and cream washed down with two bottles of Château Mouton d'Armailhacq 1934 and some excellent champagne. One of Harry Yoxall's abiding passions was wine. He became president of the International Wine and Food Society and wrote several books on the subject. He told his grandson, Richard Pietrzak, that he had kept a note of every wine he had ever tasted and that by the age of seventy the total number was 50,000 wines.

A month later, the three of them were together again when Harry picked up Audrey and Victor in his chauffeur-driven car to queue on the Mall to get into Buckingham Palace for the Investiture. They had been advised to arrive early in order to get seats close to the front so they could see the action. Audrey was taken off in one direction when they arrived and Harry and Victor managed to get a seat in the third row, where they had a fine view of proceedings, the queen's position not 20ft from them.

For forty-five minutes, they sat listening to the string quartet playing on the balcony and then, at eleven o'clock sharp, the queen arrived.

She came in in a pewter silk dress; five yeomen of the guard had previously assembled, and there was a small entourage of officers of the household, rear-admirals, major generals and so on.

Audrey, who was wearing a dark blue jacket with three-quarter sleeves and long white gloves, looked lovely, according to her two supporters in the third row.

She had never seen the queen close up and she was surprised by how small she was, but also by the way her whole face lit up when she smiled. Audrey curtseyed 'prettily' and answered the queen's questions as the sovereign clipped the blue cross with its red ribbon onto her left lapel: 'You're editor of *Vogue*, aren't you? . . . How long have you been editor? . . . I think it is a very nice magazine.' Then Audrey stepped back clutching her blue leather medal box and took her seat. The ceremony ended, and then Harry took her and Victor to Bentley's in Piccadilly for oysters and champagne to celebrate.

It was a heady and delightful few weeks, when she was feted at work and celebrated at home. *Vogue* took great pride in her honour and New York published a short feature on her, praising her for the work she had done for the coronation and adding that it was a feather in *Vogue*'s cap. Victor was the most generous and solicitous husband, with boundless energetic affection that he lavished on Audrey in a way that she had never experienced before. That summer they went to France for a three-week holiday. It was her first proper holiday for two years and she was bursting with excitement when she wrote to Edna:

> Victor and I have never had more than a weekend away together, so a whole three weeks will be simply heavenly. It is a quite extraordinary sensation to me to be able to look forward to a holiday with unmixed joy. In fact, I still cannot get used to the happiness and confidence which is now my everyday state. Sometimes it is hard to bear the thought that if it had not been for my stupidity and cowardice, we might have had thirteen more years together, and raised a family; but then I think, that without the suffering in between I could never have appreciated him as I do now.

She and Victor had received a present from *Vogue* of 100,000 French francs, which was not only a fabulously generous gift, but also a practical one. 'We shall have no currency problems,' she told Edna – a reminder that moving money from one country to another was not a simple matter in the middle of the twentieth century.

Edna had wanted to mark Audrey's wedding personally, so she had invited her to consider what sort of practical present they would like. A rare picture of Audrey's domestic arrangements emerged when she wrote to thank Edna for the magnificent electric toaster that they had decided upon, which she had had shipped from New York.

> Our breakfast table now revolves around it, and it makes perfect toast. You can think of us using it every day and

eating real American hot toast – instead of the English cold toast of which, I remember, you took such a poor view!

She added that Victor was a marvellous cook and that she merely assisted in the kitchen, chopping up food under super-vision and washing up the piles of pots and pans he used while preparing food. 'We continue to be wonderfully happy and endlessly fond of one another, so it is the greatest possible pleasure to be alive.' A month later, she wrote again about her personal happiness: 'this security in one another's love makes a solid basis to life which is to me a perpetual miracle.'

In 1954, Edna published her autobiography, *Always in Vogue*, which she had co-written with her daughter, Ilka. Audrey saw an early copy and featured a review and excerpts in *Brogue*. She wrote a personal letter to Edna, praising her for the book:

You, more than anybody in the whole organisation, are in our blood, just as if you had been our mother. We cannot think, or discuss, *Vogue* problems, without having you in our minds, and being influenced by your philosophy.

She went on:

May I rather shyly and humbly thank you very much indeed for the far too generous things you said about me. I did not expect to feature in your chronicle, and I am very honoured and happy that through it I shall take my place in *Vogue* history.

One of the joys of the book was Edna's tips on editing copy, which Audrey much appreciated. She was also highly amused by her outspoken criticism of open-toed shoes, which was a fashion Edna deplored. She had written of her one-woman campaign to educate the women of America that they were an ugly and inappropriate fashion for street-wear. She conceded that sandals could be worn on the beach but that 'the open-toed shoe is an abomination and women who have real discrimination still do not wear it.' She admitted in the book that she had probably lost the fight and her real disappointment was to see that they were favoured by the 'charming young queen of England'.

One of the things that exercised Edna more than anything else was *Vogue*'s direction of travel and its future. She constantly reminded Audrey of *Vogue*'s standard of good taste, which had been established in the last decade of the nineteenth century and in her opinion still held good sixty years on. Her greatest beef was about editors striving for a fresh look, which she felt was sometimes just a chance to be different.

> But if in order to be 'different' we have to subject our readers to the shock treatment by presenting a lot of our mannikins made up to look like tough, hard-boiled girls of dubious reputation, or poor bewildered neurotics, I think it would be better to stick to the boring banality of showing charming, simple, elegant women whose only merit may be that they look warm, alive and human – women who might conceivably love and be loved, not the type one of our readers described as looking 'like women who would eat their young if they had any'.

It was a criticism that Audrey agreed with, although for different reasons. She had received a stream of letters from male and female readers of *Vogue* complaining not about models who might eat their offspring, but rather about models who were too thin. One reader wrote to tell her she was so tired of a particular model that each time she opened her copy of *Vogue*, 'the same face haunted me, and I was so bored with the gaunt features posing in most parts of the universe that I became allergic to her photograph and finally decided to switch to another literature'.

Another correspondent was the husband of a *Vogue* subscriber who did not mind seeing models in 'frocks, costumes etc', but when it came to bathing suits he abhorred the lack of curves:

> My eye, as would the eyes of most men of my generation, flinches at the sight of the slab like figures in bathing costumes ... The *Vogue* figure may appeal to the younger generation. It is conceivable I suppose. They will grow out of it. But as it is probably the older man who pays for *Vogue* clothes, you ought in fairness to pander a little to him.

Audrey summed up the summer postbag as a worrying trend, with the words 'gaunt' and 'inhuman' used in many of the letters critical of models who were taller and thinner than the ordinary woman and who too often looked unfriendly, 'superior, aloof, hard'. The prerequisite for becoming a *Vogue* model at that time was to be between 5ft 10 and 6ft tall, at least 8 inches higher than the average British woman in the middle of the twentieth century.

Audrey urged the fashion staff and all the photographers copied in on the memo, including Beaton, Parkinson, Denney, Clarke and Deakin, to get into our pages models of a more friendly, approachable, 'normal' kind. Can we please pursue an unremitting search for such models: and in the meantime, when we have to use the 'professional', can photographers and editors do everything they can to break down their aloofness, and make them appear warm, eager, friendly and approachable.

Whether the cri de coeur from Edna and Audrey to their respective teams was heard or whether it was simply a change in the way photographers wanted to capture fashion, there was a move to more playful images. The photographers she and the editors were working with now included a handful of exceptionally talented and variously temperamental younger men who were ready to take the world by storm.

One of these was the awkward but gifted John Deakin. He had worked for *Vogue* after the war when Audrey was impressed by his street photographs of Paris and Rome, but she sacked him for losing – or possibly pawning – at least two of the studio's Rolleiflex cameras and being generally rude, indifferent and often reducing models to tears. After he was asked to leave, he wrote to Audrey enquiring whether he could have the money she had promised him as compensation for loss of office as he needed to buy a new camera, having had his stolen in Paris. He added that he had not said goodbye to anybody at the office or the studio, believing it was better that way.

However, four years later, she hired him again. She had met him in Paris and felt that he had sobered up, and his work was even better than before. She wrote to Edna to explain her thinking:

I have always thought that Deakin had qualities, especially in photographing Spotlight personalities. We accordingly took him on again on an arrangement which either side could break at a month's notice, as we did not feel inclined to be committed for a longer period. I find it very hard to get at the truth of the matter, because I have always found Deakin an interesting and easy character, and I admire some of his work, as does John Parsons. I am constantly told, however, that his manners on sittings are bad, and that editors and model girls don't want to work with him.

Deakin disliked fashion photography, preferring portrait shoots, but Audrey believed in his abilities and that was not misplaced. He is now recognised as one of the twentieth century's most influential British photographers. At the time he was at *Vogue* in the 1950s, he was spending his spare time, and a lot of his work time, in the cafés and bars of Soho. Eventually even Audrey's patience ran out and she sacked him for a second time in 1954 after Pat Matthews, head of the photographic studio, wrote a plea to let him go. Deakin is the only photographer in the history of British *Vogue* to have been hired and fired twice by the same editor.

One of Audrey's favourite photographers was the American Clifford Coffin. When Coffin was around, the studio lit up and became an even more exciting and creative place in which to work. Pat Matthews said of him: 'No one ever felt *Vogue* fashion like Coffin did. He didn't need an editor and didn't give a damn about anything except his pictures.' He was a perfectionist and drove the editors he worked with to despair and models to tears but Audrey loved having a photographer about the place whose pleasure and delight it was to take photographs for *Vogue*. They got on well and he would always address his letters to her: 'Dearest Audrey'. Often those letters were personal, describing his messy love affairs or his determination to give up alcohol because he couldn't work in the darkroom with a hangover. In one he wrote:

> I didn't mean this letter to turn into a full confession. I did mean it to convey how darling you are to want me back to do some pages. Every time one of you visits us in America I am again reminded of the really wonderful sincerity and capacities for friendship you all have. I think I love you all very, very much.

The letters between Clifford Coffin and Audrey are full of affectionate superlatives but also of exact specifics of what she wanted from him. In 1954, he was due to spend two weeks in Paris photographing the collections and then come to London to work for *Vogue* for twelve days, into which she intended to pack five photo shoots for three different editors. She planned to give him the October lead on the little black dress, 'which we feel is coming back in a big way'.

> This is the opening of a big feature which we have run in October and April for several seasons on the theme of 'What to Wear with What', so that the little black dresses will be carefully accessorised, and a set of drawn accessories will be incorporated in the lay-out of each spread. Also in the October issue we want you to do four pages of hats. Sheila Wetton, who handles our hats and whom I know you will love

working with, likes to wait until just after Paris has shown so that she can try and get Paris trends into her hat pages.

Looking ahead to the December number, she wanted him to do a wonderful glamorous spread of ball dresses in jewel colours. Pat Cunningham had five in mind in tones of emerald, sapphire, ruby, amethyst and topaz, 'but we need not include them all if you don't see it that way. Obviously, however, a theme like this is strengthened by the sort of accumulative effect of various jewel colours.' Carrying on the jewel colour theme, she wanted a single colour page featuring magnificent real jewels.

We thought that you might do a wonderful composition of any three heads wearing magnificent necklaces, earrings and so on. We thought it would be most exciting if these heads could be of actresses or ballet dancers, rather than model girls. Siriol will help you with the actresses and Lady Rendlesham, who does our jewellery features, will be looking for jewellery.

Finally there was the question of the November cover, which was to be a nod to a new Revlon make-up called Cherries in the Snow. Audrey told Coffin that Pat Cunningham and Sheila Wetton had planned to find a white fur fabric jerkin

with a flash of red in scarf or sweater neck, and possibly a streak of white Jaguar in the background, as it is among other things our motoring number. It is really a question of what type of garment they can get, and mainly of course how you see it.

In the past, New York had supplied covers to London and Paris, but that had changed and Audrey was as interested in her covers as she was in the content inside. The November cover is stunning and almost exactly as Audrey had described it.

The mention in her letter of motoring may come of something of a surprise, but *Vogue* at that time had a motoring editor, Margaret Jennings, and there were articles about all aspects of cars, including foreign holidays and celebrities and their vehicles. The actor, writer and humorist Peter Ustinov contributed a witty piece called 'Why I Love My Car', while the Olympic showjumper Pat Smythe was featured with her Standard Vanguard Sportsman with overdrive to produce greater silence and 'really excellent' petrol consumption of 30 miles to the gallon. She was also keen to tell *Vogue* readers that a redeeming feature of her car was that it did not leak. It is a reminder of the discomforts of car travel in the early 1950s, but also of Audrey's determination to address all topics of interest to the modern woman.

Meantime, there were major personnel changes at *Vogue*. In New York, Edna had stepped aside from having overall editorial control of all three *Vogue*s and had been appointed chairman of the Editorial Brand. The role had been created especially for her and it meant she still gave Audrey plenty of critique on London features and fashion.

Evelyn Forbes retired as beauty editor, which Audrey very much regretted. They had been close friends and Evelyn's professionalism and her contacts in the beauty world meant that Audrey had barely had to concern herself with the aspect of women's fashion that she found the least interesting. Losing an editor often meant a drop in advertising revenue from the sources connected with her work, so there was also concern on a professional level.

Siriol Hugh-Jones had joined *Vogue* shortly after the war and wrote the Spotlight column for almost two decades. Her contacts in the world of entertainment were second to none. Elva Carey (née Parkinson), one of Audrey's subeditors in the 1950s, described her as 'immensely glamorous. Not attractive physically but a great personality.' Siriol was out almost every night of the week and would phone in with her reports. Elva remembered Siriol's secretary was so quick at typing that she would clamp her phone to her ear and bash away at her typewriter while listening to Siriol on the other end.

Elva had come to *Vogue* from the *Ham & High*, where she had been working as a cub reporter. She was one of a series of young women who, like Pam Makin and Eileen Toll, represented a new kind of employee who was not drawn from the debutante community. She learned quickly the importance of accuracy and remembered Audrey as being fastidious about grammar. Audrey told Elva that what she liked was editing and that she would just as happily have edited the *Muckspreaders' Journal*, which made a very strong impression on the 20-year-old.

What I learned at *Vogue* stood me in great stead for the rest of my career. Audrey was very kind and the great thing about her was that she recognised what she wasn't and didn't try to be that.

Elva arrived a few years into Pat Cunningham's editorship and as such she was in a position to observe her and Audrey's relationship at editorial conferences. Audrey did not always side with her fashion editor but she was absolutely reliant on the fashion department.

'It is fair to say that the fashion editors played on it. They wanted to be powerful, but it was Audrey who had the soft power, and if they wanted to get their way they had to be nice to Audrey. When Audrey was looking dowdy, they would say: 'What are we going to do about Audrey? Send her to Hardy [Amies] again.'

One thing that impressed Elva was Audrey's insistence that women who were featured should be in *Vogue* not as wives but as women in their own right. She also liked the fact that there were features in *Vogue* for larger women, tactfully titled Above Average, and for women on tight budgets. And yet Audrey had an unshakeable belief that *Vogue* was the epitome of all fashion magazines, and that meant that she sometimes had to be ruthless. 'She had standards and people had to work to those standards. If it was not right for *Vogue* it had to be rejected or "killed".'

Audrey was always on the lookout for new contributors to keep *Vogue* fresh. One of the areas that she felt they did not cover well was cookery, so it was one of the greatest coups of her career when she managed to lure the food writer Elizabeth David away from *Harper's Bazaar* in 1957. Elizabeth had first approached *House & Garden*'s editor, but as soon as Audrey had got wind of the fact that such talent was looking for a new home, she swooped in. She liked Elizabeth's style of writing and the cachet of the woman who was regarded as in a class of her own when it came to cookery was just what Audrey needed.

Elizabeth David has been credited with lifting Britain's wartime cookery out of the doldrums and bringing continental and

Middle Eastern ingredients into the kitchens of eager cooks. Food rationing had ended in 1954, but the wartime mentality had been hard to shift. Now there were exotic ingredients such as garlic, aubergines and olive oil available, and with excellent recipes to boot. Her first published work, *A Book of Mediterranean Food*, had appeared in 1949 and sold out immediately. Suddenly people were unafraid of herbs, spices or wine-based sauces. She 'taught a whole generation of people how to think about food in ways they never had before, and how to cook the simple, authentic dishes she described'. What Audrey liked about her writing was her enthusiasm and her attitude towards cooking that meant readers were encouraged to experiment rather than being told exactly what to do. Above all she would introduce an element of fun into the cookery features, and that was just what was required.

Audrey needed her to sign an exclusive agreement with Condé Nast, and it was not an easy wooing. *Harper's* were loath to let her go and it took over three years to persuade her to make the leap. Audrey believed that if they managed to convince her to write a monthly column it could bring new readers to *Vogue* and that would be beneficial at a time when there were circulation problems. She had a battle on her hands with her colleagues in *House & Garden* who had been the first to propose Elizabeth David. There was a lengthy and at times heated exchange of nearly 250 memos and letters between the various departments of both magazines, but Audrey prevailed. Over the autumn of 1954, the pressure grew with Harry Yoxall muscling in asking if they could not get Elizabeth David 'if necessary by sheer force of finance'. Audrey told Pam Makin that getting Elizabeth David would change their lives. And it did.

In the end, Elizabeth David agreed to work for Condé Nast Publications on an exclusive basis but with permission to publish articles in newspapers from time to time. It was an unusual arrangement, as Condé Nast set great store by exclusivity, but it was a mark of how much Audrey and Harry Yoxall wanted to employ their superstar that they were able to waive their usual contract in her case.

The files on Elizabeth David in the archives of *Vogue* offer a fascinating insight into the relationship between the editorial departments within Condé Nast Publications. Exceptional courtesy and well-argued points hide a steely determination by each magazine to ensure that they had the greater access to Elizabeth David. *House & Garden* argued that they were a magazine that focused on house and home, gardens and gardening, so that it was natural that they should have the lion's share of cookery writing. Audrey argued, equally strongly, that *Vogue*'s focus was on the quality of its features, and with someone of Elizabeth David's class and pedigree it was right that she should be working on the magazine that focused on the entire woman.

Elizabeth was contracted to write twenty articles a year for Condé Nast Publications and the arguments that went back and forth were about how many articles each should have. Harry Yoxall suggested twelve for *House & Garden* and eight for *Vogue*, but Audrey stamped on that proposal firmly, arguing that her readers would notice gaps between features and conclude that it was not a regular feature. Eventually they agreed on ten articles each with the 'gaps' appearing for *Vogue* when the Paris fashions were featured.

When all the dealings had taken place and contracts had been

signed, Audrey broke the news of her new writer to Jessica
Daves in New York:

> *Brogue* is asking Elizabeth David to contribute a monthly
> article on the food that is best and most appropriate for that
> month, and our plan is to face it each time with a still-life
> colour page of food, cooked or raw, or both. Our thought is
> that a distinguished contributor on food can be of very great
> importance in building circulation, and, particularly if the
> article appears regularly, in carrying readers from issue to
> issue through the poor selling months. We want our cookery
> feature by our new contributor to claim attention and to be
> talked about.

From the outset, the column turned out to be a success. She
was twinned with Anthony Denney who was commissioned
to photograph her dishes and that developed into a creative
partnership. Audrey told Denney that she and John Parsons
saw the photographs as stylised still-life pictures with the
food looking 'simply beautiful'. The results were different
from any other kind of food photography ever reproduced in
Vogue and Audrey was delighted with them. Today they look
slightly old-fashioned, but at the time they were considered
revolutionary.

Each month, Elizabeth wrote an article entitled 'Food at
its best in . . .', with an introduction about why warm and
stimulating foods were needed to shut out the fog and damp
in November or tiny broad beans, miniature carrots and early
asparagus were harbingers of summer with all its plenty.
Although Audrey was no cook, she loved growing vegetables,

and whenever she went to have lunch with Elizabeth to discuss future issues, she would pick something from the garden to take with her as a gift. 'Your beautiful parsley has lasted a whole week, decorating my kitchen in the nicest possible way . . .' Elizabeth wrote to Audrey after one lunch in 1957.

Their most creative collaboration and the one of which Audrey was most proud resulted in a series of articles about French markets. Elizabeth David and Anthony Denney took a road trip around France, dropping in on as many markets as they could find to create half-a-dozen articles. Their two-week trip took months of planning and organising. Audrey had written to contacts in Paris who promised to get her a full list of the French markets and which days they were open. Then there were visas, currency, permissions to photograph to be acquired and at every turn an extra layer of complicated bureaucracy emerged.

Finally, in June 1959, Elizabeth David and Anthony Denney met up in Duclair near Rouen. Denney had flown in from Lydd with his driver and arrived at the hotel with English snow on his boots after a freak storm. Elizabeth's report on the trip was contained in a colourfully worded six-page letter that described some of the tribulations of the journey, including the fact that their list of French markets was out of date and inaccurate. She wrote of how difficult it had been to turn up in a hotel in France and expect the

cook and the patron to jump to attention and produce recipes and local colour before you get up the next morning at 4am to go to market. (In Italy, this can be done with less difficulty. In France, it's like trying to decipher Linear B in 15 minutes.)

That Audrey devoted so much time to her star cookery writer might seem strange given that the focus of *Vogue* was, as ever, on fashion, but it can be explained by two things. First, Pat Cunningham was such a reliable and consistent fashion editor that Audrey no longer needed to worry about the smooth running of that department. Secondly, the war was still a vivid memory and food rationing had had a devastating impact on Britain's cuisine, although a beneficial one on its waistline. A column on food that would introduce readers to something new, wholesome and, above all, delightful, was of great appeal and, as Audrey had written to her colleagues, would inspire people to buy the magazine even in the months that traditionally had lower sales.

Audrey had become much more interested in food since she married Victor and that might also have been a contributing factor. She and Victor had bought Radley Green Farm in Essex for their retirement and they spent every weekend there while they were still working. They farmed Large White pigs and Ayrshire dairy cows and grew wheat, potatoes and sugar beet. Audrey had a vegetable patch, which she tended with enthusiasm. Her relationship with Victor had changed her relationship with the world around her. She felt more whole than she had ever done when she was married to Jock and she could abandon herself with enthusiasm to the full pleasures of life: companionship, sex and food. Although she was never a gourmet, she came to love well-cooked, home-grown food. Victor introduced ingredients into their kitchen that she had only ever enjoyed while on holiday and her whole attitude to the domestic side of her life went from being one of lacklustre existence to energising happiness.

Her professional relationship with Elizabeth David turned into a firm friendship, and they spent time together away from work, often sitting around Elizabeth's table in Halsey Street, discussing travel and their love of the Mediterranean. The relationship was not one-sided. Elizabeth admired Audrey's editing skills and once wrote:

> I think it is really partly you yourself who have made me see during the past three years that a fresh approach to cookery is more important to the readers than striving after originality in the recipes, when so few people really understand even the most basic recipes.

Elizabeth David and Anthony Denney were frequent visitors to Radley Green Farm, delighting in Victor's home-made borscht, of which Elizabeth said: 'every now and again, eating a dish, one knows that it is the best of its kind that one will ever eat, and that is how I feel about Victor's Borscht.' Audrey had seldom entertained at home when she was married to Jock, preferring to meet friends in restaurants or at concerts. Victor's enthusiasm for gatherings of family and friends, always accompanied by large quantities of food and even more vodka, was a novelty, and one she greatly enjoyed, though there were times when she wondered how she could keep up with the legendary Russian hospitality.

I O

OUT OF *VOGUE*

'Audrey was very persuasive but she was also incredibly
flexible and she was always herself. Searingly honest, kind,
intelligent with a complete absence of airs and graces.'

—ANTONY PENROSE, JANUARY 2017

As the 1950s drew to a close, Audrey's long relationship with *Vogue*
came to an end. She said that she was beginning to feel out of tune
with the times and she recognised that *Vogue* needed fresh blood
and renewed energy. Edna Woolman Chase died in 1957, and
with that an era had ended. Audrey published a warm tribute to
her, describing her as a woman of passionate convictions and fiery
enthusiasm 'who stimulated, demanded and searched forever for
the best there was – and then demanded better than that.' She celebrated Edna's long service and her dedication to the Condé Nast
family and the influence she had on a generation of editorial staff:

For the *Vogue* staff and for hundreds of former associates,
there is the memory of a witty, outspoken woman whose
incisive mind and fearlessly strong character also included
an endearing, daily, affectionate warmth.

Audrey's passion for editing was still there and her enthusiasm for outstanding journalism remained, but her interest in the direction fashion was taking was diminishing. In June 1957, she told Harry over lunch at the Aperitif that she intended to retire within the next three years and that she would help him to find a successor. There was another reason for her wishing to step down, and that was her health. She had begun to have back problems in the mid-1950s. At first, she thought it was sciatica but then a doctor suggested to her that it was linked to stress. Harry sent her to Baden-Baden for a week's cure, which helped for a few weeks but the pain returned and she was often so uncomfortable that she could not sit at her desk. Being practical she had a sofa moved into her office so that if she were in too much pain she could lie down to work. In addition, Victor was keen for them to spend more time together now that he too was thinking of winding down his business and moving to Essex full time. Harry agreed to her plan and over the next eighteen months they considered who they might find as a successor.

Their first thought was Pat Cunningham, who had led the fashion team for six years, though there were many questions about the way she dealt with people. Pat did not accept the role, so they had to put out feelers into the wider fashion community. In the end, they approached Ailsa Garland, who had worked as fashion editor on the *Vogue Book of British Exports* for three years at the end of the 1940s but had been working as fashion editor of the *Daily Mirror* since 1951. She accepted the appointment in August 1959 and Harry wrote in his diary: 'Ailsa Garland, for better or worse, has accepted our offer of the editorship, to join us early next year.' That same week Audrey had a major crisis with her back when she and Victor were in Stockholm on the way back from her first trip to Russia. She was unable to move without excruciating pain and had to be brought home on a stretcher. It was a terrible disappointment to her but she managed to rally and was in the office five days later, though far from well.

One last major change happened on Audrey's watch, and that was a move from Golden Square to Vogue House on Hanover Square. In the July 1958 issue, she charted the moves from Breams Buildings on Fleet Street to Aldwych House and then to her first office at One New Bond Street, which had been the site of so much drama during the war years. Golden Square had seen an expansion of the Condé Nast publications with *House & Garden* and various special numbers edited for readers in South Africa, Australia and New Zealand. She wrote:

> The New Look – ushering in almost a decade of nipped waists and full skirts – has held sway during most of our tenancy. Then the line eased, progressively, till it reached the sack; and this spring shortened dramatically. In this Charleston mood we move, and take you, with some 300 of us, to Vogue House, Hanover Square . . .

In November 1959, Audrey opened the London fashion show at Celanese House where a reporter from the *Birmingham Post* described her as the retiring editor of *Vogue*. It was her final fashion show in her role as editor. She had been to Paris twice a year since the end of the war and to the London fashion weeks every year since she took over the managing editorship of the magazine. There were many friends who were sad to see her leave, but more who knew what an outstanding contribution she had made and how much she deserved her retirement.

Antony Armstrong-Jones, who had just become engaged to Princess Margaret, took the last photographs of Audrey at her desk in her office at *Vogue*. They show her surrounded by proofs fastened to the wall with the familiar bull-dog clips, the telephone clamped firmly to her ear, pen in hand, the desk full of papers, with a lively grin on her face. White-haired, dressed in dark blue and with three strings of pearls around her neck, she looks every bit the most powerful woman in London – but a woman of the 1950s, not of the 1960s. She said later: 'The Sixties was the beginning of something very competitive and fashion conscious. I could see that features, which had always interested me most, would be taking second place.'

Audrey's final issue appeared in December 1959. She remained on the board of Condé Nast for a further year and was given the title of editorial director. She told an interviewer later that her role was to be present in the building in case the new editor needed to consult her for anything. 'But she never in a whole year asked me a single question. I think so often people's behaviour indicates insecurity.' Rumour had it that the two women did not get on. Although there is no hint of any ill feeling in either of their autobiographies, Harry Yoxall observed a few months into Ailsa's editorship that he could sense a tension between Audrey and her successor.

Ailsa was scathing about Audrey's office, which she inherited in early 1960:

This office was a square, glass box, the walls of which did not reach the ceiling, and was part of the open plan adopted by the Company on their move from Golden Square to Hanover Square. I hated it. I could not pull up my stocking or powder my nose except in full view of anyone passing by.

Audrey would have been quite happy to be seen in her goldfish bowl. She was not interested in private personal space and had always shared an office with her assistant.

Throughout the final year at Vogue House, Audrey's back problems got ever more severe. Harry drove her to see her 'bone-setter' in June when she collapsed once again, unfortunately the day that three of Victor's relatives arrived to stay, two of them from Russia. Then in August she saw a Spanish orthopaedic specialist at Oxford who told her that she would need surgery and that he would be prepared to operate on her later in the year. In November, she went into the Radcliffe Hospital where she had a spinal operation. The surgeon took a small piece of bone from her thigh and used it to fuse three vertebrae together. She was sent home after several weeks encased in a plaster cast that covered her torso and one leg, which made moving around difficult.

Nevertheless, she was so relieved to be out of pain and able to stand without wincing that she felt able to go to the retirement party that Harry was planning for her at Quaglino's in St James's just before Christmas. She had handed in her official resignation to the board the day before and Harry wrote in his diary that it was 'the end of a long and happy chapter'.

Audrey turned out to be in tremendous form at the party. Harry gave a valedictory address, in which he summed up the twenty years of her editorship. Ailsa made a short speech as she handed over the gifts that the staff had collected for (in addition to her bonus of £350 the company gave her a leaving gift of £500) and then Audrey stood up to speak. 'She replied excellently with fine spirit, talking, and insisting on standing up, for nearly half an hour.' Harry wrote that evening in his diary. 'It was nearly 4 o'clock when, having dropped Audrey at Victor's club, I got back to the office.' In the January edition of *Vogue*, the following tribute appeared:

> The word 'retiring' seems a silly one to apply to Audrey Withers in any context. True, that after thirty years with *Vogue* (twenty as its editor), she is leaving London to live on her farm in Essex, but one thing is certain: idleness will remain unknown to her. During the years, she has helped to give the fashion industry in general – and *Vogue* in particu-lar – the place it has today, her logical mind has never been inactive; for her work for the Council of Industrial Design she was awarded the OBE. But the reason we all love her is different again; she is that rare paragon, the woman with white hair who loves and understands the young and laughs as gaily as they do.

The year after she left *Vogue* Audrey was awarded the Bicentenary Medal of the Royal Society of Arts (RSA), an award given to 'a person who, in a manner other than as an industrial designer, has applied art and design to great effect as instruments of civic innovation'. It was an honour that she was proud of as good design was something she cared about almost as much as good editing. She continued to play a role with the RSA, chairing sessions on various topics, including the history of cosmetics and the commercialisation of the theatre.

Retirement was a shock for Audrey. Victor had been pressing her to spend more time with him on the farm in Essex rather than commuting into London to work and now she was released and free to do what she wanted with her time. She had not really thought through what a difference it would make to her life, both personally and professionally, to lose the status of being editor of the most prestigious fashion magazine in Britain.

For nearly thirty years, she had lived and breathed editing. Her life had been structured around the monthly publication of *Vogue* with its traditions and deadlines. Although there had been moments of high stress and difficulty, there had been the satisfaction of seeing her magazine published once a month, year in, year out. Then there had been the professional relationships with her editorial teams, her brilliant and at times tempestuous photographers, her other Condé Nast colleagues in Paris and New York.

Suddenly it disappeared, and there was nothing to replace any of it; no freelance work, no official appointments and, at the most basic level of all, no writing to edit. Although *Vogue* offered her the opportunity to stay on the board of Condé Nast, she felt she had been pushed upstairs. She also had the sensitivity to know that it was of no use to the new editorial team to have her hanging around the offices like a ghost from a previous era.

Victor retired from his engineering business the same year Audrey stepped down from *Vogue*. He had once told her that as they had missed out on thirteen years of happiness, they had to do everything together from now onwards, even if it was something the other person was not interested in. There was a possessive element to his nature, which she later acknowledged would have made life very difficult if she had taken the bold step he had wanted her to take in 1938 and run away from Jock to marry him.

> I could not say that I had regretted what I had done. In fact, I felt that it had probably saved us from disaster. When we met, I was managing editor of *Vogue*, and hoped to go higher in my profession. Victor would have been demanding, wanting me exclusively as his wife. Looking back, I realized that I was someone who needed a career, and that without some achievement of my own I should have felt frustrated and unfulfilled.

She thought children might have been a problem as well. Victor was authoritarian, whereas she had been brought up in an atmosphere of physical and mental freedom. It would have brought a clash, as she would instinctively have let a child work things out for him- or herself, as Percy and Mamie had done when she was young, while Victor might have wanted to be more didactic. This is one of the many hints in Audrey's writing that she valued her independence at least as much as she did her happy marriage to Victor.

The other thing that marred the early years of her retirement was her back. The problems had not been resolved by the surgery and now came close to destroying both Audrey's health and her marriage. On a trip to Moscow with Victor a few months after she retired, when she was representing the Wool Marketing Board, she collapsed and was taken to a clinic. Here she had a Russian 'blockade', a pain-killing injection in the nerves in her spine. It seemed to work for a while but then the problems recurred with regularity and escalating severity. There were days when she was unable to get out of bed and could barely sit up without crying out in pain. One psychologist put her symptoms down to her regret at leaving *Vogue*; another wrote on her medical records that she was a woman who appeared to enjoy ill health.

Victor was depressed and angry that fate had dealt this terrible blow. When his friends told him that he had to accept the fact that his wife was an invalid, his anger spilled over onto Audrey. No one believed her that her pain was caused by an orthopedic problem. Audrey pleaded with Victor and Monica but her insistence that her pain had a physical cause fell on deaf ears. When her husband and sister turned away from her and sought advice from psychiatric specialists, she felt as though loneliness were feasting on her very being. This was the lowest point in her life. Never had she felt more deserted than she did over those summer months. She wrote later:

> To be disbelieved by those nearest to you, as well as by medical advisers, is a devastating experience. You feel isolated, abandoned and lose all hope. I couldn't believe that neither Victor nor Monica was prepared to fight for me.

In great pain and brought to desperation by the vast chasm between her own perception of the situation and the denial of it by others, Audrey became so depressed that the doctors and Victor agreed that she should be hospitalised for her own safety. She was detained under the Mental Health Act as a mentally disordered person, the equivalent of being sectioned today, which meant she had no rights over her care and no say in her treatment. Her freedom denied her, Audrey spent weeks in a secure psychiatric ward being observed by specialists. Here, still in the grip of intense pain, she was advised to practise chanting to calm her nerves and to take up knitting. Once the most powerful woman in London, Audrey was now reduced to impotence surrounded on the ward by other poor women in various states of mental anguish.

In typical Audrey style, she looked around her and concluded that the others were all much worse off than she was and she determined to get better and get out of hospital, whatever it took.

It was in that ward that Audrey eventually received wise advice from a psychiatrist who was really prepared to listen to her. She told him how deeply hurt she felt that neither Monica nor Victor could believe that her symptoms were physical and not mental. The psychiatrist gave Audrey time, and that was the most generous gift she could have asked for. To be listened to, and not to be belittled for believing her symptoms were physical, was a huge change, and it made her feel she was not mad but misunderstood.

Gradually she began to recover her equilibrium and was allowed to go out of the ward, and eventually out of the building to walk in the hospital gardens and beyond, to Southwark Cathedral. The doctor and Audrey talked about how she should handle the issue with Victor and Monica when she was released from hospital and she concluded that she had to let go of her feelings of abandonment and grief: 'Guilt is a powerful destroyer of people and relationships, and I was on my guard not to let it injure the two people closest to me.'

When she emerged from the psychiatric ward, Audrey finally saw a surgeon who established that she had been right all along: the original operation had resulted in a permanently trapped nerve below the grafted bone. The second operation, eight years after the first, was a complete success. Once freed from pain, she was able to resume her old life again, but she and Victor agreed to sell Radley Green Farm to avoid risking any further damage to her back.

The episode in the psychiatric ward was never discussed between them. Mental health issues were brushed under the carpet in those days, but there was another, stranger twist. Audrey knew that Victor's first wife had committed him to a mental asylum in 1938 when he told her he was planning to leave her for Audrey. He was locked up for almost a month, and one day let out with the clothes he was standing in and told there was nothing wrong with him. It is a demonstration of Audrey's immense strength of character but also her ability to compartmentalise her life that nothing more was ever said about the episode. She returned to health and the warm embrace of Victor's love for her, which continued until the end of his life.

Although they were very different personalities, Audrey and Victor had much in common. One was a passion for travel, and over the course of the next twenty years they travelled extensively, most especially to the Soviet Union, which they visited nearly a dozen times. Victor had told Audrey about his life in pre-Revolution Leningrad and the stories that kept coming out were of his bravery and determination to protect his family at all costs. After the death of Stalin in 1953, he felt it was time to return to his home country. His family was widely dispersed and he yearned to see them.

By the time they made their first trip, Victor was nearly seventy. He had a brother and sister in the USSR and two sisters in Paris, whom Audrey had already got to know. The girls had left Leningrad as teenagers in 1920 with their mother, and Lorka, the older one, had studied at the Sorbonne. Both Victor's sisters in Paris had married Ukrainian cousins who had cramped their lives and Alka, the younger one, told Audrey that she envied her for having made something of her life while she had been kept tied to the home while her husband worked long hours as an engineer. 'How could intelligent men suppose that intelligent women could find enough to occupy, let alone satisfy, them in a small flat, with only two people to shop and cook for?'

Victor had been the first of his family, other than his father, to leave Russia. He escaped on foot and by train to Switzerland via Finland where he spent a brief three weeks with his father before the old man died. After that he came to London, where he worked first as an engineer and then as a photographer. He had a passion for quality and was an expert on rugs and eighteenth- and nineteenth-century clocks. Audrey's enduring passion was for art: prints and drawings in the main, so that their homes for the first few years of their marriage were full to bursting with lovely objects. Later, many of these precious works of art and craft had to be sold to support Victor's family.

At the time they were visiting the Soviet Union, there were shortages of even the most basic necessities. Luxuries, such as books, and records were scarce. Audrey allowed Victor to buy the big-ticket items, like cars, but she took great pride and interest in supplying the English-speaking friends and university lecturers she met on their trips to Leningrad with modern novels. She would return to Britain after each visit with a list of books that they had requested or she had suggested and she would acquire them and either send them or take them the next time they visited. Being Audrey, she kept meticulous notes in a card index and she totted up that thirty years after their first visit to Russia she had gifted over 600 books. The Russians were thirsty for modern British novels and plays, which she chose for them, and the packages always included a good sprinkling of Agatha Christie, who proved enduringly popular with her friends.

After Audrey had regained her composure following the psychiatric period, she began to take on a few journalistic commissions. Her training had drummed into her the importance of records, captions and detailed information. In Leningrad, she would make copious notes on photographs that Victor took, whether of buildings or people, and these became the basis for illustrated articles in *The Guardian* or *House & Garden* about her travels. Her restless mind and her insatiable desire for intellectual stimulation was partly satisfied by this type of work.

She agreed to teach a poetry course on one of their visits, but the most fulfilling work she and Victor undertook was a large and impressive coffee-table book on the palaces of Leningrad, which was published by Thames & Hudson in 1973. Victor took the photographs and Audrey did the research, working with two Russian students who spent days in the archives of the Victoria & Albert Museum. Audrey then wrote the text and captions. It was a vast undertaking and the result is a thorough, historic account of the city's palaces and a photographic record of the remarkable post-war restoration of them in both colour and black and white.

The grandeur was extraordinary, but Audrey was aware that this was not how normal Russians lived and she made an effort to get to know the other side of life. She was impressed by the aspects of Soviet society that made better provision for women than their equivalents in the UK. She applauded the system of childcare and the health centres and rest homes for workers as well as the employment opportunities for women. Two of Victor's sisters-in-law were doctors in Leningrad and one had been a colonel in the Russian army during the war.

But she was not blind to the excesses of the KGB, and she and Victor were always aware that their luck could turn at any moment and they would be asked to leave Russia or, worse still, not be allowed to leave. While she was in Leningrad, she knew she was a prop in Victor's performance. 'I sat by the hour with a tide of Russian pouring over me . . . managing to laugh or look serious in the right places.'

Audrey and Victor continued to travel throughout the 1960s and '70s. They journeyed all over Europe by car or train and visited Bulgaria twice, but their most memorable holidays were to the United States and South America. Their longest trip, which lasted three months, took them to Caracas, Cartagena, Lima and eventually to Machu Picchu, which enchanted Audrey more than even she had expected.

A trip to India followed South America, but by the mid-1970s Victor's health had begun to fail. He was suffering from a painful heart condition called angina pectoris, which was exacerbated by a serious car accident when he had been run off the road and the steering wheel of the car had crushed several ribs. His sisters and Monica came to their new flat to help look after him but in the end it was only Audrey he wanted to care for him. He died in June 1980 at the age of eighty-six. Audrey was both sad and relieved. The pain he had suffered from his illness had been hard to watch and so difficult to manage with medication. She was glad he was no longer suffering but his death left a hole in her life that needed to be filled.

Before she could find voluntary work, Monica was badly injured in a car accident and Audrey had to switch from caring for Victor to caring for her sister. Unlike Victor, who had been at home, Monica was in hospital and Audrey spent hours every day visiting and trying to persuade her sister to eat in order to build up her strength. One evening she was visited by a Hungarian friend of Victor's and she shared her distress and frustration about her sister. He turned to her and said gently: 'At least you are needed.'

At least you are needed. Those words hit Audrey like a slap, and they made her realise how fortunate she was to be needed. The car accident had knocked Monica's confidence and wiped out her already fading memory, so she agreed to go and live in a home. This left Audrey free, for the first time in two decades, to fill her time as she chose. And fill it she did. The last twenty years of Audrey's life brimmed with activity and friendship.

She moved to a smaller flat in St George's Fields, just north of the Bayswater Road, and began an almost ten-year stint as a volunteer working for the newly formed Social Democratic Party (SDP). Although she had voted Labour for most of her working life, she liked the SDP and particularly admired its young, charismatic leader, Dr David Owen, who had been the Labour Party's foreign secretary in the late 1970s. He had left the party to found the SDP with three other politicians: Bill Rodgers, Roy Jenkins and Shirley Williams. Audrey worked in the membership department, learning how to use a computer and bringing her organisational skills to bear on the new political party's administration. When the SDP voted to merge with the British Liberal Party to become the SDLP, Audrey threw her vote behind the merger.

Steve White, who worked for the SDP at the same time as Audrey was a volunteer, remembers her as being completely involved in the day-to-day running of the office. She was as passionate about her politics as she had always been and knew that she could play a role in keeping the office ticking over while the politicians raced about giving speeches and discussing issues. She was tidy and very organised but mostly Steve remembers Audrey and her friend, Helen Sharman, laughing and enjoying their work.

On one occasion, he and his colleague became aware of great mirth in the membership office.

> There were hysterical giggles and when we went in to investigate we found Audrey reading out a letter from a man who had written to say he had resigned from the party because he was too old and could not carry on.

Audrey and the other volunteers were in fits of giggles at the idea that they, in their seventies and eighties, were still busy and active, while this man, who had reached the venerable age of sixty, had decided to step back from life.

Audrey was one of the only volunteers to keep the faith after the merger with the Liberal Party and as such she was regarded as an exceptionally loyal and much-loved member of the small team. But, as Steve White said, they knew almost nothing about her. They were aware that her surname was Kennett and that she had once been editor of *Vogue*, and that she was widely travelled, but the details were sketchy. Everyone called her Audrey and that was how she presented herself.

The impression she made on the younger employees was significant. For most, she was the first example of an elderly person being active rather than retiring to a home. To young men and women of twenty-something, it was inspirational to see a woman of over eighty still in charge of her faculties, eager to learn new skills and deeply fascinated by the world around her. She was very social and loved to join in when invited to the many parties, happily making conversation with anyone about any subject.

At one stage, towards the end of her time with the SDP, there was a discussion about getting her an honour in one of the lists. Would it be an MBE or an OBE, they wondered. Somehow Audrey got wind of this and laughed. She told them there was no point in applying for an OBE on her behalf, as she already had one from thirty years earlier. It was typical of Audrey that she would keep this side of her life private: she was inherently modest.

In the 1970s, she renewed her relationship with Somerville College, donating her father's collection of letters, papers and photographs to the college archive. At a dinner a few years later, she surprised the principal, Daphne Park, during a speech. She was speaking of the Somerville alumna Cornelia Sorabji, the first Indian woman to study at a British university who went on to become the champion of the rights of Indian women and children. Audrey surprised the gathered guests by saying, unexpectedly, 'She was my godmother.'

Audrey continued to maintain a wide social circle and had many friends from all walks of life, some old friends from her *Vogue* years, others, much younger, from her more recent activities. She was always interested in new ideas and had a prodigious memory for other people's interests. When she could no longer venture out into the world, she brought the world into her flat through the newspapers. She read them every day and kept up not only with politics but with medical developments, which had become one of her other areas of interest, and with the arts, music and theatre.

When people consulted her on matters to do with her father's artist friends, she was generous with her time and always happy to talk. Jerrold Northrop Moore was commissioned to write a biography of F. L. Griggs, one of Audrey's devoted correspondents from the 1920s. He visited Audrey on several occasions in her flat in Albion Street and described these visits as an absolute joy:

> Audrey was exceptionally intelligent and I found her warm, witty and kind. She radiated vitality. The only time I ever saw her even slightly *bouleversée* was when I gave her a copy of my Griggs book. She said, 'It's so heavy. I wonder whether I shall ever be able to hold it so as to read it.'

He remembered her flat as immaculately tidy with lovely art on the walls. On one of his visits, he told her that he had found a letter from her to Maur Griggs dating from 1924. She was initially horrified, wondering what an embarrassment it would be to read something she had written over seventy years earlier. However, she was relieved when she saw it and said, 'It turns out to be rather discerning for a 19-year-old.' He was very touched by the fact that Audrey remembered his mother was about to be ninety, and she wrote to him, asking him to pass on her best wishes and to 'welcome her to the exclusive ranks of the 90s. I have survived the first year of that decade quite successfully, and will soon be embarking on the second.'

In 1994, she published her autobiography, *Lifespan*. It is almost as interesting for what she leaves out as for what she includes, and is the most modest autobiography imaginable. She devoted less than half of the book to her remarkable career at *Vogue*, and cast her role in the war years as one of accidentally being in the right place at the right time. She wrote in *Lifespan*:

> I am very well aware that I would not have been an appropriate editor of *Vogue* at any other period of its history. I had come up through copy-writing and administration, with no fashion training . . .

That quotation has been used in every obituary that mentions Audrey Withers, but it is so very far from the truth. If Audrey had only been suitable for the war years, she would have been replaced swiftly and without sentiment upon its conclusion in 1945. She was at the helm of *Vogue* for twenty years and it was under her guidance and editorship that *Brogue* emerged from the dust of war-torn London and developed the independence and character it had gained during those war years.

Audrey's passion for *Vogue* and for everything it stood for in representing the whole woman, which she wrote to Edna Woolman Chase about with such clarity in 1946, was always there. She may not have been as knowledgeable about fashion as her outstanding fashion editor, but she did not need to be in the same way that she did not need to know every last up-to-date detail on make-up or hair, because she had a talented staff, whom she had chosen, to bring that expertise to the magazine. She understood enough about how the fashion houses worked to be on top of the seasons, and she was as aware of the importance of the beauty industry as she was of anything else. Harry Yoxall wrote:

> Audrey ... achieved her results by sheer intelligence. Fashion was something in which she was not natively interested. But by concentrated study she made herself a judge of it, and won the respect, not to mention the affection, of the fashion trade at all levels.

Of the greatest relevance and importance was her sharp-sighted editing, her eye for good design and layout and, above all, her ability to spot talent and to work with it, whatever tempestuous form it took.

Her relationships with the staff at *Vogue* as well as the superstar photographers, writers and celebrity contributors were warm and understanding. She espoused the caring family atmosphere that was promoted by Edna Woolman Chase and Harry Yoxall, and she always tried to work to get the best out of people, and if she could not, it was a matter of regret. That is not to say that Audrey could not be determined and ruthless. Pam Makin remembered watching her at a particularly feisty editorial conference. There was a row brewing over the balance between features and fashion, with opinions being aired robustly. Pam noticed how Audrey sat back and watched with apparently little interest until an impasse arrived, at which point she stepped in, said her piece, and with that the situation was resolved.

> Audrey never gave the impression of being powerful but she was most definitely in charge. She treated everyone with respect and people responded to that with respect for her. She was also instinctively kind but tried to hide this by being a little distant. She knew what she had contributed to *Vogue* but she was too innately modest to admit it publicly.

Audrey's air of composure and efficiency hid the human side of her personality. Pam was once in the lift with Audrey at the end of a long day soon after the end of the war. The lift gave a great jolt and Audrey's briefcase dropped out of her hand and flew open, scattering papers all over the floor. To Pam's amazement there, among the papers and photographs, was a pound of sausages wrapped in a paper bag. Audrey said nothing, she just picked everything up and popped it back in the case as if nothing unusual had happened. But it delighted Pam who rushed back to the studio and told the boys there that she now knew what Miss Withers had for supper: sausages!

Pam also remarked that Audrey was much more resourceful than she would admit, and she was also far more aware of everything that was going on than Pam had realised at the time. She never visited the photographic studio unannounced, but when she did turn up she was treated with great respect and courtesy. As Pam said:

> If you can impress a working-class, non-conformist group

of young men then that is impressive. Audrey could do that. She had started at the bottom and she treated everyone as a colleague and the men respected her for that.

Quality mattered and that was what Audrey stood for and strove for at all costs. *Vogue*'s reputation, its independence, its status as the pre-eminent fashion magazine in London, mattered more than anything else. If that meant killing a picture by Cecil Beaton or telling Captain Molyneux that he could not choose his own models for inclusion, then she was confident enough to deal with it. It mattered to her even more than friendship, one writer said. By the time she left *Vogue* in 1960, she had presided over 225 issues of the magazine and well over 1,000 features. It was an extraordinary achievement.

Of the people Audrey worked with closely, the greatest talent of all was Cecil Beaton. She acknowledged that both at the time and in her autobiography. He had more or less stopped working for *Vogue* in 1957, but they continued to correspond until she too left. Beaton died shortly before Victor in 1980, so Audrey had seen little of him in the last years of his life, except on occasions when their paths crossed at functions. Difficult though he had been at times, she recognised his unique importance to *Vogue*. He was, as Harry Yoxall pointed out, the only contributor to *Vogue* who could draw, write and photograph. Audrey had learned to work with him, difficult though he was, so that in the end she earned his respect and affection.

Norman Parkinson stopped working for *Vogue* at the same time as Audrey, but they had enjoyed a fifteen-year creative collaboration that had produced some of the most exceptional fashion photography from the 1940s. He moved to Tobago in 1963, and although he was a frequent visitor to London from then until his death in 1990, they did not see one another often. She always acknowledged Parkinson's innovative approach to fashion photography and she enjoyed her discussions with him, heated though they sometimes were, but theirs was a professional relationship above all else.

The single most important person who defined Audrey's war years at *Vogue* was the brilliant Lee Miller. Their collaboration has been considered by many to be the most creative of all. There is no doubt that Audrey needed Lee, but she also loved her with an understanding and affection that few others did. Audrey saw through the beauty and the bravado and she recognised Lee's humanity, her gritty courage, her immense capacity to absorb horror and represent it with a clarity and perceptiveness that made her unique. But she also recognised the enormous personal cost of this courage.

What Audrey admired as much as anything about Lee was her penmanship. She knew it was agony for Lee to write almost every word she produced, but it was worth it. How could anybody read Lee's accounts of the hospital in Normandy, or the siege of St Malo, or the campaign through Alsace-Lorraine, or the final, dramatic article about her journey through Germany in April 1945 and not have felt they were almost there, in the thick of it? If the eighteen months of Lee's war reporting were her finest hour, the articles produced from that extraordinary raw material surely represent Audrey's finest editing. She instinctively understood where the lightest of touches was required and where, in other places, more drastic cutting could be handled. The hours that she, John Parsons and Alex Kroll spent putting together Lee's seventy-seven pages of war reportage must have been the most thrilling and exceptional in all their careers combined.

After the war, Audrey tried to keep Lee interested in photographing and writing for *Vogue* but it had been sporadic. Lee suffered what would now be described as PTSD. She came back to Britain and had to try to settle down into a life that was as unfamiliar to her as it was to men who had been fighting on the battlefields she had reported from, and beyond. She found readjusting almost unbearable and sought solace in alcohol. In 1947, she fell pregnant and married her long-time lover Roland Penrose, whom she had met what must have seemed like a lifetime ago, at the end of the 1930s.

Audrey was aware of Lee's fragile state of mind and she continued to encourage her to contribute to *Vogue* on any subject that interested her. Roland Penrose had bought a farm in Sussex and the family moved there a couple of years after Antony's birth. In 1950, Audrey suggested an article on 'Taking up Gardening', which could be as funny as Lee liked. In her letter urging Lee to consider this, she wrote:

I hope you will remember how very sincere I was in telling you of my unbounded admiration for your features, and my conviction that they have made a great impression on our readers.

In April 1953, Audrey told Lee that she would be happy to let her go fully freelance rather than being tied to *Vogue* by contract. She wrote:

Siriol tells me you are in a working mood — and nothing could please me more. I have never stopped feeling that you were a 'natural' for us, and that with your tremendous zest for life in all its variety, you had something unique to give us. I would love to see if this could not be channelled in some way which we could use.

Nothing was to come of this offer. The fact was that nothing could ever replace the excitement and drama of live war reporting and eventually Roland Penrose wrote to Audrey and begged her to stop asking Lee to write for *Vogue*. The process of writing was unbearably painful, not just for Lee but for the whole family.

They continued to correspond and Audrey visited Lee and Roland at their farm in Sussex and was treated to Lee's latest passion, which was cooking. She and Victor took them a pair of tumbler pigeons as a present and Antony, who was about five at the time, looked apprehensive when he saw them. When Audrey asked him why he was worried, he said he feared they would end up in his mother's freezer.

In July 1977, Lee Miller died at the age of seventy from cancer. In 1992, Audrey gave a lecture about her work for *Vogue* at the Institute of Contemporary Arts. It was a warm and affectionate tribute to one of the most important contributors for her in all the years she edited *Vogue*. She told her audience:

Lee's reporting . . . took us into the heart of the conflict. The proper business of a magazine is to reflect the life of its times. In a time of war, we needed to report war and Lee Miller might have been created for the purpose of doing just that for us.

But she acknowledged that it had come at an almost intolerable personal cost: 'Looking back on it all, it is not surprising that the physical, professional and, above all, the emotional intensity of her work in the war period had drained her dry.'

Of her wartime collaborators, Audrey was outlived only by Alex Kroll, who had joined *Vogue* in 1942. When he left *Vogue* to become the art director of *House & Garden* in 1947, the two of them remained friends. Kroll's son, Simon, remembered Audrey's name being bandied about the house during his childhood. On one occasion, she used her connections in Leningrad to find the 13-year-old a penfriend, though that correspondence only lasted for a matter of months, Simon explained. Alex Kroll was as keen on music as Audrey and they were both regular visitors to concerts at the Wigmore Hall. Simon did not know whether her father and Audrey met at the concerts, but it would have been strange if their paths had not crossed.

After retiring from the SDLP, Audrey continued to be as active as she could. She told Jerrold Northrop Moore that she listened to music on Radio 3 most evenings, always marking up her copy of the *Radio Times* so that she would not miss something she was interested in. Visitors from all over the world, as well as family and friends, beat a path to her door and she always received them with kindness and interest.

When Carolyn Burke visited her to talk about Lee Miller, Audrey went down with her to Oxford Street after their meeting to make sure Carolyn got on the right bus. Pam Makin visited her twice in the last decade of her life. She arrived at the flat to find Audrey dressed in a raspberry-coloured lounge suit. She said to Pam: 'Of course, this is knitted cotton and Hardy [Amies] says it will become the fabric of the future.' And he was absolutely right, Pam concluded. The two of them spent happy hours reminiscing about the bright young girls and boys who had been such a key part of *Vogue*'s office in the post-war years. She loved to relive the gossip and Pam was amazed at her recollection of so much detail fifty years on. Audrey asked Pam about the finance director who had been far too familiar with the young girls in his office and had once been found having sex under his desk with one of them. Pam was highly amused. She had always thought that Audrey had been unaware of the scandals in the office or the photographic studio, but she now realised that Audrey had seen it all but had chosen not to take sides.

She created an ambience of impartiality and created for herself a role of academic observer, which she lived up to. She was straight and she disliked anything shady. Everyone knew and respected that.

She added that one of Audrey's greatest strengths was her ability to empathise with even the youngest members of staff, and, during the war, they had indeed been very young.

As Audrey reached her ninety-sixth year, her health began to fail. In autumn, she was admitted to St Mary's Hospital, in Praed Street, with an infection. The doctors treated her with antibiotics, but she succumbed and slipped away peacefully on Friday 26 October. Her grandson, Michael Kennett, was with her when she died. Her death certificate recorded old age as the secondary cause.

Ten years earlier, she had told an interviewer that she thought about death all the time and was concerned about longevity and the impact it was having on society. She worried particularly about bed-blocking elderly people in hospital and she had joined the Voluntary Euthanasia Society. She had written in her autobiography:

> I no longer feel needed. Yet I hope my life will end before I am not wanted, for then I should be forced to abandon a philosophy formed from a lifetime's experience: that with every gain there is a loss, and with every loss there is a gain. Of course, the two may be far from comparable, but I have never known either gain or loss to be total. It is when loss becomes so, that life is no longer worth living.

Obituaries followed and the consensus was that her career at *Vogue* had been distinguished and that she had been the right editor for the times. Throughout her tenure, writers acknowledged, she was one of the most influential women in London, consulted by the Board of Trade, which would inform her of any new ration restriction or piece of medical advice. She came across as a highly intelligent, articulate, able blue-stocking who, by the time she retired from *Vogue* in 1960, was out of tune with the zeitgeist.

No one got to the bottom of Audrey's character and none mentioned her passion for life, which had been one of the defining features of her personality. No one picked up the tribute in *Vogue* in 1961 that described her as that rare paragon, 'the woman with white hair who loves and understands the young and laughs as gaily as they do'. And no one ever asked themselves whether her own account of her time at *Vogue* could be believed when faced with the evidence of such an astonishingly high-quality body of work between 1940 and 1960.

It is perhaps a mark of how successfully Audrey compartmentalised her life that this should be the case, but the world deserves to know that this woman, who led the most important fashion magazine in Britain through twenty turbulent years in the middle of the twentieth century and handed it over in far better shape than when she inherited it, who championed women's issues and good design on committees when she was surrounded by men, was a woman of passion, opinions, charisma and humour.

AFTERWORD AND
ACKNOWLEDGEMENTS

Audrey Withers took over the editorship of *Vogue* in the middle of the Blitz. Over the course of the Second World War, she established the magazine as independent from its powerful New York parent. She continued as editor until 1960, seeing it through the post-war years of austerity, the jubilant Festival of Britain and the coronation of Queen Elizabeth II in 1953. Yet Audrey Withers is not a name that is familiar to many outside the world of Condé Nast. She seldom gets more than a mention in any book about *Vogue*'s history, yet arguably she did more to shape British *Vogue* than any of its previous editors, and she was the only one, until 1960, who left of her own volition.

I first came across the name Audrey Withers when I was working on a book and an exhibition on wartime clothing for Imperial War Museums, London, in 2014. It was only then that I learned that she and my grandfather were first cousins, Mamie Withers being a Summers and closest in age to my great-grandfather, Harry Summers. Over the next few years, the possibility of writing a biography of Audrey Withers began to take shape. I started at Somerville College, Oxford, where Audrey and her sister, Monica, had placed their father's archive of letters, books and albums. Percy Withers had been a professional friend to many of the literati and artists of the early twentieth century. As such, the archive has a remarkable collection of material from the likes of the poet laureate Robert Bridges, the poet A. E. Housman, the painters Paul and John Nash, and the engraver F. L. Griggs. My sincere thanks go to Kate O'Donnell, Anne Manuel, Jane Robinson, and Pauline Adams at Somerville for their help and support. Thanks also to the archivists at St John's College, Cambridge, Yale University, the Women's Library, the Tate Archives and Imperial War Museums.

A year later, I made my first visit to *Vogue* House in Hanover Square. It was there I learned that Audrey and Cecil Beaton had shredded all *Vogue*'s paper records and many of his original prints in 1942 as part of the wartime paper salvage operation. Such patriotism is magnificent, but what a blow for posterity. However, I was happy to find correspondence from the 1950s with such luminaries as Elizabeth David, who wrote for *Vogue* from 1957, Cecil Beaton and American photographers Clifford Coffin and Irving Penn. Harriet Wilson, Robin Muir and Carole Dumoulin at Condé Nast Publications have been wonderfully encouraging over the past two years and I could not have written the book without their support. Knowing I needed more material from the war years, Harriet Wilson put me in touch with Ivan Shaw at the Condé Nast archive in New York.

I visited New York in April 2018 to read the papers of Edna Woolman Chase, editor-in-chief of all three *Vogue*s until 1952. I discovered that the papers from the early war years were as sparse in New York as in London and I wondered out loud whether it was in sympathy with the British, who had pulped so much.

Marianne Brown, the archivist at Condé Nast I worked with most closely, suggested I should return to consult the papers of Condé Nast himself. Although he was only alive for two of the years that Audrey was editor of *Vogue*, there might be something worth reading. Back in Britain, I applied to the Author's Foundation for funding for a second trip to New York in the autumn of 2018 and was thrilled to receive an Antonia Fraser Grant, which would cover the costs of my entire visit. Thank you to the Society of Authors for awarding me the grant and to Antonia Fraser for her encouragement. We share a passion for marmalade as well as history.

In October, I was back in the archives at 222 Broadway poring over Condé Nast's files. It was the most enlightening read and I was struck over and over by his fastidious attention to detail and his instinct and understanding for what made and kept *Vogue* at the pinnacle of his publishing empire. He analysed every issue of his magazines, and one set in the archives is marked up with a summary of what it cost: the price of the photograph, the drawing, the caption, the feature. Line by line, he knew what had been spent on each page. Condé Nast was a prolific letter writer and he dealt with personnel matters in his correspondence. I was pleased to locate letters between him and Elizabeth 'Betty' Penrose, who had been sent to London in 1934 to see what was going on with British *Vogue*. Her reports threw light on the turbulent years of the late 1930s, when Audrey was finding her feet as a junior member of the editorial team.

Before my first visit to the US archives, I had read a comment in Edna Woolman Chase's autobiography. She wrote about Audrey: 'She is a tremendous worker, extremely intelligent and writes the longest memos known to man.' Marianne Brown and I had discussed the question of what might have happened to these memos and we had come to the conclusion that they had gone the same way as the other wartime material in Edna's archive.

On Monday afternoon of my second visit, I was sitting at a table in the archive when Marianne appeared carrying a cream archive box. A red sticker on the spine meant that it had not been archived at the time that Nast and Chase's other papers had. She opened the lid and inside I could see four A5 cloth-bound ring folders enclosed in bubble wrap. 'Marianne!' I yelped, professional coolness abandoned instantly, 'those are the memos!' Sure enough, when we removed the bubble wrap from the first folder we read: *Chase to Withers*. The second, third and fourth folders were all labelled: *Withers to Chase*.

There they were. The memos that Edna had complained about, the memos that Audrey had written throughout the Second World War. There were over 900 typewritten gems, dating from 1940 to 1947. Crisp, in perfect condition and full of so much detail about the everyday life of *Vogue* during the Second World War. The system the New York and London offices had developed was an exchange of memos once or occasionally twice a week covering all aspects of editorial and dwelling particularly on features that the two magazines would be sharing. Edna was right: Audrey had been a prolific memo writer. Some weeks she would write six or seven on a single day.

The beauty of the memos was that they are nothing like as formal as a letter. They are email-like in their quality, penned off quickly, often with spelling errors or words left out, but so vibrant and full of energy that I had, almost for the first time, Audrey's own voice. Some are funny, others apologetic and more still frustrated by anything from government red tape to women cheating the clothes rationing system. It is without doubt the most exciting find of my research career.

I do not think I have ever been so overwhelmed by archive material nor by the generosity of Condé Nast archivists who allowed me to photograph the memos so that I would be able to read them all in peace and quiet at home in Oxford. As Marianne and I examined the folders, we realised that some of the memos had been written on airmail paper. These were a third as long again as the standard sheets and had been creased and folded. As we unfolded them, with great care, it became obvious that they had not been unfolded since the late 1940s. This was pristine, first-hand, priceless material.

There were memos about Beaton's portraits of Churchill, the introduction of clothes rationing, the bombing of *Vogue*'s offices in 1940 and again in 1941, and, almost more exciting than that, memos about Lee Miller's photojournalism from France, Luxembourg, Belgium and Germany. In all, they run to about half a million words. The single most significant treasure in the collection was Withers to Chase 632, written on 4 July 1941 about the Beaton *Fashion is Indestructible* photographs in the destroyed Middle Temple in London. There, I discovered that it was Audrey who had commissioned the photoshoot. She had wanted Beaton to capture fashion against an historic backdrop and wrote: 'I felt it would show so dramatically how it is possible for *Vogue*'s entire world to carry on even amid such wreckage.' It changed my whole view of Audrey's editorship and brought her style and thinking to life. I would like to thank Ivan Shaw and Gretchen Fenston at the Condé Nast archive, for being so welcoming, and Marianne Brown for being a constant and generous support both during my two visits and subsequently.

A final piece of luck came in the form of a footnote in *All We Know*, by the American author and academic Lisa Cohen, mentioning the diaries of Harry Yoxall, Condé Nast Publications' managing director from 1921 to 1954. I wrote to Cohen and she replied that she thought they were still in the possession of Yoxall's daughter's family who lived in Suffolk. Lindsay Elizabeth Yoxall had married a highly decorated fighter pilot, Henryk Pietrzak, in 1947 and she had inherited the diaries after her father's death. I succeeded in tracking down Henryk Pietrzak, Yoxall's great-grandson, who had the diaries from the war years. The remainder I found were in Suffolk with Harry Yoxall's grandson, Richard. To both Richard and Henryk, I owe a huge debt of thanks, and also to Carol, who was so hospitable when I visited her and Richard's home in May, 2019. Harry Yoxall had written a diary every year of his life after the First World War and into his eighties. He wrote approximately 250 to 300 pages per year, sometimes in French, and these precious documents were bound and stored in cloth-covered sleeves. They gave a day-to-day account of his life, including the goings-on at his offices at Condé Nast. They were valuable in providing little injections of contemporary news or insights into people's characters, moods and behaviour. I even found a description of what the queen wore to the investiture when Audrey received her OBE in 1953.

I went from having too little material on which to draw to

almost too much, and it has been a big task to decide which memos, letters and diary entries to focus on and how to weave them into the narrative so the book does not read like an issue-by-issue story of *Vogue* in wartime. It is a biography and, as such, I wanted to cover as much of Audrey's life as possible.

I have further thanks to people who allowed me to interview them, including four remarkable women who worked for Audrey in the post-war years: Pam Makin, Elva Carey, Eileen Toll and Barbara van der Zee. Antony Penrose, Lee Miller's son, has been so generous sharing his memories of Audrey. Marion Hume, whose knowledge of Lee's life is extraordinarily valuable, has been unstinting with advice. We had great fun discussing the memos and talking about Audrey and Lee's relationship. I should also like to thank Drusilla Beyfus, Ami Bouhassane, Carolyn Burke, Lisa Cohen, Jenny Collett, Artemis Cooper, Emma Gluckstein, Jo Good, Ian and Karen Gray, Simon Kroll, Caroline Mason, Kerry Negahban, Jerrold Northrop Moore, Lynne Olson, Susan Ronald, Julian Schild, Jo Schofield, Florence Smith, Angela Tawse, Hugo Vickers and Steve White.

Edward Morrows in New York helped me to pin down Audrey and Jock's trans-America trip of 1938, while Freddie Locock Harrison in Oxford gave me valuable research assistance closer to home. He was tireless in seeking out information about the elusive Jock Stewart, Audrey's first husband. Leela Bunce transcribed dozens of memos and letters for me, which was so helpful. Caz Stuart filmed interviews with me of Pam Makin, Elva Carey and Eileen Toll, which are invaluable. Thanks, darling.

I thank my publishing team at Simon & Schuster: Iain

MacGregor, Melissa Bond, Kaiya Shang, Pip Watkins, Rich Vlietstra and Rebecca McCarthy. Catherine Clarke at the Felicity Bryan Agency has been, as ever, a tower of strength, and Michele Topham a sane and calm voice when I got into a spin. Richard Leon at Richard Leon PR has believed in Audrey from the moment we discussed her, and has been a great help to me.

On a personal level, thanks go to Andy Ballingall, Graham Ives and Fiona Morrison for their quiet support and invaluable friendship. Thanks also to my brilliant rowing friends Lisa Cochrane, Sos Eltis, Tina Farr, Alison Gruenwald, Alison Salvesen, Camilla Scarf, Naomi Sharma and Suzanne Holmes Smith, who keep me sane at busy periods by reminding me that there is more to life than writing. To Simon, Richard and Sandy, thanks, boys, for your encouragement, and to Chris, the most heartfelt thanks of all. I could not have written this without you.

One person remains to be mentioned. Diane Setterfield, to whom this book is dedicated, is my closest writing companion. Brilliant and busy writer though she is, she has been with me every step of the way: from the moment I stood in the car park at the Lee Miller Archives and shared my excitement about the quality of the material to the morning when the copy-edited version came back to my desk. We have regular 'staircase meetings' to discuss our writing, and stomps along the riverbank to let off steam. Without her wise advice, outstanding way with words and infectious enthusiasm, this book would not have been such a pleasure to write.

NOTES

1. GREEN SHOOTS

8 **its dirty-mindedness, its terrors and deceits** ... Excerpt from Percy Withers' unpublished autobiography

8 **I seem never to have known** ... Ibid.

9 **learned all too soon and too grossly** ... Ibid.

14 **the massive jaws of Borrowdale** ... Percy Withers, op. cit., 'Abbot's Bay', pp. 36–7

14–15 **I risked and enjoyed** ... Ibid., p. 26

21 **no just reason for excluding girls** ... http://www.oxforddnb.com/view/10.1093/ref:odnb/9780198614128.001.0001/odnb-9780198614128-e-51744?rskey=MHASrI&result=1#odnb-9780198614128-e-51744-div1-d1335685e447

22 **We picture you radiantly happy and prosperous** ... Percy Withers (PW) to Audrey Withers (AW), 14 May 1922

22 **What would your early Victorian grandmothers think of it?** ... PW to AW, 11 June 1922

24 **Chick is here; you and Mick follow** ... PW to AW, 15 July 1923

25 **such friendships have crowned a life with happiness** ... PW to AW, 5 June 1922

25 **seeing nothing but gleams of friendly fun** ... F. L. Griggs to AW, 15 September 1934

25–26 **I loved him for his sincerity, his heartfelt principles** ... AW to Jerrold Northrop Moore, 12 December 1994

26 **My relationship with Paul was more complicated** ... Ibid.

27 **No, I don't mind how often you write to me, Audrey** ... Paul Nash to AW, undated c. 1924

28 **Paul Nash was the first person I had met who** ... AW to Jerrold Northrop Moore, 12 December 1994

28 **You know quite well that I do not think of you as** ... Paul Nash to AW, undated c. 1923

28–29 **I like your frank confessions** ... Paul Nash to AW, undated c. 1923

29 **You take things so dangerously, so gloriously to heart** ... Hugh I'Anson Fausset to AW, April 1923

30 **The promised land is yours!** ... Hugh I'Anson Fausset to AW, 26 March 1924

32 **to which the English onlooker goes** ... *The Fritillary*, p. 4

33 **Doubtless the modern generation** ... Isabelle Watkins, unpublished memoir, Somerville College Archives

35 **At the sound of the tin being opened** ... Audrey Withers, *Lifespan* (London: Peter Owen Publishers 1994), pp. 29–30

35 **You seem very earnest about human relationships** ... Paul Nash to AW, undated c. 1927

35–36 **I warn you of one thing – you're not to get too hearty** ... Paul Nash to AW, spring 1926

36–37 **I suppose you'll get above yourself** ... Paul Nash to AW, 2 October 1926

37 **You are rather like a very young animal** ... Paul Nash to AW, 1927

38 **A second is the degree that all the really best people take** ... Hugh I'Anson Fausset to AW, 27 July 1927

39–40 **Meals were an ordeal for us all** ... Audrey Withers, op. cit., p. 34

40–41 **He seemed to have no ability to use either hand or brain** ... Ibid., p. 35

2. NEW SHOES

43 **When our social life was in full swing** ... Audrey Withers, op. cit., p. 37

44 **As one of my contemporaries said** ... Isabelle Penwick, unpublished memoir, Somerville College Archives

46 **as long as it contributes the softening** ... Paul Nash to AW c. 1929

46 **It is comforting to hear you are more** ... Ibid.

46 **Don't stand any nonsense from old Wilson** ... Ibid.

49 **In her meticulous and unsentimental journalism** ... Lisa Cohen, *All We Know* (New York: Farrar, Straus and Giroux 2012), p. 200

51 **a dignified, authentic journal of society** ... Edna Woolman Chase, *Always in Vogue* (London: Victor Gollanz Ltd 1954) p. 23

51 **a well-bred atmosphere** ... Ibid., p. 39

52 **'Burning with shame,' she wrote** ... Woolman Chase, *Always in Vogue* (London: Victor Gollancz Ltd 1954), p. 33

53 **shy, meticulous, highly numerate** ... Susan Ronald, *Condé Nast* (New York, St Martin's Press 2019), p. 25

54 **Condé's "maddening sense of detail"** ... Susan Ronald, *Condé Nast: The Man and His Empire* (New York, St Martin's Press 2019) p. 63

54–55 **He lusted over mathematics** ... Woolman Chase, op. cit., p. 57

55 **Beginning with spring fashion forecast number** ... Ibid., p. 59

57 **In France the couture is both an art and a vital industry** ... Ibid., p. 99

59 *Vogue* **is about women and their frills** ... Ibid., p. 129

60 **a tour-de-force of fashion** ... https://www.dazeddigital.com/ fashion/article/38933/1/the-1920s-lesbian-couple-transformed-british-*Vogue*-dorothy-todd-madge-garland

60 **The atmosphere she created** ...Woolman Chase, op. cit., p. 131

61 **I say 'asking' but really** ... Harry Yoxall, *A Fashion of Life* (New York: Taplinger Publishing 1966), p. 2

62 **So poor Todd is silenced** ... Cohen, op. cit., p. 266
63 **The old bitch has some right on her side** ... Harry Yoxall, Diary, 13 December 1933
64 **those knickers of yours** ... Audrey Withers, op. cit., p. 39
68 **Our friends had assumed that Jock** ... Ibid., p. 8
69 **You know, dear Audrey, that in terms of mere money** ... R. L. Griggs to AW, 29 August 1933

3. STEPPING UP

73 **given a freer rein** ... Betty Penrose to Condé Nast, 6 August 1935, Memo
74 **Withers has a ready pen** ... Ibid.
74 **I couldn't in a life-time duplicate her performance** ... Ibid.
75 **is tremendously good at her job, but** ... Ibid.
75 **With the above, plus an adequate supply of secretaries** ... Ibid.
77 **who should by all means invent stories** ... AW to Edna Woolman Chase, 26 February 1946
82 **Even the waste-paper basket** ... Audrey Withers, op. cit., p. 41
83 **Sky-rocketing across the horizon** ... *Vogue*, June 1935, p. 50
85 **the most completely individual** ... Anne Boston, *Lesley Blanch: Inner Landscapes, Wilder Shores* (London: John Murray 2010), p. 43
85 **above all, the most determined** ... Ibid.
87 **It is a matter of record** ... Condé Nast to Betty Penrose, 11 November 1938
87 **Particularly during the past year** ... Ibid.
92 **With the consistent grind and detail** ... Betty Penrose to Condé Nast, 5 November 1937
93 **I now learn that Audrey Withers** ... Betty Penrose to Condé Nast, 5 November 1937
94 **tall, slender, swaying like a reed** ... Woolman Chase, op. cit., p. 186
95 **Oh, Mrs Chase, Nannie does it for me** ... Ibid.
95 **He, more than any other photographer or artist** ... Ibid.
96 **We're in a tough spot** ... Hugo Vickers, *Cecil Beaton* (London: Weidenfeld & Nicolson 1985), p. 210
97 **I was reduced to pulp** ... Ibid., p. 211
98 **I would be eternally grateful** ... Betty Penrose to Condé Nast, 5 November 1937
98 **is needed if the organization** ... AW to Condé Nast, 11 February 1938
98–99 **it is delightful to think** ... Percy Withers to AW, 9 January 1938
101 **of willingness to take a chance** ... Woolman Chase, op. cit., p. 305
104 **enormous showcase windows 5ft wide** ... https://en.wikipedia.org/wiki/Coast_Daylight#/media/File:Southern_Pacific_Coast_Daylights_1945.jpg
106 **Later I realized that Jock was desperate** ... Audrey Withers, op. cit., p. 79
107 **Of course if there had been nothing else in my life** ... Ibid., p. 80

4. *VOGUE* UNDER FIRE

143 **I think Audrey, while showing a very proper firmness** . . . Harry Yoxall to EWC, 31 March 1944

143 **because he has great power** . . . Harry Yoxall to EWC, 31 March 1944

144 **She had absolute authority** . . . Pam Makin, November 2018

144 **In the build-up to an issue** . . . Eileen Toll, December 2018

145 **I knew that all of them cared** . . . Audrey Withers, op. cit.

145 **The subject for us really has to be handled** . . . Withers to Chase, Memo 567, 14 February 1941

149 **We went through such a transitional stage** . . . Lady Audrey Stanley to Condé Nast 18 December 1940

5. FASHION IS INDESTRUCTIBLE

152 **Ford Madox Brown's emigrants** . . . *Vogue*, January 1941

153 **America is going flat out** . . . *Vogue*, January 1941, pp. 34–5

154–155 **The trees are still there** . . . *Vogue*, January 1941

155 **The Fetter Lane business** . . . Harry Yoxall, Diary, 13 May 1941

156 **where they found the steel bins** . . . Withers to Chase, Memo 623, 16 May 1941

156 **He is still determined to go back** . . . Ibid.

156 **how our British staff is carrying on** . . . Condé Nast to American businessmen, 10 February 1941

157 **One of the amazing things about this war** . . . Ibid.

158 **I had long wanted to get Cecil Beaton** . . . Withers to Chase, Memo 632, 4 July 1941

159 **Your series of summer covers was of course specially unsuitable** . . . Withers to Chase, Memo 651, 19 August 1941

161 **In war the term 'battle-stained'** . . . Oliver Lyttelton, BBC Home Service Radio Broadcast, 1 June 1941

161 **His rationing scheme drives home** . . . *Vogue*, July 1941

162 **They allow us ample material** . . . Ibid., p. 18

163 **I am afraid it has not got a very exciting appearance** . . . Withers to Chase, Memo 680, 18 December 1941

163 **The shops themselves protest to us in confidence** . . . Withers to Chase, Memo 667, 17 October 1941

164 **I used to get so angry** . . . Interview in the *Evening Standard*, March 1991, p. 64

164 **You may be amused to know** . . . Withers to Chase, Memo 680, 18 December 1941

166 **One of our new turners** . . . Sue Bruley (ed.), *Working for Victory: A Diary of Life in a Second World War Factory*, Kathleen Church-Bliss, Diary, 5 November 1942

167 **Neat Heads. War work, whether in the services or factories** . . . *Vogue*, February 1942

167–168 **No sooner was I beginning** . . . Cecil Beaton, 'Winged Squadrons', *Vogue*, July 1941, p. 29

168 **in a community where the presence of death** . . . Ibid.

169 **the macabre recruiting scenes, the fanfares** . . . Ibid.

170 **This pile of pictures – treasure-trove for the waste-paper ...** *Vogue*, March 1942

170 **This flood must be kept in spate ...** *Vogue* frontispiece, March 1942

171 **Barbara Castle and I, as housewives ...** Audrey Withers, op. cit., p. 49

172 **It seemed unbelievable, but of course we knew ...** EWC to Harry Yoxall, 3 February 1942

172 **We all keep well in spite of everything ...** Ibid.

172–173 **take many leaves ...** Condé Nast to EWC, 20 February 1942

173 **I cannot overemphasize ...** Condé Nast to EWC, 20 February 1942

173 **style percolating downwards ...** Harry Yoxall to Iva Patcévitch, 8 January 1942

174 **if we started to conserve ...** EWC to Condé Nast, Memo, 7 January 1942

174 **with new boîtes and bistros ...** *Vogue*, Spotlight, March 1942, p. 44

174–175 **We have great allies ...** Audrey Withers in *Vogue*, March 1942

6. AUSTERITY WITHERS

177 **What fun it will be ...** Paul Nash to AW, November 1941

177 **All had individual beauty ...** *Vogue*, March 1942, p. 43

178 **I am so very glad ...** Paul Nash to AW, 19 December 1941

178 **childish desire to muscle in ...** Ibid.

178–179 **Be enveloped in mystery ...** Mamie Withers to Paul Nash 23 December 1941

179 **Why shouldn't I write at fairly regular intervals ...** Paul Nash to AW, January 1942

179 **We do not like the Paul Nash feature ...** EWC to AW, Memo 591, 2 March 1942

182 **I am now becoming the merest wreckage ...** Percy Withers to Paul Nash, 4 May 1944

187 **Fashion is undergoing a compulsory course ...** *Vogue*, July 1942, p. 27

188 **were passionately anxious to show ...** *Vogue*, October 1942, p. 24

188 **is the society woman who pays 30 guineas ...** Julie Summers, *Fashion on the Ration* (London: Profile Books 2015), p. 104

189–190 **To us, who have worked with him ...** *Vogue*, November 1942, p. 23

191 **As the Germans swept through Europe ...** *Vogue*, November 1942, p. 23

193 **the pioneer of the lively, caugh-you-in-action ...** Anne Scott-James in *Vogue*, September 1958, p. 61

193 **Parks has got a little bit of hypnotism about him ...** Louise Baring, *Norman Parkinson* (New York: Rizzoli International Publications 2009), p. 8

195–196 **Parkinson, you have done a very bad thing ...** Norman Parkinson, *Lifework* (London: Octopus Books Limited 1983), p. 62

198 **They were both honest, intelligent, quick witted, erudite ...** Antony Penrose in conversation with JS, 22 January 2018

201 **Lee Miller, the new photographer ...** Harry Yoxall, Diary, 26 December 1939

202 **eyes blazing with ecstasy ...** Antony Penrose, *The Lives of Lee Miller* (London: Thames & Hudson 1985), p. 99

203 **she has borne the weight of ...** Withers to Chase, Memo 638, 18 July 1941

203–204 **I am always impressed afresh ...** Ibid.

205 **No woman could have arrived at the peak of her career ...** *Vogue*, January 1943, p. 43

205–206 **is it worth me spending five working days ...** Antony Penrose, op. cit., p. 112

7. *VOGUE* AT WAR

209 **Convoys pass in procession ...** *Vogue* editorial, July 1944

210 **'Prisoners of war, prisoners of opinion, of race' ...** *Vogue*, July 1944, p. 39

210 **France has been the heart of Europe ...** *Vogue*, July 1944, p. 43

210 **As we flew into sight of France ...** *Vogue*, September 1944, p. 35

211 **The wounded are not ...** 'Unarmed Warriors', *Vogue*, 1944

211 **As you may not have yet received ...** AW to EWC, 1 August 1944

212 **We are making an important four-page feature ...** Ibid.

212 **tangible proof of our appreciation ...** AW to Lee Miller, 28 July 1944

213 **Hope our message through Yoxall ...** Iva Patcévitch to Lee Miller, December 1944

213 **I was never more jealous ...** Withers to Chase, Memo 825, 6 September 1944

213 **I've spent fifteen or so years of my life ...** Lee Miller to AW, June 1944

214 **We were so short staffed ...** Audrey Withers, lecture on Lee Miller, Institute of Contemporary Arts, London, 1992

214–215 **Lee must have asked innumerable intelligent questions ...** Ibid.

215 **Her clothes will be rich and rather grand ...** *Vogue*, August 1944, p. 86

216–217 **At this moment, and for months afterward, I chuckled ...** David E. Scherman, in Foreword to Antony Penrose (ed.), *Lee Miller's War* (New York, Thames & Hudson 2005), p. 10

217 **St. Malo ... the siege and the assault ...** *Vogue*, October 1944, p. 51

217 **I thumbed a ride to the siege of St. Malo ...** Ibid.

217 **I had the clothes I was standing in ...** Ibid.

217–218 **couples with babies, prams ...** *Vogue*, October 1944, p. 80

218 **We jeeped down to a corner on the quai ...** *Vogue*, October 1944, p. 84

219 **ready to go into action, grenades hanging ...** Ibid., p. 85

219 **We waited, then we heard them ...** Ibid.

219 **sweeping them away, a pity ...** Ibid., p. 86

220 **We spread out the photos in the art department ...** Audrey in her lecture at the Institute of Contemporary Arts

220 **It does represent a great achievement of Lee's ...** Withers to Chase, Memo 832, 11 September 1944

221 **I hope you like it ...** Lee Miller to AW, 26 and 27 August 1944

222 **Lee darling, we are all sick with excitement ...** Sylvia Redding to Lee Miller, 29 August 1944

222 **Every word I write is as difficult as 'tears wrung from stone'** ...
Lee Miller to AW, early December 1944

223 **The girls are fantastically pretty** ... Lee Miller to AW, August 1944

224 **so don't pay too much attention to the negs** ... Lee Miller to AW,
September 1944

224 **As you can imagine, I am pretty bitter** ... Withers to Chase, Memo
825, 6 September 1944

225 **Almost everything with Lee depends on how she is feeling** ...
Ibid.

225 **I would like to emphasise once more my own conviction** ...
Ibid.

225 **Nearly every woman there was conjecturing** ... Women's Press
Club newsletter, October 1945

226 **Beyond that its aim was to enhance the status** ... Ibid.

226 **Glasses clinked, sandwiches disappeared** ... Ibid.

227 **to that dazed but valiantly determined Establishment
Committee** ... Ibid.

227 **'A fitting patron saint for the Women's Press Club of London'** ...
Women's Press Club newsletter, front cover, October 1946

228 **the equivalent of running up the flag** ... Women's Press Club
newsletter, 1 October 1945

229 **There can be no comparison between magazine and
newspaper** ... Audrey speaking at the launch of the Women's Press
Club, July 1944

229 **The idea for such a magazine as mine** ... Ibid.

230 **We don't so much live as manage** ... *Vogue* (US), October 1944,
p. 126

230–231 **She wears suits almost all the time** ... *Vogue* (US), October 1944,
p. 128

231 **upon whom executive and organizing work** ... Ibid., p. 128

231 **She is small, miraculously groomed** ... Ibid., p. 130

232 **The fact is that we simply are not staffed** ... Withers to Chase,
Memo 825, 6 September 1944

232 **Lee and all the *Life* people** ... Ibid.

233 **It seems a little hard** ... Withers to Chase, Memo 892, 11 October 1944

233–234 **Remember them when you turn to the seeming normality** ...
Vogue, October 1944, p. 33

235 **Some of their triumphs over barbarism are preserved** ... *Vogue*,
October 1944 p. 33

236 **We were prepared to do without food, fuel, light, soap,
servants** ... *Vogue*, October 1944

236 **goggle-eyed, dark-glassed girls whirling** ... Ibid., p. 98

237 **women have shown they don't need a gun** ... Ibid.

237 **Our office is completely out of touch with** ... Withers to Chase,
Memo 844, 20 September 1944

237 **their present standing and particular tendencies** ... Ibid.

238 **I feel it is only people on the spot and can sense these** ... Withers
to Chase, Memo 840, 18 September 1944

238 **I believe you are likely to agree with my view** ... Withers to Chase, Memo 859, 29 September 1944

238–239 **as my impression is that she types** ... Withers to Chase, Memo 844, 20 September 1944

239 **It was Dave who alternately comforted and badgered Lee** ... Antony Penrose, op. cit., p. 126

241 **Perhaps it is that we here are nearer the scene** ... Ibid.

241 **There seems to be a very mixed feeling** ... EWC to Lee Miller, 5 October 1944

242 **when our women have spent the war in uniforms** ... Withers to Chase, Memo 845, 21 September 1944

242 **I think that now Paris fashions are being published** ... Withers to Chase, Memo 944, 24 November 1944

243 **The handling of the Paris material** ... AW to EWC, 13 November 1944

243 **I am sure they would find it very helpful** ... Withers to Chase, Memo 858, 28 September 1944

243 **I feel it is very important** ... Ibid.

244 **If you manage to send anyone else** ... Ibid.

245 **a real field day** ... Withers to Chase, Memo 864, 2 October 1944

245 **rigged his dryers to stove pipes** ... *Vogue*, October 1944, p. 78

246 **Edna critical snapshot fashion reportage** ... Withers to Lee Miller, telegram, 13 October 1944

246 **I find Edna very unfair** ... Lee Miller to AW, 14 October 1944

247 **The undercurrent of tragedy is appalling** ... Withers to Chase, Memo 880, 6 October 1944

247 **I get bits and pieces of these stories** ... Ibid.

247-248 **This is a very difficult piece** ... Lee Miller to AW, 4 December 1944

248 **I, myself, prefer describing the physical damage** ... Ibid.

8. IN THE SHADOW OF DEATH

251 **the unhealed cicatrice of humiliation** ... *Vogue*, January 1945, p. 35

252 **They chose their moment well** ... Ibid., p. 86

253 **In the United States, these careers** ... Ibid., p. 64

254 **The Condé Nast judges** ... 'From Culture to Couture' by Penelope Gilliatt in the *London Review of Books*, Vol. 7, No. 3, 21 February 1985, p. 12

254 **We are rushing one off to you** ... Withers to Chase, Memo 1001, 2 February 1945

256 **It was the women who spoke French** ... *Vogue*, April 1945, p. 80

256 **Camouflaged in night-gowns, petticoats, hand-woven sheets** ... *Vogue*, April 1945, p. 51

257 **you will remember the retiring habits** ... Withers to Chase (Penrose) Memo 1000, 2 February 1945

257 **I am really warming up** ... Chase to Withers, Memo 640, 20 February 1945

257 **a really outstanding feature** ... Withers to Chase, Memo 1066, 23 March 1945

258 **I know it is always somewhat irritating** ... Ibid.

258 **Audrey's political beliefs are strong ...** Woolman Chase, op. cit., p. 320

259 **When it comes to reporting ...** Withers to Chase, Memo 1084, 16 April 1945

260 **I am most anxious that we should do nothing ...** Ibid.

260 **I am sure he would bring a personal point of view ...** Chase to Withers, Memo 650, 23 April 1945

261 **We have two young men ...** AW to EWC, 13 November 1944

262 **There was no difficulty ...** Audrey Withers at a lecture, ICA, 1992

263 **I don't take pictures of these things ...** Burke, op. cit., p. 252

263 **Her photographs, which we could hardly bear to look at ...** Audrey Withers, ICA lecture, 21 August 1992

263 **In this case the camp is so close to the town ...** Penrose, op. cit., p. 182

264–265 **But where were those pictures ...** Audrey Withers, ICA lecture, 21 August 1992

265 **We hesitated a long time ...** Woolman Chase, op. cit., p. 312

265 **In Frankfurt, amid complete devastation ...** *Vogue*, June 1945, p. 41

266 **My fine Baedecker tour of Germany ...** Ibid.

266 **The 600 bodies stacked in the courtyard ...** Ibid., p. 42

266-267 **for the end of the war ...** Lee Miller to AW, May 1945

267 **It was in an old-fashioned building ...** Antony Penrose, op. cit. p. 140

267 **He became less fabulous ...** Lee Miller to AW, May 1945

268 **Dave Scherman and I took off from Dachau ...** Ibid.

269 **It was the swansong of Lee's ...** Antony Penrose, op. cit., p. 175

269 **Lee's courage was never in doubt ...** Audrey Withers, ICA lecture, 1992

271 **Visiting Germany briefly after the war ...** Speech at the Institute of Contemporary Arts, 1992

271 **I do not know exactly how you feel ...** Harry Yoxall to EWC, 1 June 1945

272 **now an experienced editor ...** EWC to Harry Yoxall, 6 July 1945

272–273 **How could you? How could you? ...** EWC to AW, 20 March 1945

273 **I haven't had time to make a considered judgment ...** Chase to Withers, Memo 655, 14 May 1945

274 **You are right about the American reactions ...** EWC to AW, 1 August 1945

275 **And hereby hangs what is ...** AW to EWC, 27 July 1945

275 **I am telling you all this ...** Ibid.

276 **My mother was the kindest ...** Audrey Withers, op. cit., p. 36

278 **I want you because, Audrey, you really loved Paul ...** Margaret Nash to AW, 1948

279 **Yet all these minor trials ...** Audrey Withers, op. cit., pp. 63–4

280–281 **exposing Audrey to a great deal of ...** EWC to Harry Yoxall, 11 January 1946

283 **A visit to America ...** AW to EWC, 1 January 1946

284 **It was very encouraging ...** Ibid.

284 **I do thank you for it with all my heart ...** Ibid.

9. FIGHTING FOR FREEDOM

285–286 **I do nothing** ... *Vogue*, September 1946, p. 65

286 **On what shall I feed my husband** ... *Vogue*, September 1946, p. 92

286 **I switch on the news. No longer 'Three hundred Lancasters** ... Ibid.

286 **Instead of payment direct I think** ... Withers to Chase, Memo 1286, 8 April 1946

288 **since the days I first began to have responsibility** ... AW to EWC, 17 October 1946

288-289 **for with the 'incorporation of Vanity Fair'** ... Ibid.

289 **I think *Vogue* should be like the complete woman** ... Ibid.

290 **One is being every whit as political, for instance** ... Ibid.

290-291 **one of the clearest indexes to the political** ... Ibid.

291 ***Vogue*, in addressing women, constantly emphasises intelligence** ... Ibid.

291 **Our emphasis on dual purpose and interchangeable clothes** ... Ibid.

292 **Courage almost always pays. I think *Vogue* should always** ... Ibid.

292–293 **I have always realised** ... Ibid.

293 **This is a day of specialization** ... Woolman Chase, op. cit., p. 139

293 **it is just to her, socialist theory is self-evident** ... Harry Yoxall to EWC, 1 September 1946

295 **The psychological effect** ... Dorothy (Darcy) Braddell, 'General Notes. Designing an Exhibition', *Journal of the Royal Society of Arts*, pp. 898–9

295–296 **Design in clothes has all the elements** ... Britain Can Make It, 1946, p. 45

296 **How often one sees a nondescript dress** ... Ibid.

296 **an art resembling painting** ... Ibid., pp. 45–6

297 **exceptionally wearable and becoming** ... Ibid., p. 47

297–298 **But the fashion designer needs to be up and about** ... Ibid., p. 48

298 **There is even a plan, perhaps a little nebulous** ... Pathé News

299 **I want to congratulate you most sincerely** ... Marghanita Laski to AW, 10 February 1947

299 **I think that famous tenet of 'gracious living'** ... AW to EWC, 10 November 1946

299 **I have tried to put down everything** ... AW to EWC, 17 October 1946

300 **I want to say what a joy it is** ... Harry Yoxall to EWC, 23 November 1946

300–301 **And where do they go** ... *Vogue* editorial, June 1945

301 **such a good mother while having** ... AW to EWC, 3 May 1951

302 **Mrs Forbes you said quite a lot** ... AW in the Chair at the Royal Society of Arts, 9 May 1962

303 **Handsome red leather jacket** ... *Vogue*, January 1947, p. 50

304 **It's quite a revolution, Dear Christian** ... Summers, op. cit., p. 175

304 **retrieved the general situation by reviving** ... *Vogue*, March 1947, p. 47

305 **I wanted my dresses to be 'constructed'** ... www.dior.com

306 **These human situations that must arise** ... EWC to Harry Yoxall, 28 March 1951

307–308 **It would have been easy** ... Draft Statement to the House of Commons, March 1949, by the president of the Board of Trade, Harold Wilson

308 **Rationing has never been the means** ... Board of Trade, internal document, 3 March 1949

308–309 **The road runs from the black-plumed funeral** ... *Vogue*, January 1950, p. 27

309 **Exhaustion, bewilderment, loneliness** ... Ibid.

309 **We who live in the open** ... Ibid.

310 **She has the taste, intelligence and ambition** ... Harry Yoxall to EWC, 15 June 1951

310 **fell in with a bohemian crowd** ... Robin Muir, Obituary to Patricia Cunningham, 2007

311 **My one real doubt is** ... AW to EWC, 28 June 1951

311–312 **colleagues and collaborators valued her judgement** ... Robin Muir, op. cit.

312 **but Audrey didn't want anything to do** ... Pam Makin in conversation with JS, 1 November 2017

314 **Of course we are all eternally striving** ... EWC to AW, 13 June 1950

314 **I think all of us here** ... AW to EWC, 2 September 1952

315 **There are usually some features** ... AW to EWC, 16 May 1950

316 **I cannot stress too much my main anxiety** ... Ibid.

316 **I shall wear it constantly** ... AW to EWC, 13 November 1950

316 **dramatize, for our home and overseas readers** ... *Vogue*, February 1951, p. 47

317 **I liked especially the "small trades"** ... EWC to AW, 17 February 1951

318 **From the title, one gathers that they are man and wife** ... Ibid.

318 **Conceived among the untidied ruins of a war** ... The Festival of Britain catalogue, 1951, p. 3

319 **I do not think anyone who saw it** ... AW to EWC and Jessica Daves, 26 October 1951

319 **For the occasion of our arrival** ... EWC to AW, May 1952

321 **from our selfish point of view** ... Harry Yoxall, Diary, 6 February 1952

321 **put the demands of his country** ... *Vogue*, March 1952

321 **We knew that the train had drawn in at Windsor** ... AW to EWC, 2 March 1952

322 **I am delighted to find** ... AW to EWC, 22 January 1953

323 **Harry tells me you are not quite well** ... EWC to AW, 2 October 1952

324 **I'm so glad!** ... Audrey Withers, op. cit., p. 81

325 **I did not grudge him the money** ... Ibid., pp. 107–8

325 **Audrey is to be made an honest woman of** ... Harry Yoxall, Diary, 16 February 1953

326 **She came in in a pewter silk dress** ... Harry Yoxall, Diary, 10 March 1953

326 **You're the editor of *Vogue*, aren't you?** Ibid.

327 **Victor and I have never had more** ... AW to EWC, 15 June 1953

327–328 **Our breakfast table now revolves** ... AW to EWC, 26 December 1953

328 **We continue to be wonderfully happy** ... AW to EWC, 15 November 1953

328 **this security in one another's love** ... AW to EWC, 26 December 1953

328 **You, more than anybody in the whole organisation** ... AW to EWC, 22 October 1954

328 **May I rather shyly and humbly** ... Ibid.

329 **But if in order to be 'different'** ... EWC to AW, 2 October 1952

330 **the same face haunted me** ... Quoted in AW's memo to staff, 17 October 1952

330 **My eye, as would the eyes of most men** ... Ibid.

331 **get into our pages models** ... AW to Fashion Staff, Studio and Beaton, Parkinson, Denney, Deakin, Clarke, 17 October 1952

332 **I have always thought that Deakin** ... AW to EWC, 11 November 1953

332 **No one ever felt *Vogue* fashion** ... Quoted in National Portrait Gallery blurb for Clifford Coffin exhibition, 1997

333 **I didn't mean this letter to turn into a full confession** ... Clifford Coffin to AW, 9 July 1954

333–334 **This is the opening of a big feature** ... AW to Clifford Coffin, 23 July 1954

334 **but we need not include them all** ... Ibid.

334 **We thought that you might do a wonderful composition** ... Ibid.

334 **with a flash of red in scarf or sweater neck** ... Ibid.

336 **What I learned at *Vogue* stood me in great stead** ... Elva Carey in conversation with JS, 6 June 2018

337 **It is fair to say that the fashion editors** ... Ibid.

337 **She had standards** ... Ibid.

338 **taught a whole generation of people** ... Cooper, Artemis, *Elizabeth David: Writing at the Kitchen Table* (London: Michael Joseph, 1999), p. xiii

340 **Brogue is asking Elizabeth David** ... AW to Jessica Daves, June 1956

341 **Your beautiful parsley has lasted** ... Elizabeth David to AW, May 1957

341 **cook and the patron to jump to attention** ... Elizabeth David to AW, 6 July 1959

343 **I think it is really partly you yourself** ... Elizabeth David to AW, May 1959

343 **every now and again, eating a dish.** .. Audrey Withers, op. cit., p. 93

10. OUT OF *VOGUE*

344 **who stimulated, demanded and searched forever** ... *Vogue*, May 1957, p. 81

344 **For the *Vogue* staff** ... Ibid.

345 **Ailsa Garland, for better or worse** . . . Harry Yoxall, Diary, 20 July 1959

346 **The New Look** . . . Audrey Withers, *Vogue*, July 1958, p. 65

347 **The Sixties was the beginning of something** . . . Interview in the *London Evening Standard* with Pauline Peters

347 **But she never in a whole year asked me a single question** . . . Ibid.

347–348 **This office was a square, glass box** . . . Ailsa Garland, *Lion's Share* (London: Michael Joseph, 1970), p. 141

348 **The end of a long and happy chapter** . . . Harry Yoxall, Diary, 23 December 1960

349 **She replied excellently with fine spirit** . . . Harry Yoxall, Diary, 23 December 1960

349 **The word 'retiring' seems a silly one to apply** . . . *Vogue*, January 1961

351 **I could not say that I had regretted** . . . Audrey Withers, op. cit., p. 85

352 **To be disbelieved by those nearest to you** . . . Audrey Withers, *Lifespan*, p. 105

353 **Guilt is a powerful destroyer** . . . Ibid., p. 106

355 **How could intelligent men suppose that intelligent women** . . . Ibid., p. 82

357 **I sat by the hour with a tide of Russian pouring over me** . . . Ibid., p. 124

359 **There were hysterical giggles** . . . Steve White, interview with JS

361 **Audrey was exceptionally intelligent** . . . Jerrold Northrop Moore in conversation with JS, 14 May 2019

362 **It turns out to be rather discerning** . . . AW to Jerrold Northrop Moore, 12 February 1996

362 **I am very well aware** . . . Audrey Withers, *Lifespan*, p. 55

363 **Audrey . . . achieved her results** . . . Harry Yoxall, op. cit. p. 88

364 **Audrey never gave the impression** . . . Pam Makin to JS, 1 November 2017

365 **If you can impress** . . . Pam Makin in conversation with JS, 1 November 2017

367 **I hope you will remember how very sincere I was** . . . AW to Lee Miller, 2 June 1950

368 **Siriol tells me you are in a working mood** . . . AW to Lee Miller, 1 April 1953

368 **Lee's reporting . . . took us into the heart of the conflict** . . . ICA lecture, 1992

369 **Looking back on it all, it is not surprising** . . . Ibid.

370 **She created an ambience of impartiality** . . . Pam Makin in conversation with JS, 1 November 2017

371 **I no longer feel needed** . . . Audrey Withers, op. cit., p. 210

371 **the woman with white hair who loves** . . . *Vogue*, January 1961

BIBLIOGRAPHY

BOOKS

Baring, Louise, *Norman Parkinson* (New York: Rizzoli International
    Publications, 2009)

Beaton, Cecil and Pope-Hennessy, James, *History Under Fire* (London:
    B. T. Batsford Ltd 1941)

Beaton, Cecil, *The Glass of Fashion* (New York: Doubleday &Company
    1954)

Bilbey, Diane (ed), *Britain Can Make It: The 1946 Exhibition of Modern
    Design* (London: Paul Holberton Publishing in association with
    V&A Publishing 2019)

Boston, Anne, *Lesley Blanch: Inner Landscapes, Wilder Shores* (London:
    John Murray 2010)

Bruley, Sue (ed), *Working for Victory: A Diary of Life in a Second World War
    Factory* (Stroud: The History Press 2010)

Burke, Carolyn, *Lee Miller* (London: Bloomsbury Publishing 2005)

Chase, Edna Woolman, *Always in Vogue* (London: Victor Gollancz Ltd
    1954)

Cohen, Lisa, *All We Know* (New York: Farrar, Straus and Giroux 2012)

Cooper, Artemis, *Elizabeth David: Writing at the Kitchen Table*
    (London: Michael Joseph 1999)

Dorner, Jane, *Fashion in the Forties and Fifties* (London: Ian Allan 1975)

Garland, Ailsa, *Lion's Share* (London: Michael Joseph 1970)

Hartley, Jenny (ed), *Hearts Undefeated: Women's Writing of the Second
    World War* (London: Virago Press 1994)

Holborn, Mark (ed), *Cecil Beaton: Theatre of War* (London: Jonathan Cape 2012)

Howell, Geraldine, *Wartime Fashion: From Haute Couture to Homemade, 1939–1945* (London: Berg 2012)

Huff, Alexandra B. with Sharf, Frederic A., *Beauty as Duty: Textiles on the Home Front in WWII Britain* (Boston: Museum of Fine Arts 2011)

Muir, Robin, *Unseen Vogue* (London: Little, Brown 2002)

Muir, Robin, *Vogue 100: A Century of Style* (London: National Portrait Gallery 2016)

Parkinson, Norman, *Lifework* (London: Octopus Books limited 1983)

Penrose, Antony, *The Lives of Lee Miller* (London: Thames & Hudson 1985)

Penrose, Antony (ed), *Lee Miller's War* (New York: Thames & Hudson 2005)

Ronald, Susan *Condé Nast: The Man and His Empire* (New York: St Martin's Press 2019)

Ross, Josephine (ed), *The Vogue Bedside Book* (London: Vermilion 1984)

Ross, Josephine (ed), *The Vogue Bedside Book II* (London: Century Hutchinson 1986)

Seebohm, Caroline, *The Man Who Was Vogue: The Life and Times of Condé Nast* (New York: Viking Press 1982)

Settle, Alison, *English Fashion* (London: Collins 1948)

Sladen, Christopher, *The Conscription of Fashion* (Aldershot: Scolar Press 1995)

Summers, Julie, *Fashion on the Ration* (London: Profile Books 2015)

Vickers, Hugo, *Cecil Beaton* (London: Weidenfeld & Nicolson 1985)

Walford, Jonathan, *Forties Fashion: From Siren Suits to the New Look* (London: Thames and Hudson 2011)

Waller, Jane and Vaughan-Rees, Michael, *Women in Wartime: The Role of Women's Magazines 1939–1945* (London: Macdonald Optima 1987)

Withers, Audrey, *Lifespan* (London: Peter Owen Publishers 1994)

Withers, Percy, *Friends in Solitude* (London: Jonathan Cape 1923)
Yoxall, Harry, *A Fashion of Life* (New York: Taplinger Publishing 1966)

EXHIBITION CATALOGUES

Design 46: Survey of British Industrial Design displayed in the 'Britain Can Make It' Exhibition (London: His Majesty's Stationery Office 1946)

NEWSPAPERS AND PERIODICALS

Daily Sketch, 20 September 1940
London Review of Books, 1985
The Fritillary (magazine of the Oxford Women's colleges)
The Times
Vogue (UK)
Vogue (USA)

CREDITS AND PERMISSIONS

INDEX

Cunnington, Dr Cecil Willett, 215
Curie, Eve, 148
Cyclax, 79

D-Day, 208–9
Dachau, 263, 267–8
Dahl-Wolfe, Louise, 272, 273
Daladier, Edouard, 108
Dalí, Salvador, 282
Dalton, Hugh, 184
'dark room magic', 192
Davenport, Bill, 119
Daves, Jessica, 99–100, 100–1, 131, 146,
   230, 281, 340
David, Elizabeth, 337–41, 343, 374
Davies, Lillie, 313, 319
Deakin, John, 330, 331–2
Deakin, Phyllis, 226
Dean, Basil, 32
Debenham & Freebody, 79
Denney, Anthony, 330, 340, 341, 343
Descartes, René, 34
Descombes, Roger, 209
Detolle, 111
Dietrich, Marlene, 282
Dig For Victory! 151
Dior, Christian, 304–5
'*directoire* knicker', 79
DIY knitting leaflets, 157
Dome of Discovery, 318
domestic service, 17–18, 22
'Down with Diets' feature, 84
du Maurier, Daphne, 285–7
Dumoulin, Carole, 374
Dunkirk, 121
Durst, André, 83

editorial conferences, 1, 80, 129, 140, 144,
   336–7, 363
editorial control, 126, 142–3, 335
editorial direction, 75
editorial implementation, 55–6
editorial independence, 51, 65
editorial judgement, 180
editorials, 60, 75, 116, 123, 152, 161,
   163–4, 174, 187, 194, 209, 234–5,
   251, 265, 308
Education Committee, Oxford, 34
Edward VIII (Duke of Windsor), 81
Eiffel Tower, 233, 247
Elizabeth Arden, 79, 113
Elizabeth II, 115, 321, 325–6, 329, 378

coronation of, 322, 373
marriage of, 257
Elizabeth, Queen, 113, 115, 139, 147
Elster, General, 240
Éluard, Nusch, 233
Éluard, Paul, 233
Epwell Mill ('The Mill'), 108, 152, 181,
   187, 254, 275, 276
Erickson, Carl ('Eric'), 78, 124
Erickson, Lee, 124
Establishment Committee, 226–7, 228
Euston, Lord, 257
evacuation, 111, 121, 130, 134, 137, 151,
   211

Falstaff Club, 225
'fancy dress' women, 184
fashion anarchy, 242
fashion fête, first-ever (1914), 58–9
'Fashion is How You Wear It' feature, 80
'Fashion Policy' memo, 242
'Fashionable Intelligence' feature, 188
Fausset, Hugh I'Anson, 7, 29, 30, 38, 42
Fellowes, Daisy, 294
Fenston, Gretchen, 377
Festival of Britain (1951), 318–19
Fetter Lane, 3, 129–30, 155, 157, 158,
   204
Fields, Gracie, 45
firewatchers, 127, 154
First World War, 2, 19–20, 26, 56, 61, 111,
   115, 140, 141, 169, 189, 215, 378
Fleet Street, 63, 225, 346
flying bombs, 227, 250, 250–1
Forbes, Evelyn, 301, 302, 335
Forbes, Rosita, 127
Fortnum & Mason, 3, 79
free-thinking, 16–17, 21–2
freelancing, 67, 95, 201, 350, 367
Frissell, Toni, 84

Garland, Ailsa, 345, 347–8
Garland, Madge, 49, 60, 61, 62, 63, 82, 94,
   110, 119, 294
George V, 321
George VI, 107, 320–2
Gervais, M., 245
Gestapo, 233, 251
Gielgud, John, 32
Gilliatt, Penelope, 253, 254
Ginger (cat), 155
Goering, Hermann, 107